S0-AYF-573

PRIVATE CHURCHES
AND
PUBLIC MONEY

To Christopher,
Peter,
and Benjamin

PRIVATE CHURCHES AND PUBLIC MONEY
Church-Government Fiscal Relations

Paul J. Weber and
Dennis A. Gilbert

Contributions to the Study of Religion, Number 1

GREENWOOD PRESS
WESTPORT, CONNECTICUT • LONDON, ENGLAND

Library of Congress Cataloging in Publication Data

Weber, Paul J   1937-
    Private churches and public money.

    (Contributions to the study of religion ;
no. 1 ISSN 0196-7053)
        Bibliography: p.
        Includes index.
        1.   Religious liberty--United States.
2.   Church finance--United States.   3.   Church and
state in the United States.   I.   Gilbert, Dennis A.,
joint author.   II.   Title.   III.   Series.
KF4865.W4   342.73'087   80-1793
ISBN 0-313-22484-6 (lib. bdg.)

Library of Congress Catalog Card Number: 80-1793
ISBN: 0-313-22484-6
ISSN: 0196-7053

First published in 1981

Greenwood Press
A division of Congressional Information Service, Inc.
88 Post Road West, Westport, Connecticut 06881

Printed in the United States of America

10 9 8 7 6 5 4 3 2 1

COPYRIGHT ACKNOWLEDGMENTS

    For permission to reproduce materials, we are grateful to the following:

Portions of chapters 2 and 7 were originally published by Paul J. Weber in "Building
on Sand: Supreme Court Construction and Educational Tax Credits," 12 *Creighton
Law Review*, pp. 531-65. © 1979 by Creighton University School of Law, Omaha,
Nebraska. Reprinted in slightly revised form by permission of the publisher.

Tables 4-2 and 4-3 from Martin A. Larson and Stanley C. Lowell, *The Religious
Empire*, © 1976 by Robert B. Luce, Washington, D.C. Reprinted by permission of
the publisher.

Table 4-11 from Daniel J. Sullivan, *Public Aid to Nonpublic Schools*, 1974, D.C. Heath, Lexington, Mass., p. 93. Reprinted by permission of the author.

Table 4-7 from Howard R. Bowen and W. John Minter, *Private Higher Education*, p. 40, copyright 1974, Association of American Colleges, Washington, D.C. Reprinted by permission of the publisher.

Tables 5-2, 5-3, 5-4 from Manning M. Patillo, Jr. and Donald M. Mackenzie, *Church-Sponsored Higher Education in the United States* copyright 1966, American Council on Education, Washington, D.C., pages 32, 34, 35. Reprinted by permission of the publisher.

CONTENTS

TABLES

SERIES
FOREWORD

American church-state relations are not a simple matter, either in historical practice or current policy. The notion that religiously affiliated institutions should receive no public funding is a simple and reassuring theory, but the facts prove otherwise, especially in our own day. Contemporary activities in this area follow no single legal doctrine or interpretive logic, and they are expanding without any coherent policy behind them. This volume challenges us to review past government actions and integrate those actions into concepts that will treat all religious groups equally.

The authors, Paul J. Weber and Dennis A. Gilbert, have broached a subject rarely treated in the voluminous church-state literature, even though it involves millions of tax dollars annually. Despite its importance, this subject has not received many discussions of this sort in contemporary scholarship. Legal documents are relatively inaccessible. Standard works on religion and public policy generally ignore fiscal implications. By highlighting fiscal policy, the authors focus on a neglected aspect of the church-state question and discuss it with admirable clarity. They use financial considerations to correlate standard interpretations into a new synthesis, and through statistical tables and appendixes connect data from many related fields.

This volume makes three contributions. It provides a succinct overview of American experience regarding the First Amendment, pointing out that there has been no univocal agreement on government attitudes about religious groups. Then, in more detailed analysis, it shows the difficulties and inconsistencies with which public regulations have treated religious affiliations. As political scientists the authors are particularly helpful in revealing the legal deficiencies of church-state case law and the economic consequences of today's often contradictory practices. Throughout the text, they demonstrate how difficult it is to act knowledgeably in an area without fully understanding the implications of public support for religious organizations and their educational institutions. Finally, they suggest tentative guidelines for solving such a dilemma.

Without treating their conclusions as definitive solutions, Weber and Gilbert follow guidelines that may prove useful in redressing the situation. Concerned primarily with maximum freedom and equal treatment for all citizens, they offer the present study to stimulate thought and provoke further analysis in the area. This volume not only provides a historical summary of past and present interpretations, demonstrating various uncertainties, but also it moves ahead to urge intelligent action in a controversial area that is still in its formative stages. Studies such as this may help us determine future church-state fiscal relations that incorporate traditional habits with deliberate efforts to be legally acceptable and economically viable. Whether such policies continue to revise former practices, this book makes it possible to act with a clearer understanding of the alternatives.

Past action and current diversity show that there is no final answer or single panacea in church-state financial questions. Interested in encouraging debate, Weber and Gilbert do not terminate their deliberations with a conclusive statement. Their concern for equity opens new questions about the rationale for aid to religious groups, the circumstances involved, and the wider results of distributing financial benefits. Within that context they relate all questions to constitutional law, sound economics, and other public programs. Their work is relevant to general classroom use, university and law libraries, government advisors, and all persons interested in contributing effectively to the course of public policy.

INTRODUCTION

Religion in America has become a complex economic enterprise. To be sure, many small groups of religious believers subsisting on meager budgets still dot the country from border to border, conducting their affairs simply. Far more significant from an economic perspective are the very large religious organizations with enormous assets, far-reaching affiliations, and highly complex financial arrangements. Organized religion is not the same now as it was when the First Amendment was written. If one is to focus primarily on fiscal issues, precisely what does it mean that "Congress shall make no law respecting an establishment of religion, or prohibiting the free exercise thereof. . . ."?

One classic school of thought, the separationist, argues that the Establishment Clause forbids Congress to provide any form of economic assistance whatever to religious or religiously affiliated organizations.[1] It does not matter what form aid takes, whether direct or indirect, nor does it matter whether all religious sects benefit equally. All aid from the public sector to religious organiztions tends to establish religion and is therefore unconstitutional. The principle more fervently invoked by separationists is, of course, the "separation of church and state," or as Jefferson called it, "the wall of separation."[2] One of the uncomfortable facts separationists must face is that an enormous amount of aid, both direct and indirect, is given by government each year to religious and religiously affiliated organizations. Such aid has existed since well before the establishment of the Republic, has repeatedly been upheld as constitutional by both legislatures and courts, and therefore has the weight of legal tradition and established practice behind it. Even more disturbing from their perspective, the dollar amount of such aid continues to expand at a significant rate.

A second classical school of thought, the accommodationist, takes a quite different stance. The Establishment Clause, argue accommodationists, should not be allowed to obliterate the Free Exercise Clause. Government has an obligation to accommodate the desires of Americans to exercise their religious beliefs. In accommodating those desires, the government may find it appropriate or even necessary to provide economic assistance to religious and religiously affiliated organizations.[3] What the First Amendment prohibits, they argue, is not aid, but privilege, coercion, and civil disabilities based on religious belief or practice.[4] Economic aid may be given, they insist, if it is shared equitably and does not favor one religious group over another. One of the uncomfortable facts accommodationists must face is that in popular culture, "separation of church and state" is a deeply ingrained value and aid is looked upon with suspicion. In addition, courts in general and the Supreme Court in particular have repeatedly declared select forms of aid unconstitutional.

What we are saying is that despite nearly two hundred years of interpretation, explanation and—let's face it—downright propagandizing, there is simply no common agreement about the meaning of the religion clauses of the First Amendment. Neither of the classical approaches has been accepted nor rejected in its entirety. What has developed as a practical matter through our history is a kind of marble cake mixture with several certainly distinguishable areas but few clear lines. As a result, policymaking in church-government fiscal relations is by and large jerryrigged from issue to issue.

Yet, determining consistent policies for church-governmental fiscal relations that are legally acceptable, cognizant of traditional practice, and grounded in sound economic theory is not easy. Is it constitutionally permissible for the public sector to supply aid in any form to religious or religiously affiliated organizations? On that question absolute separationists clearly do not reflect economic realities. Religious organizations do indeed receive economic aid from the public sector, in many forms and in substantial amounts. Is aid given equally to all religious groups constitutionally permissible? On that question accommodationists have been unable to persuade either the populace at large or the courts. Other questions remain. In what circumstances can aid be given? What types of aid are allowable? How many dollars may be involved? What is the constitutional rationale? The major institution called upon to answer such questions authoritatively has been the Supreme Court. Its members have labored over these questions at length and have created an inconsistent and unsatisfactory case law tradition. The constitutional justifications for their decisions are deficient and the various dicta, taken together, are—to put it charitably—confusing and disingenuous.

The writing on church-government *fiscal* relations is neither extensive nor very helpful. The field has been left largely to polemicists. Objective analysis is the rare exception. When legal scholars venture into the area, they tend to focus on narrow legal issues and fail to take salient fiscal factors sufficiently into account. Economists tend to avoid the area altogether. A proper understanding of church-government fiscal relations requires bringing together constitutional law, economics, and general public policy considerations. Nowhere has that been satisfactorily done. Nowhere is there an objective and systematic effort to integrate all aspects of church-government fiscal relations around a cohesive and coherent policy. Practice has now outstripped theory. Fundamental constitutional issues and billions of dollars each year are at stake, and yet policymakers stumble along without clear direction. This book is an attempt to take a hard, objective look at the problems involved in church-government fiscal relations and suggest how those problems might be solved.

Having said that, it is important to make clear what this book is *not* trying to do. First, and perhaps most important to keep in mind throughout the analyses here, this book is not an effort to catalog every possible fiscal relationship that does or might exist between governments and religious organizations. Instead, the object is to explain a basic principle that we believe can and should be applied to church-government fiscal relations in whatever form they may take. We will illustrate the application of the principle in particular problem areas as a way of demonstrating how the principle would work, but we will not try to apply the principle in every possible circumstance. To do so would be unnecessary for establishing the point to be made and too tedious for the reader whose interest may already be heavily taxed.

Second, this book is about church-government *fiscal* relations in particular, not church-government relations in general. The focus, as the title of the book indicates, is on the relationship between governments and religious organizations where money, especially public sector money, is involved. While there is a considerable body of case law on church-government relations, the central concern of our inquiry here will limit our investigation primarily to those cases where public money is an important issue.

Third, this book is not trying to examine every possible aspect of the public policy issues involved in church-government fiscal relations. Public policy can be evaluated along four different dimensions: efficiency; effectiveness; equity; and responsiveness. Efficiency is a cost-benefit concept. What is the return on the investment in the public sector? Effectiveness is getting the job done. Are the policy objectives met? Equity is whether the policy is fair. Responsiveness is whether the people paying the bill and receiving the service get what they desire. Every public policy can be evaluated against each of these criteria. Policies are more or less efficient, effective, equitable or responsive. Often these objectives are traded off against one another; a policy that is most efficient may not be at all what the public wants.

Efficiency, effectiveness, and responsiveness will get some attention here, but the central concern of this book is *equity*, because equal treatment is the keystone of the policy of fiscal neutrality that will be propounded here. In the literature currently available equity has been given less attention than the other three aspects of public policy. Part of the reason, no doubt, is that equity is the most difficult of the four to define and measure. As Oppenheim notes, some of the more traditional definitions of equity or egalitarianism have included: (1) equal shares to all; (2) equal shares to equals—that is, equal with respect to some property such as all adults voting or equal income being equally taxed; (3) proportional equality—that is, the more the characteristic, for example, poverty, the more the benefit or burden; (4) unequal shares corresponding to relevant differences—that is, the inequality in allotment being based on relevant differences in personal characteristics such as restricting voting on the basis of age or citizenship but not sex or race—which obviously involves very normative judgments; (5) to each according to his desert—which Oppenheim says goes back to Aristotle arguing that "a person's desert is the only characteristic relevant to allocations."[5]

Before jumping to any conclusions about which of these alternative formulations is best, it is well to keep Lakoff's observation in mind:

> The philosopher who propounds a particular understanding of equality is free to consider it absolute and universal; but the historian of ideas, faced with conflicting claims, can only consider them all valid in their own terms. *Formally* there is one idea of equality; *substantively* there are many.[6]

And if that is not sobering enough one can reflect on the couplet Tawney quotes:

> High Heaven rejects the lore
> Of nicely calculated less and more.[7]

Oppenheim warns that agreement on equality will not come easily, not only because of the nature of the concept, but also because equality conflicts with other worthy social goals such as maximization of self-interest, higher production, fewer government restrictions, minority freedoms, cultural excellence, individualism, and the like.[8]

All of these factors have contributed to the malleability of the equal protection guarantees of the Constitution. While equal protection has most often been sought as a remedy in the area of civil rights, it has also been the objective of litigation in cases involving the financing of elementary and secondary education[9] and the provision of municipal services.[10] Although in both instances the Supreme Court refused to expand the equal protection guarantees to the extent desired by the plaintiffs, state legislatures and courts have in other instances broadened equal protection guarantees.[11] The point is simply that our understanding of the need to expand equal protection and the activities to which it is applicable is still in the formative stage.[12] It is our belief that the exigencies of existing political and economic relationships, as well as constitutional requirements, dictate that we apply the standards of equal protection to church-government fiscal relations.[13]

The proposed policy, called fiscal neutrality, would treat religious and all similarly situated organizations equally. Essentially it is a policy of equal treatment for equals, designed to implement the two religion clauses of the First Amendment together rather than separately. This approach is suggested because present case law and public policy are both inconsistent and lack a common rationale. Chapter 1 of this book is historical and examines the evolution of church-government fiscal issues from the earliest American settlements to the present. Chapters 2 through 5 constitute a critique of prevailing practices and their justifications. To demonstrate weaknesses in existing case law on the topic, chapter 2 discusses important Supreme Court cases dealing with church-government fiscal relations. This critique is carried further in chapter 3, which describes the inconsistencies in the Court's economic reasoning. Chapter 4 turns to a broader question of public policy, showing how little reliable information we actually have about church-government fiscal relations and the problems encountered in gathering it. Chapter 5 also challenges many current distinctions between religiously affiliated and secular organizations. Given the difficulties and deficiencies of the status quo as documented, chapter 6 offers fiscal neutrality—defined as government treatment of religiously affiliated groups in the same manner as similarly situated groups—as a more desirable alternative.[14] Chapter 7 explores some general policy implications of fiscal neutrality, particularly the limitations and control of aid acceptable under a policy of fiscal neutrality. A general summary and concluding remarks follow.

It may be appropriate to end this introduction with a disclaimer. The authors are writing as political scientists, not as advocates of any religious point of view. We have taken as our fundamental values the scholarly commitment to objectivity and accuracy and the human commitment to maximizing freedom and equality of treatment for all persons. As political scientists we are concerned that public policy decisions be based on full, accurate information and a consideration of the possible alternative policies. In the course of this book we may have offended some people within each of the several religious traditions; our only hope is that we have offended all in an evenhanded manner.

In a more serious vein, it has been our objective to present a particular interpretation of the First Amendment religion clauses not so much as a definitive statement of what ought to be but as an invitation to dialogue and debate. Our interpretation is, we believe, well grounded in constitutional history and economic theory. But it is not set in concrete. Hopefully it is a work that will stimulate insights, criticisms, and additions from other scholars within the political, economic, and religious professions. Out of that exchange may come the beginnings of sound public policy.

NOTES

1. The classic separationist work is Leo Pfeffer, *Church, State and Freedom*, 2d ed. (Boston: Beacon Press, 1967).

2. Thomas Jefferson, "Letter to Danbury Baptists' Association," in Saul K. Padover, *The Complete Jefferson* (New York: Duell, Sloan and Pearce, 1943), pp. 518-19.

3. There is no single classic accommodationist work. Perhaps the best brief statement is Edward S. Corwin, "The Supreme Court as National School Board," *Law and Contemporary Problems* 14 (1949): 3.

4. For an exhaustive defense of this interpretation of the Establishment Clause, cf. C. J. Antieau et al., *Freedom From Federal Establishment* (Milwaukee: The Bruce Publishing Co., 1964).

5. Felix E. Oppenheim, "The Concept of Equality," *International Encyclopedia of the Social Sciences*, s.v. "equality."

6. Sanford A. Lakoff, *Equality in Political Philosophy* (Boston: Beacon Press, 1964), p. 6.

7. R. H. Tawney, *Equality*, 4th ed. (London: George Allen & Unwin, 1952), p. 27.

8. Oppenheim, "The Concept of Equality."

9. San Antonio Independent School District v. Rodriquez 411 U.S. 1 (1973).

10. Hawkins v. Shaw 461 F. 2d 1171 (5th Cir. 1972).

11. e.g., Serrano v. Priest I, 5 Cal. 3d 584 4s, 7 P. 2d 1241, 96 Cal. Rptr. 601 (1971); Serrano v. Priest II, 18 Cal. 3d 728, 557 P. 2d 929, 135 Cal. Rptr. 345 (1976).

12. For a more general philosophical discussion of equality see Ronald Dworkin, *Taking Rights Seriously* (Cambridge, Mass.: Harvard University Press, 1977) especially pp. 266-278. For the application of equal protection to the First Amendment, see Kenneth Karst, "Equality as a Central Principle in the First Amendment," *University of Chicago Law Review* 43 (1976): 20.

13. This policy can be applied to other church-government relations as well, but will not be discussed here. For a wider examination of neutrality see Paul J. Weber,

"Religion and Equality: Understanding the First Amendment," (Ph.D. diss., University of Chicago, 1977).

14. One substantial difficulty the authors have not resolved to their own satisfaction is that of terminology. Much of the language in church-government relations has gathered ideological baggage over the years (the old Latin word for baggage, *impedimenta*, expresses it well). As a result, clarity and freshness are difficult to attain. We have opted to use the more commonsense term "church-government relations" rather than the traditional but stilted "Church-State relations." In most contexts Americans speak of their federal or state governments, not of a philosophical entity called "the state." We think church-government is the most appropriate term.

Likewise we have struggled to find a proper name for the fresh interpretations of the First Amendment we propose. While we are uncomfortable with the term "fiscal neutrality" (like motherhood and apple pie, who can be against it?), we could find no satisfactory substitute. Our only caveat is that when we use the term we mean a very distinct kind of legal principle which we shall explore more fully in chapter 6.

PRIVATE CHURCHES
AND
PUBLIC MONEY

1

HISTORICAL
ROOTS

THE COLONIAL PERIOD

It is difficult if not impossible to appreciate fully the current stage
of religious-government fiscal interaction without an understanding
of the immensely rich and varied path the nation has trod. Since the
Mayflower Compact, the threads of religion and government have
been interwoven in a myriad of different patterns. Or perhaps a
vine metaphor is more appropriate, for the relationship was and is
ever growing, ever changing, drawing nourishment from the spiritual climate and political soil in which it must grow. As a result, and
contrary to popular myth, there has been no common, long-estab-
lished standard against which to measure current practices. Growth
and change have been the rule.

Much of the impetus for change in political ideology and religious
principle (in church-government affairs these are often two sides of
the same coin) has come from the pocketbook connection. Historians of American church-government relations tend to focus on the
development of principle, culminating in the First Amendment
religion clauses. This can be misleading. It is our purpose to show
that economic considerations gave birth to noble principles, and
that as economic conditions changed, so did the principles. This is
not to argue the case for economic determinism, for there was
precious little of the inevitable in the early development of church-
government relations. It is rather an argument for two things: that
church-government relations and theory have both undergone
frequent and dynamic change, and that as economic conditions

changed, so did Americans' understanding of the proper relationship of church and government.

One concern of the early colonists that tends not to be appreciated by contemporary audiences was the perceived need for moral instruction in general and for religion in particular. Their concern is more easily understood when one recalls that there was no public education, free or otherwise, in the colonies, no mechanisms beyond the family for what we might now call moral development, few processes for political socialization, and no publicly supported social services. Among colonists struggling to develop a sense of common identity and political cohesion, religion was seen as a *sine qua non*. This was true not only among the pious, but among secular leaders as well. It was only in the late eighteenth century that a few southern gentlemen, especially James Madison and Thomas Jefferson, began to perceive that society's social fabric was not so interwoven with religion after all. To that developing awareness we now turn.

In his classic study *The Garden and the Wilderness* the late Mark DeWolfe Howe pointed out that two major colonial influences led the Founding Fathers to frame the First Amendment religion clauses as they did.[1] The first and least familiar influence was that of the New England dissenters, exemplified by Roger Williams; they longed for a separation of church and government on the theological premise that once the wall was broken down, the authority and power of government would corrupt the churches. The second influence, that emphasized by the courts and legal historians, and hence more familiar to us, is that of the Virginia deists as captured in the writings of James Madison and Thomas Jefferson. It was Jefferson who immortalized the "wall of separation" metaphor when he wrote to some New England Baptists, "I contemplate with sovereign reverence that act of the whole American people which declared that their legislature should 'make no law respecting an establishment of religion or prohibiting the free exercise thereof,' thus building a wall of separation between church and state."[2] Jefferson's concern, quite the opposite of Williams's, was to protect the powers of government from the corruption which would come if churches were allowed to extend their control.

Ironically, within both traditions, taxation was a catalyst for developing a church-government bond that spread far beyond monetary matters.

New England Tradition

The tangled history of New England's struggle to establish religious liberty is best pictured as a smoldering campfire from which occasional flames shot up for a few short gulps of air, then sank back to form the coals from which came ever stronger blazes. The Puritans fled an established Church of England in the name of religious liberty. After a short stay in Holland they migrated to the New World to be free at last to practice their own faith peaceably. But it was a self-centered freedom, to say the least. The settlers of both the Plymouth and the Massachusetts Bay colonies were self-righteous Puritans who proved harshly intolerant of other views. They were not interested in religious freedom as such, but only "in their freedom to establish an exclusive monopoly of religion in the territories they occupied."³ Quakers, Baptists, and Roman Catholics who dared to settle in Massachusetts were persecuted and exiled. But as immigration increased, population grew and the established church was torn by internal disputes. Attempts to break free of established religions and allow for toleration of pluralism grew apace. In 1649 a small group of colonists in Maine formed an independent "democracy" and proclaimed a policy of religious toleration. The noble experiment flourished for three years until the territory was seized by neighboring Massachusetts and the policy cancelled.

Although not New England colonies, Maryland and Pennsylvania were similar with respect to religion. Religious freedom flamed briefly in Maryland under the personal rule of Catholic Lord Baltimore. In his effort to populate the colony and make it economically profitable, Lord Baltimore welcomed all religious sects, although in 1649 the General Assembly passed an "Act Concerning Religion" which specifically limited toleration to those persons "professing to believe in Jesus Christ." In 1654, Puritans captured a majority in the assembly and proceeded to withdraw toleration from Roman Catholics and other non-Puritans in the population. Ironically enough, this establishment eventually gave way to a Church of England establishment in 1692.

Similarly, in Rhode Island, during the leadership of Roger Williams and for a considerable time afterwards, all Protestant denominations were tolerated, although again Catholics and Jews were not permitted.

Pennsylvania too exemplifies the pragmatism of the middle colonies with their mix of idealism and economic shrewdness. As Leo Pfeffer points out,

Undoubtedly toleration in Pennsylvania was based on Penn's idealism, but, as in Calvert's Maryland, it also coincided with the proprietor's desire to reap substantial profits from his province, and this necessitated attracting large numbers of settlers. Penn's widespread advertisements for settlers prominently promised religious toleration.. These brought immigrants from the continent as well as from Britain, and resulted in a more rapid population growth than in any of the older colonies.[4]

As important as Maryland and Pennsylvania were for setting precedents and demonstrating that religious toleration was good economics, one must return to New England and Massachusetts in particular to understand the theoretical development of the concept of religious liberty. The Massachusetts colony began with a fusion of religious and civil law. Its religion provided the very meaning and purpose of the colony. It provided the common identity for a community in the wilderness. "During its first generation, Massachusetts recognized the Lord's Supper, not baptism, as the central symbol of church and state alike. Full membership required the baptised to demonstrate the manner and effect of their conversion. Once admitted to communion, they possessed the right to vote in both ecclesiastical and civil affairs."[5] Taxes were levied to support both the civil and the ecclesiastical establishments.

One difficulty that continually plagued the colony was that too few inhabitants were able to hurdle the high spiritual barriers to civil membership. This applied not only to dissenters, but to solid citizens unable to recount a "conversion" experience. In 1662 the Half-Way Covenant was proposed as a practical solution. The Lord's Supper gave way to infant baptism as the basis for the right to vote. Here began the difficulty for the Baptists. Originally an obscure offshoot of Puritanism, they believed adult baptism was a key doctrine, and spiritual conversion a requisite, for any clergy whom they would consent to support. As the number of Baptists grew, so did the problem.

The monetary connection with the development of religious liberty theory is best exemplified in the works of Isaac Backus (1724-1806), a prolific Baptist preacher, historian, and writer, who was deeply influenced by the works of Roger Williams. "Isaac Backus began his career of protests with an apparently simple demand for freedom from taxation for the support of clergymen that Baptists would not receive."[6] By Backus's time, Massachusetts law was nominally tolerant, allowing dissenting congregations to elect their own clergy by majority vote provided such clergy met the educational standards set by the Puritans, or as they came to be known, Congregationalists.[7] Individuals in such congregations would then be granted certificates of exemption from the common tax and be free to support their own clergy. Few of the Baptist preachers could meet the educational requirement and the dissenters found themselves forced not only to support their own ministers, but to pay an assessment for the support of the Congregational ministers they rejected. Not surprisingly, many refused. What was at issue, of course, was the entire religious tax system of Massachusetts upon which the established church depended.

In presenting the Baptist position, Backus raised the issue from the level of an inequitable tax to a question of religious liberty. The more he reflected on the matter the more Backus became convinced that the very concept of certification for tax exemption must be rejected" . . . [b]ecause it implies an acknowledgement that civil rulers have a right to set up one religious sect above another, which they have not . . . [and] because they are representative in religious matters and therefore have no right to impose religious taxes. . ."[8] Backus was an avid student of John Locke and, under pressure to justify Baptist opposition to governmental interference of any kind, he found in Locke powerful support for the idea that government's role is limited primarily to the protection of property. But he also radically developed the earlier Puritan concept of covenant as a justification for separation. For Backus the social con-

tract which produced the state was a necessary evil, the result of
human sinfulness. It stood in unbridgeable opposition to the covenant of faith which existed between God and each individual. The
two covenants had little in common, and faith demanded the absolute separation of the two. Whereas supporters fo the status quo
saw religion as the adhesive binding society together, the dissenters
led by Backus conceived of society as the result of two independent
covenants. That between the state and individuals was held together by force exercised by the gathering of taxes. The covenant
between churches and individuals was held together by faith expressed in voluntary support. Backus's principal insight was that
faith and force are incompatible.

In brief, the development of the theoretical discussion of a proper
church-government relationship was stimulated by and interwoven
with the tax issue. Shortly after his arrest for refusal to pay a tax in
support of the established church, Backus penned a retort to John
Adams, who had argued that an establishment based on majority
vote and supported by taxation did not violate religious liberty:

> I fully concur with your grand maxim that it is essential to liberty that
> representation and taxation go together. Well then, since people do not
> vote for representatives in our legislature from ecclesiastical qualifications,
> but only by virtue of those which are of a civil and worldly nature, how can
> representatives thus chosen have any right to impose ecclesiastical taxes?
> Yet they have assumed and long exercised such a power. For they assume a
> power to compel each town and parish in the Province to settle a minister,
> and have empowered the majority of the inhabitants to give away as much
> of their neighbor's estates as they please to their minister; and if they refuse
> to yield it to them, then to take it by force. And I am bold in it that taxes
> laid by the British Parliament upon America are not more contrary to civil
> freedom than these taxes are to the very nature of liberty of conscience,
> which is an essential article in our character. . . .[9]

Virginia Tradition

The struggle for religious liberty and separation in Virginia had
quite different roots from the stuggle in New England. Unlike the
Massachusetts settlers, the planters of Virginia identified themselves
with the British crown and were content to be governed by English
law, including the establishment of the Anglican church. The first

guiding rule was the English Act of Toleration of 1689, confirmed for Virginia by a 1699 statute. Basically the Act provided that those protestant dissenters who had sided with the Anglican establishment in the Glorious Revolution of 1688 were to be given the right to hold religious services, provided their ministers and places of worship were registered with the government. Dissenters were still disqualified from public office, and the Anglican church retained its privileges. Among the privileges granted were the exclusive right to perform weddings and funeral services, as well as to keep baptismal records and control the levies for the care of the poor. The fees collected for such services were a major source of ecclesiastical revenues.

The struggle for religious liberty began with reaction against this Act of Toleration. The first movement, meeting with considerable success, was to interpret the Act so broadly that it would accommodate most sects. But in the 1740s, the Great Awakening crossed the Blue Ridge Mountains in the form of evangelical preachers. The rather diffident, and by most accounts thoroughly corrupt, Anglican clergymen were no match for the Baptist and Presbyterian enthusiasts. As the dissenters grew in number and strength, the established clergy pressed for a more restrictive reading of the Act of Toleration. Their reasoning was that the enthusiasts tended to undermine the social fabric of the colony. A number of resolutions, all proporting to spell out the meaning of the Act of Toleration, were proposed—namely, to require that each new meetinghouse be registered, to limit the number of dissenting preachers who could be licensed and the number of dissenters' meetinghouses to be allowed in each county, and to limit the freedom of itinerent preachers to move from place to place. In addition to this attempt to read the Act of Toleration in an exceedingly narrow light, "[t]here were also many petitions from advocates of establishment, urging a new toleration bill which would check night meetings, preaching among slaves, and other new dangers."[10]

The attempt to limit toleration backfired for all practical purposes, and the struggle to extend toleration was transformed into a struggle to destroy establishment. That effort was helped immensely by the advent of the Revolutionary War. While the Anglican clergy by and large remained loyal to the crown, the Virginia Baptists declared their loyalty to the Continental cause as early as August 1775. 1776 was a turning point for religious liberty in Virginia, for in that year was written article 16 of the *Virginia Declaration of Rights*. Drafted by George Mason, an unusually liberal Episcopalian, and amended by James Madison, the *Declaration* signaled a shift from toleration however broadly conceived to religious liberty grounded in freedom of conscience. Intrinsic to the idea of toleration was the right of government to establish a church and to compel, if not religious belief, at least religious observance. The *Declaration* destroyed the basis for this coercion by declaring:

> That religion, or the duty which we owe to our Creator, and the manner of discharging it, can be directed only by reason and conviction, not by force and violence; and therefore, all men are equally entitled to the free exercise of religion according to the dictates of conscience; and that it is the mutual duty of all to practice Christian forbearance, love and charity toward the other.[11]

This remarkable document was in many senses the beginning of the intellectual legacy of the Virginia deists. But the issue was not merely one of principle. As a petition from the Presbyterians of Hanover to the Virginia Assembly makes clear, there were financial interests at stake. In October of 1776 the legislators were considering whether the principles of the *Virginia Declaration of Rights* were to be translated into statutory law. Basing their petition on the words of the *Declaration*, the presbyters included a request for relief from taxation to meet the operating expenses of the (Presbyterian) clergy and properties and the purchase of glebes (lands which would yield revenues for the maintenance of churches). But as the last phrase of the petition indicates, the Presbyterians were not quite ready to repudiate all religious taxation: ". . . and exempted from all taxes for the support of any church whatsoever *further than what may be agreeable to their own private choice*, or voluntary obligation."[12] In a time when money was scarce, the population scattered, and regular church-goers a distinct minority, one can understand the hesitancy of the Presbyterians to cut the strings entirely.[13] Nevertheless, a year later the Hanover Presbytery resolved the issue to its own satisfaction, petitioning the legislature to cease all taxation for support of religion.

While they were not totally successful, for all practical purposes the financial aspects of establishment ended in Virginia in the fall of 1776 when the legislature enacted a statute holding that "all dissenters of whatever denomination from the (Anglican) church shall from and after the passing of the Act be totally free and exempt from all levies, taxes and impositions whatever toward supporting and maintaining the said church."[14] In addition, the legislature temporarily suspended the Act for the Support of Clergy, thereby relieving Anglicans as well of existing religious taxation. The suspension was renewed each session until 1779.

The Revolutionary War interrupted further debate, and it was not until 1784 that further advance was made in developing the concepts of religious liberty. Appalled by the social chaos left by the war and by an apparent increase in crime, numerous leaders cast about for way to reknit the social fabric of Virginia. One urgent necessity was considered to be the replacement of the religious and educational functions performed by the now largely discredited and dispirited Anglican clergy. In 1784 no less a person than Patrick Henry introduced into the legislature the *Bill Establishing a Provision for Teachers of the Christian Religion.* According to Henry, the purpose of the bill was to obligate all citizens "to pay a moderate tax or contribution annually for the support of the Christian religion, or of some Christian church, denomination or communion of Christians, or for some form of Christian worship."[15]

In one sense the bill itself represented a substantial advance in the understanding of religious liberty. Surely its purpose as stated in the preamble was a noble one, and could be justified in secular as well as religious terms: "The general diffusion of Christian knowledge hath a natural tendency to correct the morals of men, restrain their vices, and preserve the peace of society; which cannot be effected without a competent provision for licensed teachers."[16] Even more significantly, the bill would have allowed each taxpayer to designate which Christian church would receive his tax support or, if a citizen objected to even that broad discretion, the money could be earmarked "for the encouragement of seminaries of learning within the Counties where such sums shall arise, and to no other use or purpose whatsoever."[17] Finally, the bill did, at least in the opinion of George Washington, allow persons to obtain an exemption by declaring themselves to be "Jews, Mohametans, or otherwise."[18]

But the assessment bill was not to be. In order to rally opposition among the populace, James Madison hurriedly penned one of the classic documents of religious liberty, *The Memorial and Remonstrance Against Religious Assessments*. Once again we witness the movement from a fiscal concern to a far more profound ideological argument. Some have seen the *Memorial* as an attack on religion; it is rather an attack on privilege, coercion and disability based on religious belief—the elements of religious establishment. Madison felt it was important to distinguish political support for religious freedom from financial support for religious practice and education. Because the document is critical to an understanding of later theoretical formulations of the proper relationship of church and government, it merits analysis.

In his first argument Madison asserted that "the religion . . . of every man must be left to the conviction and conscience of every man; and it is the right of every man to exercise it as these may dictate. This right is, in its nature, an unalienable right."[19] Because the right was inalienable, it was prior in order of time and degree of obligation to any claims of civil society, and "in matters of religion no man's right is abridged by the institution of civil society."[20] Madison explicitly put religion as such not only beyond the reach of the majority but also beyond the reach of state legislatures, which might or might not be truly representative of the majority. After stating that not even a small infringement of our liberties could be countenanced, but that the principle itself must be defended, Madison made the crucial linkage between taxes and the broader issue of religious liberty:

Who does not see that the same authority which can establish Christianity in exclusion of all other religions may establish with the same ease, any particular sect of Christians, in exclusion of all other sects? That the same authority that can call for each citizen to contribute three pence only of his property for the support of only one establishment, may force him to conform to any one establishment, in all cases whatsoever?[21]

The linkage is twofold. Madison tied taxation to other forms of coercion. If the principle of taxation for religious purposes was allowed to be established, the same principle would suffice for other forms of coercion. In other words, if the principle of coercion were established, it only remained to determine at what point to draw the line. Madison's first argument was that beyond the point of the principle, there was no uncrossable line. Madison's second argument was that religious liberty is intimately tied to equality:

> The bill violates that equality which ought to be the basis of every law . . . Above all [all men] are to be considered as retaining an equal right to the free exercise of religion, according to the dictates of conscience. While we assert for ourselves a freedom to embrace, to profess, and to observe, the religion which we believe to be of divine origin, we cannot deny an equal freedom to those whose minds have not yet yielded to the evidence which has convinced us . . . As the bill violates equality by subjecting some to peculiar burdens, so it violates the same principle by granting to others peculiar exemptions.[22]

Madison proceeded to reason that religion does not need the support of civil government in any unique way, nor does a just government need the prop of religion. This was, at the time, a radical and daring position for any politician to take. A just government, he wrote, would be best supported . . . by protecting every citizen in the enjoyment of his religion with the same equal hand that protects his person and property; by neither invading the equal rights of any sect, nor suffering any sect to invade those of another.''[23] In one sense this reduction of religion to the level of other natural rights is startling. Did Madison believe religion could be regulated by government just as other natural rights of property and person could be? The answer lies in Madison's understanding of the limited and essentially negative purpose of government— the protection of individual rights. Clearly, natural rights, including religion, can be regulated but not in a manner which will abridge or deny them. Government can regulate natural rights only to protect and promote them equally among citizens. Citizens in a political society give up unlimited but ineffective rights for limited but effective ones.

The *Memorial* was an overwhelming success, stirring tremendous opposition and leading to a sound defeat of the Assessment Bill. Madison and Jefferson quickly took advantage of the victory to bring up Jefferson's *Bill for Establishing Religious Liberty*. Although it had been tabled in 1779 in the face of certain defeat, the mood of Virginia had been so changed by the *Memorial* that the bill became law in 1785. Once again the theoretical tie of religious liberty and taxation to support religious teaching was affirmed. Jefferson urged in the preamble that,

. . . to compel a man to furnish contributions of money for the propagation of opinions which he disbelieves, is sinful and tyrannical; that even forcing him to support this or that teacher of his own religious persuasion, is depriving him of the comfortable liberty of giving his contributions to the particular pastor whose morals he would make his pattern, and whose power he feels most persuasive to righteousness, and is withdrawing from the ministry those temporal rewards, which proceeding from an approbation of their personal conduct, are an additional incitement to earnest and unremitting labors for the instruction of mankind . . .[24]

With the acceptance of Jefferson's *Bill for Establishing Religious Liberty* as binding on all Virginians, the preconstitutional development of a church-government philosophy was ended. The next major development came on a national level with the passage of the Bill of Rights.

In summary, the roots of American church-government theory provide interesting contrasts. The New England experience was far more theological, focused on the nature of covenants and determined to protect the faith covenant from the force of the government. The Virginia experience was humanistic, focused on natural rights, particularly liberty and equality.[25] Yet the similarities are far more striking. In both traditions the growth of new, dissenting religious groups was the catalyst for change. While those who clung to religious establishment in both traditions feared social disintegration without government aid to religion, the dissenters saw taxation as a critically divisive factor. Both paths led from situations of intolerance, coercion, disability, and privilege based on religious belief toward acceptance of diversity, the secular nature of government, and the abolition of taxation to support religious institutions.

THE FOUNDING

It was in the development of the Bill of Rights in 1787 that the New England and Virginia experiences were integrated into a single principle that was to dominate all later discussion of church-government issues in the United States. For that reason the seldom told tale of the development of the First Amendment of the Bill of Rights bears repetition here. There are several other reasons to emphasize this critical period for church-government theory. One is to emphasize that the amendment was not casually accepted, but was rather the result of a long, often agonized debate over proper wording and possible implications. More important, an analysis of the debate will highlight the goals and assumptions of the amendment. First among these was religious liberty. After the linkages established in *The Memorial and Remonstrance*, it was assumed that taxation was a form of coercion and a violation of that liberty. But in addition to liberty were the concerns of maintaining a separation of federal and state issues, that is, federalism, and of ensuring equality of treatment, not only between religions, but between religion and other natural rights.

On June 8, 1787, Madison rose to introduce his long awaited amendments in the House of Representatives:

> The amendments which have occurred to me, proper to be recommended by Congress to the State legislatures, are these. . . . Fourthly, that in article 1st, section 9, between clauses 3 and 4 be inserted these clauses, to wit: The civil rights of none shall be abridged on account of religious belief or worship, nor shall any national religion be established, nor shall the full and equal rights of conscience be in any manner, or in any pretext, infringed . . . Fifthly, that in article 1st, section 10, between clauses 1 and 2 be inserted this clause, to wit: No state shall violate the equal right of conscience . . .[26]

If one is looking into the mind of James Madison on laws and religion and what he hoped to secure in the Bill of Rights, it is reasonable to assume that he expressed it in the proposed amendment. In the first phrase he would forbid any and all disabilities springing from religious belief or worship. In the second he would forbid any national religion from being established. In the third and fourth phrases he would not allow either the national or state governments to create privilege or inequality in dealing with the rights of conscience.

It is clear from his long battle in Virginia that Madison utterly opposed state religious establishments as well as a national one, but in the offered amendments he forbade only national religious establishment while protecting the rights of conscience against state infringement, i.e., the prohibitions were not parallel. Two conclusions may be drawn from this. First, Madison took federalism seriously. He acknowledged two separate jurisdictions and saw that the problems of national and state establishments were two different problems. Bearing in mind that Madison wanted the amendments written into the text, and not appended at the end, this distinction was shown by the placement of phrases one through three and separate placement of phrase four.

Second, one may conclude with equal certainty that Madison's primary concern was religious liberty. His proposal to protect liberty of conscience was broader than his proposal to limit establishment of religion. The probable explanation for this lies in his sense of the politically possible. The Bill of Rights was conceived by its proponents as a limitation on the national government. Madison went beyond this proscription to propose a limitation on the states in the name of liberty of conscience. He walked a narrow path; he was aware that any attempt by the first Congress to propose that the federal government should have the power to forbid state establishment as such would be seized by opponents of the Constitution to win support from those already fearful of the central government's power. Yet he was distrustful of the states, fearing that the liberty secured on the federal level could be destroyed on the state level. Hence he proposed a limitation which, while not forbidding establishment, did forbid its most noxious consequences, coercion and disabilities based on religious beliefs.

On August 15 the House considered the proposed wording of article 1, section 9 as amended: "No religion shall be established by law, nor shall the equal rights of conscience be infringed."[27] What is clear from the debate which followed is that both Madison and the other congressmen were struggling to find the proper balance between protecting religious liberty and prohibiting the harmful consequences of establishment.

Mr. Sylvester of New York indicated that he had some doubts about the propriety of the mode of expression used in the sentence. He felt that it was liable to a construction different from what had been decided in the committee, that is, that it might be thought to have a tendency to abolish religion altogether. In other words, if religion could not be recognized by law (and the difference between recognition and establishment was at this time by no means clear) it could not be protected by law nor have the right to engage in those civil tasks necessary for institutional existence, such as receiving gifts and endowments, buying and selling property, or entering into contracts enforceable in court. Mr. Gerry of Massachusetts believed the amendment would read better if it stated that no religious doctrine should be established by law. Mr. Sherman of Connecticut indicated that the amendment was altogether unnecessary inasmuch as Congress had no delegated authority whatever to make religious establishments. He would strike the amendment altogether. Mr. Carroll of Maryland responded that the rights of conscience were, in their nature, of peculiar delicacy, and would little bear the gentlest touch of a governmental hand, and as many sects had concurred in the opinion that they were not well secured under the present constitution, he was much in favor of adopting the words. He thought it would tend to conciliate the minds of the people to the government more than almost any other amendment he had heard proposed.

Rising to take advantage of Carroll's endorsement, Madison stressed that the amendment meant that Congress could not establish a religion and enforce the legal observation of it by law, nor compel men to worship God in any manner contrary to their consciences. Whether the words were necessary or not he did not say, but they had been required by some of the state conventions which seemed to believe that the clause of the Constitution which gave power to Congress to make all laws enabled them to make such laws as might infringe on the rights of conscience, and to establish a national religion. He presumed the amendment was intended to prevent this and thought it was as well expressed as possible.

Mr. Huntington of Connecticut responded that while he understood the amendment in the same sense as Madison, he feared the words might be taken with such latitude as to hurt the cause of religion. For example, the ministers in many congregations were maintained by the contributions of those who belonged to their societies; the expense of building meetinghouses was met by contributions in the same manner. Both were regulated by the bylaws of the congregations. If an action were brought before a federal court on any of these cases, he feared that the person who had neglected to perform what he had committed himself to could not be compelled to do so, for a support of ministries or building places of worship might be construed as religious establishment.[28] Madison hoped to answer that problem by inserting the word "national" before "religion" in the phrase, but when it was objected that such phrasing might lead people to consider the government to be a national, and not a federal one, he withdrew the proposal.

Unable to come to a final conclusion on section 9, the House, still working as a committee of the whole, turned to the 5th proposition, section 10. Madison moved to insert between the first and second paragraphs the words "no State shall infringe the equal rights of conscience, nor the freedom of speech or of the press, nor of the right of trial by jury in criminal cases." Tucker of South Carolina quickly pointed out that while this was offered as an amendment to the Constitution of the United States, it went only to alter the constitutions of the particular states. He moved to strike the amendment altogether. Madison was not easily dissuaded, however, and argued that this was the most valuable amendment in the whole list. If there were any reason to restrain the government of the United States from infringing upon these essential rights, it was equally necessary that these rights be secured against state governments. He was not able to persuade the House, however, and his cherished amendment was dropped.

The debate continued. Finally on August 20 the House agreed to an amendment which read, "Congress shall make no law establishing religion, or to prevent the free exercise thereof, or to infringe the rights of conscience." The amendment was sent to the Senate, which promptly rejected it in favor of its own version, "Congress shall make no law establishing articles of faith or a mode of worship or prohibiting the free exercise of religion; or abridging the freedom of speech or of the press." This version did not prohibit establishment as such, but only that establishment mandating certain articles of faith, and it dropped the crucial protection of the rights of conscience. By September 21 it was clear that the House and Senate could not agree on wording and a conference committee was named, including Senators Ellsworth (Connecticut), Carroll (Maryland), Paterson (New Jersey), and Representatives Madison (Virginia), Sherman (Connecticut), and Vining (Delaware). It was this committee that hammered out the version of the First Amendment as we now have it, "Congress shall make no law respecting an establishment of religion, or prohibiting the free exercise thereof . . ."[29] As chairperson of the House members in the conference committee Madison was in an ideal position to shape the final draft. Neutralizing the House language by inserting the word "respecting," dropping the final phrase as redundant, and adding the speech and press phrase of the Senate version, he probably wrote the amendment as it now stands. While it did not protect individuals against state establishment, as he would have wished, Madison never voiced later opposition to the wording and apparently judged it capable of sustaining his perception of the proper relationship of religion and government.[30]

Several points must be made about this most important debate. It shows beyond doubt that the New England fear of government interference with religious liberty was as powerful a force as Madison and Jefferson's fear of religious establishment. Included here was a desire to insure that religious *institutions* would have the protections and rights needed to function freely in a civil society. That is, the freedom they wished to protect was broader than simply freedom of conscience for individuals. It shows that federalism, and the right of the states to make their own arrangements for both protecting religious liberty and maintaining or ending religious establishments, was absolutely critical for passage of the amendment.[31] The wording "respecting an establishment of religion" was carefully chosen to ensure that Congress could neither establish a religion nor interfere with state establishments. Financial or economic interests were not at the forefront of this debate, although as Sylvester's comments indicate, they were very definitely present. The tax issue had reached the level of settled principle, at least for the national government, and federalism was the critical issue. Huntington and Sylvester raised the issue of protecting the right of religious institutions in their normal financial dealings. No one disputed this in principle; the only concern was how to provide adequate clarity in the wording of the amendment to insure that protection.

Finally it should be noted that nowhere in the debate was the issue of "aid to religion" raised. That interpretation of the estab-

lishment clause is a later and inaccurate gloss. What "establishment" meant to those who wrote and to those who later ratified
the amendment was coercion, privilege, and disability based on
religious belief or affiliation.[32] This distinction will be important
later when we discuss the neutralist approach to the religion clauses.

THE NATIONAL PERIOD

The authors consider the national period to be that time in
American history between the First Congress's submission of the
Bill of Rights to the states for ratification and the end of World
War II, roughly a century and a half.[33] In the area of church-
government theory this was both a period of consolidation and of
application. To an amazing degree the compromises that resulted in
the First Amendment marked an end to controversy over the basic
structure of church-government relations. Religious controversy
was by no means ended, but its roots were primarily economic and
depended little on the interpretation of the First Amendment.
Indeed, since it was seen as exclusively a limit on federal action and
most controversies were on a state level, the amendment was seldom
invoked. One rather substantial change in the national period is
that the development of theory, thin though it was, passed from the
hands of theologians and statesmen to those of the legal community. It was lawyers and judges working through legal disputes
in the legislatures and courts who developed church-government
theory, a phenomenon that quickened and intensified in the period
since World War II.

As in the colonial period, changes in theory were largely tied to
changes in economic circumstances, that is, in most cases there was
a fiscal connection that was pivotal in the development of the law.
This may be seen in five distinct areas of cases: church property,
polygamy, school aid, hospitals and tax law.[34]

The church property cases began with a rather unique Virginia
case, *Terrett v. Taylor*. The facts have been summarized quite well
by Richard Morgan:

. . .in 1776 the Virginia Legislature had passed an act incorporating all
Episcopal parishes in Virginia and confirming all titles to property then

held. These parishes owned buildings, of course, but also glebes. . . .In 1801, at the end of the process of disestablishment, the Legislature declared its 1776 act null and void, held the Episcopal churches disincorporated, and no longer seized their glebes. The new law directed that these glebes be sold by the overseers of the poor in each county and the proceeds used to help the needy. The justification for this action was that strict separation of church and state, now written into the Virginia Constitution, required it.[35]

Story held that the legislature erred in its interpretation of the Virginia constitution and could not lawfully withdraw the titles to property from the church. Story's reasoning is of particular interest for he argued that religious titles must be held as valid as those of other corporations and voluntary organizations, thus providing an early precedent for what the authors will discuss in chapter 6 as fiscal neutrality.[36]

By far the most common property title disputes to come before the courts during the period arose from the dynamic nature of American Protestantism. As doctrinal disputes erupted and schisms occurred within denominations and even local churches, the inevitable question was: who gets the church property? Almost as inevitably, the question was ultimately answered in the civil courts.[37]

The growth of the law in this area is instructive. The original approach, adopted from English common law, was called the "implied trust" doctrine. It assumed that those who originally donated the property did so on the implied condition that it be used to perpetuate and spread the religious doctrine to which they adhered at the time of the donation. In a schism, one or the other faction adopted a doctrine at variance with that of the donors. When the issue came to court, ran the theory, it would be the duty of the judiciary to determine which of the factions was closest to the original doctrine and which had strayed. The property would go to the former. The difficulties of the "implied trust" for the courts was obvious: the judiciary would find itself studying and judging religious dogma. The decision was based on an assumption which might or might not have been valid, and the court could award large amounts of property to distinct minorities.

A second approach was initiated by the Judicial Court of Massachusetts. In a case involving an Episcopal church in Boston where a majority decided to become Unitarians, the court followed a majority rule rationale and avoided the doctrinal dispute altogether.[38] But this position had its own difficulties. Majoritarianism fit snugly into certain religious beliefs, primarily Congregationalists, Unitarian, and Baptist, but it ran counter to the religious beliefs of hierarchically organized churches such as Presbyterian, Catholic, and Episcopalian. Was one set of religious beliefs to be written into law and another suppressed in relationship to property ownership? A second problem was to determine who could and who could not be considered a church member for purposes of determining a majority. To determine that would again put the courts in the middle of religious policymaking.

A third and for a long time dominant approach appeared when the Court decided *Watson v. Jones* in 1871.[39] A Presbyterian church in Louisville, Kentucky had been split by the Civil War. The majority decided to continue affiliation with the northern-controlled General Assembly, which expelled those members who believed in slavery or had aided in the rebellion until such time as they agreed to "repent and forsake their sins." A minority voted to join a new assembly, the Presbyterian Church of the Confederate States, and seized the church building. In the ensuing court battle the Kentucky Appellate Court upheld the minority on the basis of an implied trust reasoning.

The majority appealed to the federal district court for relief.[40] The Supreme Court upheld the northern faction, rejecting both the "implied trust" and the majority rule principles. Instead, the Court, in an opinion written by Justice Miller, argued that the basic principle was that the internal rules of the religious organization were to govern the disposition of property. The role of the Court was merely to discover the facts (what were the internal rules and how did they determine the power to dispose of property?) and then enforce the decision made. While *Watson* was not a First Amendment case, and therefore not a precedent in that regard, it was important in that it handled religious property just as it did that of any other voluntary organization, that is, by following and enforcing the internal rules of the organization.

The effect of *Watson* was that if a religious organization had a congregational structure, the Court would follow the congregational principle in settling disputes. If the organization had a hierarchical structure, the Court would follow a hierarchical principle. *Gonzales v. Archbishop*[41] reaffirmed that the *Watson* ruling was binding on federal courts, but Justice Brandeis weakened the neutrality by suggesting that civil courts might give marginal review to the decisions of church authorities to determine if there had been "fraud, collusion or arbitrariness." In brief, *Watson* established the rule for a century of religious property disputes. The Court's more recent cases will be discussed in chapter 2.

A second area of church-government dispute in which economics played a significant, if less central and less well known part, was that of polygamy. The Church of the Latter Day Saints was born in the midst of controversy, suffering, and persecution in the 1820s and 1830s. After it had moved to Salt Lake in the Utah territory, Brigham Young in 1852 published Joseph Smith's revelation on plural marriages. Congress, as overseer of the territory, passed a law prohibiting polygamy and providing severe civil penalties. An act of 1884 added economic penalties, and in 1887 Congress finally disincorporated the Mormon Church in Utah and confiscated all property except that used strictly for worship. The Court upheld this action of Congress in *Mormon Church v. United States* and *Romney v. United States.*[42] Writing for the majority, Justice Bradley stated that when a charitable organization unremittedly defied the law of the land, Congress as overseer of the federal territories was well within its powers to take over control of the property and devote it to other charitable purposes.

Chief Justice Fuller dissented, not on religious liberty grounds, but on what he considered an insufficiency of congressional power to take over property. The majority was not persuaded, however. The problem was finally resolved for the Mormons when they reversed their stand on polygamy in 1890. Two things are of note for our purposes. First is the government's use of an economic sanction, successfully as it turned out, to exert enormous pressure on a religiously motivated action, and Justice Bradley's reasoning, which treated religion on a level with other charitable organizations.

The third and most significant issue faced in the national period was the public-private school controversy. Although the issue was not prominent in the courts until after World War II, its roots

reached back as far as the 1840s. In the 1830s free public education
became an objective in most states and many cities. Tax funding
became, if not a commonplace, at least a popular form of support.
The first state board of education was founded in Massachusetts in
1837 under the guidance of Horace Mann. One major problem was
that the so-called public schools were dominated by Protestants
and the education they provided included a large measure of Protestant moralism, to say nothing of anti-Catholic propaganda.[43]

Horace Mann proved to be more enlightened in his educational
objectives than most of his contemporaries, even if his motivation
left something to be desired. As Morgan observes,

> Mann was very fearful of Roman Catholicism and argued that if its
> teaching were to be kept out, Protestant sectarianism must be kept out as
> well. He urged rather, that non-controversial biblical and moral teachings
> be made the basis of instruction. In the transition from private to public
> patterns, however, many of the new governmentally funded schools pre-
> scribed for their students heavy doses of Protestant piety, and even the
> supposedly non-controversial biblical and moral teachings created problems
> for Catholics.[44]

Catholic suspicions that Protestants planned to use the public
schools to convert young Catholics were widespread and not without foundation. The first bruising battle to break into open political
conflict was in New York City. In the late 1830s and early 1840s a
private, Protestant-controlled group, the Public School Society,
was given control of the tax-raised public school fund. The schools
they chose to finance were overtly Protestant in orientation. Many
Catholics refused to send their children and began to build their
own schools at considerable sacrifice, given their low economic
status. In an appeal for Catholic votes, Governor Charles Seward
suggested that Catholic schools might have some claim to public
funds. With the encouragement and under the leadership of Bishop
John Hughes, the New York Catholics began a three-year grass
roots campaign to break the power of the Public School Society
and have Catholic schools included in a new system of publicly
funded schools. The campaign came at the height of a surging
nativist movement and reinforced the worst Protestant fears of a
Catholic power grab. The Catholics won a partial victory insofar as

the Public School Society was replaced by an elected board of education and Protestant proselytising was sharply reduced in the schools. They suffered a defeat in that Catholic schools were adamantly refused a share in available public funds.

After an interlude provided by the Civil War, Catholics renewed their twofold effort to eliminate Protestantism from the public schools and to gain funds of their own. As Professor Higham describes the effort:

About 1869. . .Catholics in many parts of the northeast and midwest opened a campaign to eliminate the Protestant tinge the Bible reading gave to the public schools, to secure for their own parochial schools a share of the funds that the states were providing for education, and to get for Catholic charitable institutions public subsidies comparable to those traditionally awarded to Protestant charities.[45]

Catholic efforts brought a predictable reaction from Protestant groups. Distrustful of legislative politics, they attempted to write into state constitutions absolute prohibitions against funding church-related schools. James G. Blaine (R.–Maine) introduced an amendment in the House of Representatives that would have expanded the religion clauses of the First Amendment to read:

No state shall make any law respecting an establishment of religion or prohibiting the free exercise thereof; and no money raised by taxation in any state for the support of public schools, or derived from any public fund therefore, nor any public lands devoted thereto, shall ever be under the control of any religious sect, nor shall any money so raised or lands so devoted be divided between religious sects or denominations.[46]

The amendment passed the House easily and finally failed narrowly in the Senate.[47] Similar "Blaine Amendments" passed in numerous states and there the matter rested until after World War II, when Catholics shifted tactics and began campaigning for public funding of auxiliary services to parochial schools, and the battle was again joined.

Throughout the national period it was commonly assumed that the First Amendment applied only to the federal government, so while state court cases were abundant, federal court cases were rare.[48]

In *Quick Bear v. Leupp*[49] the Supreme Court upheld the right of
the federal government to use funds held in trust for an Indian
tribe to pay tuition at Catholic mission schools. The Court reasoned
that since the money belonged to the Indians and not the government, the establishment clause was not violated by a contract made
between the mission schools and the federal government at the
request of the Indians. A decade and a half later, in the patriotic
fallout from World War I, came *Meyer v. Nebraska*.[50] Nebraska
outlawed the teaching of foreign languages to children in private,
denominational or parochial schools. Meyer and his codefendants
taught German in Lutheran and Reformed schools and were duly
arrested and convicted. The Supreme Court reversed, reasoning
that the term "liberty" in the 14th Amendment's ban on state
denial of life, liberty, or property without due process of law included the right "to contract, to engage in any of the common
occupations of life, to acquire useful knowledge. . .and generally to
enjoy those privileges long recognized at common law as essential
to the orderly pursuit of happiness by free men."[51] In other words,
the issue was decided on the due process claim of the 14th Amendment and on the defendant's right to earn a living. Two years later
in *Pierce v. Society of Sisters*[52] the Court struck down an Oregon
statute requiring all parents to send their children between the ages
of eight and sixteen to public schools. This case too was decided on
the basis of the due process clause of the Fourteenth Amendment.
Justice McReynolds wrote for the Court that ". . .enforcement of
the statute would seriously impair, perhaps destroy, the profitable
features of appellee's business and greatly diminish the value of
their property."[53] Five years later the court addressed a somewhat
different issue in *Cochran v. Louisiana State Board of Education*.[54]
Louisiana passed a statute providing secular textbooks for use by
all schoolchildren, including those in church-related schools. The
appellants sued on the grounds that the Fourteenth Amendment
forbade states to deprive any person of property without due
process of law, and that providing textbooks for private school
students was a tax for a private rather than a public purpose and
therefore a collection of taxpayers' money without due process.
The Court gave short shrift to this contention, ruling that the
benefits did not go to any schools, but rather to all the children of

the state and consequently to the state. The private schools received nothing from the appropriations nor were they relieved of a single obligation. Therefore the taxing power of the state had been used for a public, not a private purpose, and the Fourteenth Amendment due process clause had not been violated.

The school aid question would reappear with a vengeance, as we shall see in chapter 2, but during the national period it appeared in the federal courts infrequently. The one thing each of the federal cases had in common was an issue and a holding that turned on an economic concern, whether taxes, spending, or simply a property right.

What was most significant during this period was the change in popular perceptions of the school issue. The public versus private school debate became a symbolic battleground. Protestant desires to proselytize the new immigrants and their fears of growing Catholic power clashed with Catholic fears of "losing the faith" and their hunger for economic, social, and political equality. What had begun with Catholic and Protestant leaders arrayed on both sides of the issue hardened through years of sermons, newspaper tracts, and political battles into sectarian cleavage. Rooted in bigotry, the issue rose to a struggle over constitutional principle.

Two areas remarkable for the lack of litigation and public dispute during the national period are those of hospitals and other service facilities built and operated under the auspices of religious groups, and the area of tax exemption of religious property. The former is striking because the national period witnessed a phenomenal growth in religious hospitals across the nation, particularly after the Civil War. The one significant case was *Bradfield v. Roberts*, decided in 1899.[55] In order to understand its significance it is helpful to go back to an incident during Madison's presidency. In 1811 Congress passed a bill incorporating the Episcopal Church of Alexandria into the District of Columbia and authorized it to provide for the support of the poor and the education of poor children. Madison vetoed the bill and in his subsequent message to Congress reasoned that aside from giving legal force and sanction to certain articles of the church's constitution and administration, "the bill would be a precedent for giving to religious societies as such a legal agency in carrying into effect a public and civil duty."[56]

Bradford presented a somewhat similar issue to the Court. In a general appropriation bill for the District of Columbia, Congress included $30,000 to build two hospital units for the care of indigents. One of the units was to be an addition to a Catholic hospital run by the Sisters of Providence and would be administered by the hospital. A District taxpayer sued to void the construction contract, alleging that this was an appropriation of federal funds for the use and support of a religious society and contrary to the First Amendment. It was also, he continued, echoing Madison, a dangerous precedent in that it gave to a religious society a legal agency for performing a public and civil duty. In a unanimous decision the Court, voting that the hospital was incorporated by an act of Congress, rejected Bradfield's allegations in a decision worth quoting at some length:

. . . Assuming that the hospital is a private eleemosynary corporation, the fact that its members . . . are members of a monastic order or sisterhood of the Roman Catholic Church, and the further fact that the hospital is conducted under the auspices of said church, are wholly immaterial, as is also the allegation regarding the title to its property. . . . The facts . . . do not in the least change the legal character of the hospital, or make a religious corporation out of a purely secular one as constituted by the law of its being. Whether the individuals who compose the corporation under its charter happen to be all Roman Catholics, or all Methodists, or Presbyterians, or Unitarians, or members of any other religious organization, or of no organization at all, is of not the slightest consequence with reference to the law of its incorporation, nor can the individual beliefs upon religious matters of the various incorporators be inquired into . . .[the hospital] must . . . be managed pursuant to the law of its being. That the influence of any particular church may be powerful over the members of a non-sectarian and secular corporation, incorporated for a certain defined purpose and with clearly stated powers, it surely not sufficient to convert such a corporation into a religious or sectarian body. That fact does not alter the legal character of the corporation, which is incorporated under an Act of Congress, and its powers, duties and character are to be solely measured by the charter under which it alone has any legal existence.

. . . It is simply the case of a secular corporation being managed by people who hold to the doctrines of the Roman Catholic Church, but who nevertheless are managing the corporation according to the law under which it exists.[57]

The Court, in brief, made the rather startling and, in the authors' opinion, perceptive argument that although the hospital was owned and operated exclusively by Catholic sisters, it was incorporated just as any other private eleemosynary organization was, and in that respect should be considered as a purely secular corporation. The Court's approach was quite the opposite of Madison's and yet not incompatible. The appropriations bill did not give to religious societies *as such* a legal agency to carry out a civil duty. Rather, it treated a religious society as part of a broader, nonreligious class-ification—private eleemosynary organization—and found no impediments to government contracting with such a group for a purely secular purpose. *Bradfield v. Roberts* has never been over-ruled and forms the constitutional precedent for later federal aid to all, including religious, hospitals under the Hospital Survey and Construction Act of 1946, more commonly known as the Hill-Burton Act.

The final area to be considered in the national period is that of tax exemption granted to religious organizations.[58] To understand its development we must go back to the English Statute of Chari-table Uses of 1601, which is the beginning of the modern law on charity. For many centuries prior to this, of course, the church had encouraged and often controlled donations for "corporal and spiritual works of mercy." The purpose of the English Statute was twofold: to give some specificity to what would or would not be considered "charitable," and to reform the administration of charity. Two aspects of the statute are of note here. The first is that it is decidedly secular. Churches are mentioned, but only as part of a long list of recipients; they are in no way singled out for special privileges. As later controversy was to show, Parliament, while not wishing to burden religious giving, was deeply concerned with the accumulation of land and other wealth by religious groups, and therefore wished to maintain control over that possible effect of charitable giving. The second aspect is that state action and private giving were seen as complementary, not competitive, means to meet societal needs. While from time to time American leaders also fretted about the possible accumulation of "clerical" wealth,[59] their emphasis on the whole was on the cooperative aspects of philanthropy:

The colonists who settled America brought with them the English legal and social tradition of an active private philanthropy. This tradition, coupled with the needs of the colonists and the encouragement of charitable activity by the colonial churches, created an environment favorable to the formation of charitable organizations designed to meet the needs for social services within the primitive frontier society.[60]

As one commentator has pointed out, distinguishing the areas of public and private philantropic responsibility was not a burning issue for the colonists. The two were intertwined, and the laws regulating them reflected more pragmatism than ideology.

Colonial assemblies went out of their way to remove obstacles in the way of charities. The courts, valuing social betterment about legal technicalities, asserted a permissive charity doctrine that supported donors' benevolent intentions, even when the formulation of their plans was clearly imperfect.[61]

As a result of this general attitude of encouragement and legal indifference, religious, educational, and other charitable institutions were usually granted total exemption from property and other forms of taxation. As noted earlier, concern among the colonists was to stop taxation for religious purposes; they seldom addressed the issue of taxing religion for governmental purposes. Established churches were exempted on the same basis as other public property and as establishment gave way to toleration, dissenting churches were given the same exemption. Following the move from toleration to full religious liberty, the policy of exemptions continued, being "so entirely in accordance with public sentiment that it universally prevailed."[62]

After the forming of the union, the individual states and localities upon whom fell the burden of providing for the poor, sick, elderly, orphans, and others, continued to exempt from state and local taxes the religious and charitable institutions. The process was more the practical implementation of an assumption—charitable institutions perform valuable public services and so should not be burdened—than a consciously debated and chosen policy. As as result, during the national period every state in the union provided some form of property tax relief. Many also provided relief from inheritance, sales, and income taxes, although there were great inconsistencies between, and even within, states.

Exemptions from federal taxation are of much more recent origin and far easier to trace. Until well after the midpoint of the nineteenth century, federal revenues came primarily from import duties and excise taxes and so the question of charitable exemptions did not arise. The first federal income taxes were emergency measures adopted during the Civil War and were, from the very beginning, aimed at specific classes of business "such as railroads, canal companies, and banks."[63] The first comprehensive federal income tax law was passed in 1894. It is important to note that while the tax was levied on the income and profits of corporations in general, the framers of the law explicitly exempted certain classes of corporation, stating

[t]hat nothing herein contained shall apply to . . . corporations, companies, or associations organized and conducted solely for charitable, religious or educational purposes, . . . nor to the stocks, shares, funds, or securities held by any fiduciary or trustee for charitable, religious, or educational purposes. . . .[64]

While the 1894 Revenue Act was declared unconstitutional a year later, the Sixteenth Amendment to the U.S. Constitution was passed in 1913 and an income tax was reimposed almost immediately. The new law again included an exemption, this time broadened to include scientific organizations. The further development of federal tax law during the national period was primarily a matter of broadening coverage.[65] In the expansion of federal taxation there is a consistent pattern of establishing a general taxable category and either immediately or shortly thereafter providing an exemption or deduction for charitable, religious, and educational organizations.[66]

CONCLUSION

Chapter 1 has provided an overview of the development of public policy in the area of church-government relations during the formative and national periods as well as the development of the most influential church-government theory by legislators and justices as they confronted problems in the areas of church property, education, polygamy, hospitals, and taxation. We have shown that in each area there was a substantial economic interest and that developments in theory reflected economic developments or understandings current at the time. With the exception of polygamy, where the rather highhanded confiscation of property was used as a political weapon to change a religious practice, and education in religious schools, there has developed a remarkable strong and consistent tradition of fiscal neutrality in which religious organizations have been treated like similarly situated charitable and educational institutions. The notable exception was the school question. This tradition has not been adequately developed or followed in the post-World War II period, particularly by the courts. The result has been a growth of bad law, bad economics, and bad information.

NOTES

1. Mark DeWolfe Howe, *The Garden and the Wilderness* (Chicago: University of Chicago Press, 1965).

2. *The Writings of Thomas Jefferson*, ed. Andrew A. Lipscomb, Thomas Jefferson Memorial Association of the United States (1903), vol. 16, pp. 281-82.

3. Joseph L. Blau, ed., *Cornerstones of Religious Freedom in America* (Boston: The Beacon Press, 1949), p. 32.

4. Leo Pfeffer, *Church, State and Freedom*, 2d ed. (Boston: Beacon Press, 1967), p. 89.

5. Elwyn A. Smith, *Religious Liberty in United States* (Philadelphia: Fortress Press, 1972), p. 8.

6. Ibid.

7. The best example is the Massachusetts Constitution of 1780. See Ronald M. Peters, Jr., *The Massachusetts Constitution of 1780* (Amherst: University of Mass. Press, 1978). See also Charles H. Lippy, "The 1780 Massachusetts Constitution: Religious Establishment or Civil Religion," *Journal of Church and State* 20 (Autumn 1978): 533.

8. Isaac Backus, *A History of New England, With Particular Reference to the Denomination of Christians Called Baptists*, vols. 1-3 (Boston: n.p., 1777), vol. 2. As cited in Smith, *Religious Liberty in United States*, p. 15.

9. As quoted in Edward F. Humphrey, *Nationalism and Religion in America, 1774-1789* (Boston: Chipman Law Publishing Co., 1924), p. 363.

10. Smith, *Religious Liberty in United States*, p. 33.

11. Irving Brant, "Madison on the Separation of Church and State," *William and Mary Quarterly*, 3rd ser. 8 (January 1951): 16.

12. As quoted in W. H. Foote, *Sketches of Virginia, Historical and Biographical* (Philadelphia: n.p., 1850), p. 323. Emphasis added. It might also be noted that the Presbyterians had a tradition of establishment in Scotland. This may explain some of their caution.

13. Voluntary financing was easy only for the Baptists who at this time had no salaried clergy at all, and no tradition of establishment anywhere.

14. Julian P. Boyd, ed., *The Papers of Thomas Jefferson*, vol. 1 (Princeton: Princeton University Press, 1950-), p. 334.

15. N. J. Eckenrode, *The Separation of Church and State in Virginia* (Richmond: Virginia State Library, 1910), p. 86.

16. Ibid.

17. Ibid.

18. Anson Phelps Stokes, *Church and State in United States*, vol. 1 (New York: Harper & Row, 1950), p. 390.

19. Marvin Meyers, ed., *Mind of the Founder: Sources of the Political Thought of James Madison* (New York: Bobbs-Merrill, 1973), p. 9.

20. Ibid.

21. Ibid.

22. Ibid., p. 10-11.

23. Ibid.

24. Blau, *Cornerstones of Religious Freedom*, p. 77.

25. The middle colonies such as Pennsylvania and Maryland tended to mix religious principle with economic interest. Perhaps due to this practical bent they produced very little theory.

26. *Annals of Congress* I: 450-52.

27. Ibid., p. 757. The following paragraphs summarize the proceedings of the Congress on this topic.

28. Professor Berns interprets this as a fear that the amendment would "forbid state laws requiring contributions in support of ministers of religion and places of worship." Walter Berns, "Religion and the Founding Principle," in *The Moral Foundations of the American Republic*, ed. Robert H. Horwitz (Charlottesville: University Press of Virginia, 1977), p. 161. We respectfully disagree. The "bylaws" refer to the laws of individual congregations and not to state laws. What Huntington feared was that contracts, simply because they were made with a religious body, might not be enforceable in a civil court. That is, he feared an extreme form of separation.

29. It is informative to note that on the same day the Senate concurred on the amendments, a significant exchange took place in the House. Doudinot of New Jersey announced that "he could not think of letting the session pass over without offering an opportunity to all the citizens of the United States of joining . . . in returning to Almighty God their sincere thanks for the many blessings he had poured down upon them." He then moved that both houses request the president to recommend a day of public thanksgiving and prayers, to be observed by "acknowledging . . . the many signal favors of Almighty God." Tucker of South Carolina suggested wryly that the people might not be quite that grateful for the new constitution, at least not until they found it promoted their safety and happiness. But, he added, "whether this be so or not, it is a business with which Congress has nothing to do; it is a religious matter, and as such proscribed to us." Sherman, who had just returned from the conference committee, justified the practice as laudable, and the motion passed the House. *Annals of Congress*, vol. I, p. 914f.

30. See the argument of Brant, "Madison on Separation," p. 16. In light of the evidence there seems little ground for the late Professor Corwin's statement that

Madison "was not the author of the amendment in the form in which it was proposed to the state legislature for ratification." Edward Corwin, "Supreme Court as National School Board," *Law and Contemporary Problems* 14 (Winter 1949): 13.

31. For an interesting account of the ideological and political tensions surrounding the framing of the Bill of Rights, and particularly article 6, section 3 (no religious test as a qualification for public office), see Morton Borden, "Federalists, Antifederalists, and Religious Freedom," *Journal of Church and State* 21 (1979): 469.

32. The title of the subsection calls for some explanation, since few historians would sweep this roughly one hundred fifty-year period under one caption. This period of history saw the consolidation of national power, the enormous growth and expansion of religious institutions, and the establishment of certain principles in church-government relations. There were however, no significant "breakthroughs" or "turning points" until after World War II. Therefore we judge it appropriate to treat this extended time period as a single era.

33. Property cases do not normally involve the allocation of public money. We include them, however, because they illustrate the role of property disputes in the development of law and provide the rudiments of a fiscal neutrality type analysis.

34. 9 Cranch 43 (1815).

35. Richard Morgan, *Supreme Court and Religion* (New York, The Free Press, 1972), p. 37. Emphasis in the original.

36. In his later years Justice Story adopted a far more accommodationist interpretation of the First Amendment. See Joseph Story, *Commentaries on the Constitution*, vol. 3 (Boston: Hilliard, Gray and Co., 1833).

37. There are no hard figures available, since most cases were resolved in state courts. Morgan states that in New England alone the Unitarian break from Congregationalism disrupted hundreds of churches between 1800 and 1830. Ibid., p. 32. The author of a note on the subject estimated that as late as 1962 there were still roughly 25 church-property dispute cases a year in the courts. Note "Church Property Disputes," *Harvard Law Review* 75 (1962): 1142.

38. *Rector of King's Chapel v. Pelham*, 9 Mass. 501 (1813).

39. 13 Wallace 679 (1871).

40. Since some members lived in Indiana, they successfully argued federal jurisdiction on the basis of a disparity of citizenship.

41. 280 U.S. 1 (1929).

42. Decided together at 132 U.S. 1 (1889). The more widely known cases are *Reynolds v. United States*, 98 U.S. 145 (1878) and *Davis v. Beason*, 133 U.S. 33 (1889). The issues in these cases were religious liberty claims and not property.

43. This is hardly surprising, granted the upsurge of nativism at the time. For a fascinating account of the period, see John Higham, *Strangers in the Land* (New Brunswick, New Jersey: Rutgers University Press, 1955).

44. Morgan, *Supreme Court and Religion*, pp. 48-49.

45. Higham, *Strangers in the Land*, p. 28.

46. Quoted in Stokes, *Church and State in United States*, vol. 2, p. 723.

47. The meaning of the failure of the Blaine Amendment is a matter of some dispute. Professor Morgan opines that the failure was due in part to the belief of at

least a few senators that the Establishment Clause already prohibited aid to church-related schools. See Morgan, *Supreme Court and Religion*, p. 55. Senator Moynihan argues the contrary interpretation, that opponents of aid "were clear that the Constitution would have to be amended to [make aid unconstitutional]." Daniel Patrick Moynihan, "Government and the Ruin of Private Education," *Harper's*, April 1978, p. 33.

48. It is of historical interest to note than many of the early state cases were brought by Catholic parents to stop Protestant proselytizing in the public schools. See *Ring v. Board of Education*, 245 Ill. 334, 92 N.E. 251 (1910); *Harold v. Parish Board of School Directors*, 136 La. 1034, 68 S.W. 116 (1915); *Weise v. District Board*, 76 Wis. 177, 44 N.W. 967 (1890); *Freeman v. Scheue*, 65 Neb. 853, 91 N.W. 846 (1902); *Finger v. Weedman*, 55 S.D. 343, 226 N.W. 348 (1929).

49. 210 U.S. 50 (1908).

50. 262 U.S. 390 (1923).

51. Ibid., p. 400.

52. 268 U.S. 510 (1925).

53. Ibid., p. 512.

54. 281 U.S. 370 (1930).

55. 175 U.S. 291 (1899).

56. *Annals of Congress* 22: 983.

57. 175 U.S. 291 at 293.

58. For much of the following material the authors are indebted to the *Research Papers* sponsored by the Commission on Private Philanthropy and Public Needs, vol. 4: *Taxes* (Washington, D.C.: Department of the Treasury, 1977). Hereinafter referred to as *Research Papers*.

59. Madison, in his twilight years, wrote an essay, "Monopolies, Perpetuities, Corporations and Ecclesiastical Endowments" in which he voiced the fear of "the silent accumulation and encroachments by Ecclesiastical Bodies. . . ." In Elizabeth Fleet, "Madison's Detached Memoranda," *William and Mary Quarterly*, 3d ser. 3 (1946): 551-562. Both Virginia and Maryland passed acts restricting the right of churches to acquire property. Kentucky utilized a mortmain statute to achieve the same end. See Howard S. Miller, *The Legal Foundation of American Philanthropy 1776-1844* (Madison: The State Historical Society of Wisconsin, 1961), p. 8. Also, Acts of 1805-1806, ch. 74 in Code of Virginia (1949), ch. 77, Sec. VIII, 362; Maryland Constitution 1776, Declaration of Rights, Act 34; Paul J. Weber and Janèt R. Olson, "Religious Property Tax Exemptions in Kentucky," *Kentucky Law Journal* 66, no. 3 (1978): 651.

60. *Research Papers*, p. 1920.

61. Howard S. Miller, *The Legal Foundations of American Philanthropy 1776-1844* (Madison, Wisconsin: The State Historical Society of Wisconsin, 1961), p. xi.

62. *State v. Collector of Jersey City*, 24 N.J.L. 108 at 120 (1853).

63. *Research Papers*, p. 1993, n. 110.

64. Revenue Act of 1894, ch. 349, #32, 28 Stat. 556 (1894).

65. "The phrase 'or the prevention of cruelty to children or animals' and the word 'literary' were added to the list of exempt purposes in 1918 and 1921, respectively,

and the phrase 'testing for public safety' was added in 1954.'' *Research Papers*, p. 1924-25.

66. For example, in 1898 a tax was placed on legacies, and the exemptions came in 1901. In 1913 the income tax amendment was ratified and in 1917 a deduction was allowed for contributions to charitable, religious, and educational organizations; in 1916 a tax was placed on estates and in 1917 a deduction was allowed for charitable, religious, and educational bequests; in 1926 a federal gift tax law was passed which included a tax deduction for gifts to the charitable, religious, and educational organizations.

2

CASE LAW CONFUSION

After World War II a whole new era began across the broad domain of civil liberties. Roughly a decade after the near disaster of President Roosevelt's court packing plan, the Supreme Court justices turned their attention away from economic regulations and toward the protection and expansion of individual rights. It was also an era of rapid government expansion at all levels. Both federal and state governments began far more liberal policies of funding and regulating a wider range of institutions and activities than ever before in American history. In a number of states, legislators began to respond to constituent efforts to obtain funding for private schools. Opponents of such aid took to the courts, claiming violation of their rights under the Establishment Clause of the First Amendment. Thus, the Supreme Court became the primary architect of church-government constitutional theory. Separationist and accommodationist approaches were intermingled, but never quite successfully.

During this period other church-government problems arose or returned as well: religious property tax exemptions, religious property ownership, charitable tax deductions, and employment in religious institutions. While the Court has not yet developed a single, consistent underlying theory of the religious clauses of the First Amendment (and has made a number of false starts) it has laid a relatively solid foundation in non-school aid questions. Whether the Court will be able to build further remains to be seen. This chapter focuses on case law since World War II, drawing attention to the strengths and weaknesses of the Court's work, emphasizing in particular the foundations it has developed for a theory of fiscal neutrality.[1]

AID TO EDUCATION

It may be ironic that contemporary case law began with that problem on which the least consensus was reached during the national period: aid to private education. The precedent-setting case was *Everson v. Board of Education.*[2] *Everson* assured later controversy when Mr. Justice Black utilized the language of strict separation—no aid to *uphold* busing for parochial school children:

The "establishment of religion" clause of the First Amendment means at least this: Neither a state nor the Federal Government can set up a church. Neither can pass laws which aid one religion, aid all religions, or prefer one religion over another. . . .No tax in any amount, large or small, can be levied to support any religious activities or institutions, whatever they may be called, or whatever form they may adopt to teach or practice religion.[3]

Despite Mr. Justice Black's protestation that busing went to the "verge" of constitutionality, the precedent was set so that in future cases the issue would be both where to draw the line and how to draw it. Mr. Justice Black defended bus transportation on two grounds: it was public welfare legislation and it was peripheral to the private education involved.

The issue of aid to parochial school children came before the Court a second time in *Board of Education v. Allen.*[4] New York had legislated a program whereby state-approved secular textbooks were loaned to all secondary school children. According to the statute, all books would be processed through local public school districts, but for children who attended private schools, the books would then be distributed by their respective schools and returned there for storage. Mr. Justice White, writing for a majority of six, held that the program did not violate the establishment clause. Applying the test developed in *Abington School District v. Schempp,*[5] he found that the New York law, like the New Jersey law in Everson, had a "secular legislative purpose and a primary effect that neither advances nor inhibits religion."[6] The law's purpose was furtherance of the educational opportunites available to the young. Appellants have shown us nothing about the necessary effects of the statute that is contrary to its stated purpose. . . .Thus, no funds or books are furnished to parochial schools, and the financial benefit is to parents and children, not to schools. Perhaps free books make it more likely that some children choose to attend a sectarian school, but that was true of the state-paid bus fares in Everson. . . .[7]

Mr. Justice White made two distinctions between the secular and religious aspects of education. Concerning the selection of textbooks he observed that "absent evidence, we cannot assume that school authorities, who constantly face the same problem in selecting textbooks for use in public schools, are unable to distinguish between secular and religious books, or that they will not honestly discharge their duties under the law."[8]

Secondly, responding to the appellant's contention that free textbooks must be distinguished from free bus fares because the former are critical to the teaching process, "and in a sectarian school that process is employed to teach religion,"[9] he pointed out that "this Court has long recognized that religious schools pursue two goals, religious instruction and secular education."[10] Mr. Justice White, in short, developed two new tests, the child benefit and the secular-sectarian test, as an alternative to Mr. Justice Black's central-peripheral test.

Mr. Justice Harlan's concurrence emphasized that the law does not employ religion as its standard for action or inaction, and does not involve the state "so significantly and directly in the realm of the sectarian as to give rise to . . . divisive influences and inhibitions of freedom."[11]

Two separate dissents were filed. Mr. Justice Black rejected the majority view that his *Everson* decision was being followed. He argued that bus fares provide a general and nondiscriminatory transportation service in no way related to substantive religious views and beliefs, whereas a state's furnishing of books "actively and directly assists the teaching and propagation of sectarian religious viewpoints."[12]

Mr. Justice Douglas' dissent reflected a profound suspicion of educators in religiously attached schools: "Can there be the slightest doubt that the head of the parochial school will select the book or books that best promote its sectarian creed?"[13] He then made two somewhat startling assertions. First, he stated that the textbook goes to the very heart of education in a parochial school and that "there is no reliable standard by which secular and religious textbooks can be distinguished from each other."[14] Second, he stated that "the result of tying parochial school textbooks to public funds would be to put nonsectarian books into religious schools, which in the long view would tend towards state domination of the church."[15]

The dissenting opinions point out a major difference between approaches to the problem. Mr. Justice White and the majority accepted a secular/sectarian distinction within the private schools, whereas the two dissents insisted on a peripheral/central-to-education distinction. Unfortunately, the rationales for each position were not clearly reasoned in the case. Another weakness of Justice White's majority opinion in *Allen* was that it did not clearly indicate the *limits* of his individual benefit test, or of the secular purpose and primary effect tests. The lines began to be drawn in several 1971 cases, two of which involved statutes enacted in Pennsylvania and Rhode Island.

In *Lemon v. Kurtzman*,[16] Mr. Chief Justice Burger had a chance to expand upon a test of excessive entanglement which he had developed a year earlier.[17] Rhode Island had enacted a Salary Supplement Act for teachers of secular subjects in nonpublic elementary schools. The Act included numerous conditions and restraints, including a written statement by any teacher applying for the supplement that he or she would not teach a course in religion during such time as he or she was receiving the supplement.

In the Pennsylvania case, a 1968 education act provided for direct reimbursement to nonpublic schools "solely for their actual expenditures for teachers salaries, textbooks and instructional materials."[18] According to the provisions of the statute, a school seeking reimbursement had to maintain prescribed accounting procedures that identified the separate cost of secular educational services. Its accounts were to be subject to state audit, and reimbursement limited to courses in mathematics, modern foreign languages, physical science, and physical education. Both the Rhode Island and the Pennsylvania legislatures had depended heavily on the *Allen* decision and carefully separated aid for secular services from the religious services in church-related schools. But the legislators failed to recognize the significance of Mr. Chief Justice Burger's non-entanglement test. He concluded that "the cumulative impact of the entire relationship arising under the statutes in each State involves excessive entanglement between government and religion."[19]

Mr. Chief Justice Burger's opinion hammers on the inadequacies of the *Allen* argument. Mr. Justice White reasoned in *Allen* that secular and religious aspects of education in parochial schools must be strictly separated for the schools to qualify for aid. But, said the Chief Justice, because of the religious character and purpose of the Roman Catholic elementary schools and the inescapable fact that parochial schools constitute an integral part of the religious mission of the Catholic Church, there is a grave potential that "a dedicated religious person, teaching in a school affiliated with his or her faith and operated to inculcate its tenets, will inevitably . . . find it hard to make a total separation between secular teaching and religious doctrine."[20]

In order to avoid that potential violation of the establishment clause, a comprehensive, discriminating, and continuing state surveillance would inevitably be required. And, concluded the Chief Justice, "[u]nlike a book, a teacher cannot be inspected once so as to determine the extent and intent of his or her personal beliefs and subjective acceptance of the limitations imposed by the First Amendment. These prophylactic contacts will involve excessive and enduring entanglement between state and church."[21]

Mr. Justice White, not surprisingly, protested this addition to his religious-secular distinction.

> The Court thus creates an insoluable paradox for the State and the parochial schools. The State cannot finance secular instruction if it permits religion to be taught in the same classroom; but if it exacts a promise that religion not be so taught—a promise the school and its teacher are quite willing, and on this record, able to give—and enforces it, it is then entangled in the Court's Establishment Clause jurisprudence.[22]

In a companion case decided on the same day, *Tilton v. Richardson*,[23] Mr. Chief Justice Burger again announced the judgment of the Court. This time, however, the facts and outcome were different. At issue was a federal program providing construction grants for buildings and facilities at church-affiliated universities and colleges used exclusively for secular educational purposes.[24] Again he rested his holding on the cumulative impact of the grant program. But this time the record showed that on college and university campuses the religious and secular educational functions are in fact separable. Indeed, observed the Chief Justice, "the parties stipulated in the District Court that courses at these institutions are taught according to the academic requirements intrinsic to the subject matter and the individual teacher's concept of professional standards."[25]

Since in the *Lemon* case another district court had made a similar finding on the elementary and secondary school level which the Chief Justice had found insufficient, the distinction loses much of its persuasiveness.[26] Was the Chief Justice stating a lesser regard for or trust in the professionalism of elementary school teachers? Or was he denying that in lower grades courses will be taught "according to the academic requirements intrinsic to the subject matter"? It is only when he turned to a consideration of entanglement that one finds a more plausible foundation. College students, it seems, are less susceptible to religious indoctrination; college courses tend to limit the opportunities for sectarian influences, and colleges and universities are characterized by a high degree of academic freedom.

Aid to higher and lower education in church-related institutions, apparently, does not depend on a school's ability to perform secular services well. Rather, it depends on a religious test. Institutions of higher learning are assumed to distinguish, or are allowed to prove that they distinguish, secular courses from religious courses, and assumed to teach the former according to professional standards. Elementary and secondary schools, however, are assumed to be incapable of such separation and are not given an opportunity to prove otherwise.[27]

Finally, the Chief Justice continued in *Tilton*, government entanglements with religion in this case were minimal because "unlike the direct and continuing payments under the Pennsylvania program, and all the incidents of regulation and surveillance, the Government aid here is a one-time, single-purpose construction grant."[28] In short, substantial brick and mortar facilities (libraries, language laboratories, science buildings, and a fine arts complex) given directly to church-related institutions of higher education to not infringe on the Establishment Clause, but salary supplements to teachers of secular subjects and physical materials given to teach secular subjects on the elementary and secondary level do.

The distinction was too much for Messrs. Justices Douglas, Black, and Marshall, who said, "The public purpose in secular education is, to be sure, furthered by the program. Yet the secular purpose is aided by making the parochial school system viable."[29] This twist of the nonestablishment doctrine did not satisfy more objective critics either. Not only is there a double standard for lower and higher education, but there is a double standard for church-related institutions and secular recipients of government grants. As Donald Giannella observes:

The question still remains whether religiously neutral periodic auditing in and of itself constitutes excessive entanglement. In *Walz* the Court eschewed the administrative entanglements of tax valuation of church property, tax liens, and tax foreclosures, *none of which requires differentiating the religious from the secular*. In distinguishing the post-construction audits required by the Higher Education Facilities Act, the Chief Justice in *Tilton* relied only in part on the fact that no segregation would have to be made between secular and religious expenditures. He referred also to the absence of continuing financial relationships and annual audits. Nonetheless, it is difficult to believe that the periodic auditing requirement is crucial. If so, it would lead to anomalous results. Although the state could subsidize the construction of a new hospital wing or college facility for a religiously affiliated institution, it could not finance continuing health programs for indigents or an experimental education program carried on within a subsidized building.[30]

"In addition," Giannella adds, in obvious reference to the political divisiveness argument, "any confrontation or conflicts that might arise from auditing would be of the kind and order as those involving secular recipients of state subsidies."[31] The test of entanglement is unsatisfactory in other respects as well. Initially, its implications are unclear, and secondly, the Court admitted in *Walz* that entanglement is a matter of degree.[32] The uncertainty of the test may well lead to increased confrontations and the suspicion of arbitrariness or even prejudice on the part of the justices.

Finally, the need for surveillance raises several questions. Why, in the teaching of secular subjects, or by the use of secular materials, must religiously affiliated schools be subjected to a different standard of surveillance from public schools? One reason some parents choose religiously affiliated schools is their fear that public school teachers impose a "religion of secularism."[33] Granted that the legislation is for a clearly secular purpose, and as in *Lemon*, recipients of aid agree *not* to teach religion, should not the same standard of surveillance be applicable to both public and religiously affiliated schools? The Chief Justice notwithstanding, a double standard of surveillance does not indicate an assumption of bad faith and most assuredly poses an equal protection question. Further, a possible "potential hazard" differs from an actual violation of the Constitution. Speaking later in *Roemer v. Board of Public Works*,[34] Mr. Justice Blackmun wrote that "[i]t has not been the Court's practice, in considering facial challenges to statutes of this kind, to strike them down in anticipation that particular applications may result in unconstitutional use of funds."[35] Yet it seems that this is precisely what the Court did in *Lemon*.

Most critical to the Court's divergent holdings in *Lemon* and *Tilton* is the distinction between elementary and secondary schools on the one hand, and colleges and universities on the other. The reasoning was based again on a religious test and drew a line that did not accurately reflect the problem. Giannella comments that:

> The Court's point is probably well taken that religion is more central to the activities of parochial schools than to those of most church-related colleges. But it is highly questionable to conclude that the risk of sectarian instruction creeping into a parochial school's physics course is greater than the risk of a similar entry into a college history course. One must look to the nature of the aid as well as the nature of the recipient in evaluating the need for surveillance.[36]

Indeed, commenting on a later case decided on the basis of *Tilton*,[37] one Court critic points out that the aided Baptist college had *more* required religious courses and stricter chapel attendance requirements than most Catholic grammar schools.[38]

The seeds of the *Lemon-Tilton* distinctions were not long in bearing fruit. In 1973 the Court decided *Committee for Public Education and Religious Liberty v. Nyquist*.[39] The state of New York provided financial assistance in several ways to nonpublic schools serving a high concentration of pupils from low-income families. Among other restrictions, the grants could not exceed forty dollars per pupil nor fifty percent of comparable expenses in the public school system. Mr. Justice Powell, writing for the Court, struck down a portion of the statute, holding that:

> No attempt is made to restrict payments to those expenditures related to the upkeep of facilities used exclusively for secular purposes, nor do we think it possible within the context of these religion-oriented institutions to impose such restrictions. . . . [I]t simply cannot be denied that this section has a primary effect that advances religion. . . .[40]

He admitted that the legislature might have supposed that at least fifty percent of the ordinary public school maintenance and repair budget would be devoted to purely secular facility upkeep in sectarian schools, but he dismissed this as a mere statistical judgment inadequate to guarantee separation.[41]

The second program allowed direct grants of fifty to one hundred dollars per child (but not more than fifty percent of the tuition actually paid) as reimbursement to poverty-level parents who send their children to nonpublic schools. Mr. Justice Powell used the effect test, claiming that in this case parents acted only as conduits of unrestricted funds to religious schools, since the grants contained no restrictions to guarantee the separation between secular and religious educational functions.[42]

The third program provided state income tax credit to parents of nonpublic school children whose annual family income was over five thousand but less than twenty-five thousand dollars. Believing that there was no relevant distinction between this tax forgiveness statute and the direct grant program, Mr. Justice Powell would have none of it: "The qualifying parent . . . under either program receives the same form of encouragement and reward for sending his children to nonpublic schools."[43] He then struggled to differentiate this case from *Walz*, concluding that "it should be apparent that in terms of the potential divisiveness of any legislative measure, the narrowness of the benefited class would be an important factor."[44]

Nyquist, despite its weaknesses, is most likely to be the controlling precedent in any federal tax credit challenge, and in examining that issue an analysis of the majority opinion will be useful. Mr. Chief Justice Burger, with Mr. Justice Rehnquist, joined the Court's opinion with respect to the maintenance and repair provision, and with Mr. Justice White, dissented as to the tuition grant and tax credit program. The Chief Justice focused on three weaknesses of the majority position. Concerning the first he wrote that

[i]t is beyond dispute that the parents of public school children in New York and Pennsylvania presently receive the "benefit" of having their children educated totally at state expense; the statutes enacted in those states and at issue here merely attempt to equalize that "benefit." . . . It is no more than simple equity to grant partial relief to parents who support the public schools they do not use.[45]

Concerning the conduit theory, Mr. Chief Justice Burger noted that there are numerous forms of governmental assistance that can legitimately be channelled to religious ends, such as social security benefits or G.I. Bill payments, which are not subject to "non-religious use" restrictions, and which the majority of the Court would not find unconstitutional. In addition, he argued that

[f]or purposes of constitutional adjudication of that issue, it should make no difference whether 5%, 20%, or 80% of the beneficiaries of an educational program of general application elect to utilize their benefits for religious purposes. The "primary effect" branch of our three-pronged test was never . . . intended to vary with the *number* of churches benefited by a statute under which state aid is distributed to private citizens.[46]

Mr. Justice Rehnquist, joined by the Chief Justice and Mr. Justice White, found "both the Court's reasoning and result all but impossible to reconcile" with *Walz, Allen*, and *Everson*.[47] Mr. Justice White, joined by the Chief Justice and Mr. Justice Rehnquist, also dissented on the tuition grant and tax credit laws, arguing that these had a clearly secular legislative purpose.[48]

While the dissenters seem clearly to have had the better argument, the majority was not persuaded, and the results may not have been altogether what they had in mind. In an excellent analysis of *Nyquist*,[49] Richard E. Morgan pointed to one probable result:

Mr. Justice Powell's argument, that allocations will be fought over no matter the route they take to the sectarian institutions, is surely sound. The outstanding problem with all this is that the premise is almost universally unexamined. If the involvement of fighting religious groups in the political process is the danger to be avoided, does it obviously follow that the least risky strategy is to deny aid and avoid entanglements? Is it not at least possible that the obdurate exclusion of church-related institutions from governmental programs which utilize other governmental entities will produce higher levels of strife than would be created through hard bargaining for shares if the religious institutions were included in the program?[50]

Whatever else one may say of *Nyquist*, it was a far more effective trigger for political division along religious lines than any other single case in the aid to religious schools sequence.[51] Nevertheless, the Court has continued to follow the directions set in the *Lemon-Tilton-Nyquist* cases.

In *Levitt v. Committee for Public Education and Religious Liberty*,[52] Mr. Chief Justice Burger, relying explicitly on *Nyquist*, invalidated New York payments to nonpublic schools as reimbursement for the expenses of keeping various records, making reports, and administering tests to pupils—all of which were required by state law.[53] The appellants had argued that the state should be permitted to pay for any activity mandated by state law,[54] but the Chief Justice rested his opinion on the lack of an identifiable and separable secular function.[55] The presence of state audits would, of course, have run afoul of the excessive entanglement test. In addition, the element of suspicion of a possible potential infringement became critical. As Mr. Chief Justice Burger observed:

[N]o attempt is made under the statute, and no means are available, to assure that internally prepared tests are free of religious instruction.

We cannot ignore the substantial risk that these examinations, prepared by teachers under the authority of religious institutions, will be drafted with an eye, unconsciously or otherwise, to inculcate students in the religious precepts of the sponsoring church.[56]

In the 1975 case, *Meek v. Pittenger,*[57] Mr. Justice Stewart, writing for the Court, held invalid two Pennsylvania programs for children enrolled in nonpublic schools. The first had authorized the lending of secular instructional materials and equipment. The second had supplied auxiliary services, including counseling, testing and psychological services, speech and hearing therapy, teaching and related services, for exceptional children, for remedial students and for the educationally disadvantaged. Mr. Justice Stewart went a long way toward rejecting the secular-sectarian distinction worked out in *Schempp* and *Allen* without actually repudiating those holdings.[58] Concerning the first program, he wrote that "[e]ven though earmarked for secular purposes, 'when it flows to an institution in which religion is so pervasive that a substantial portion of its functions are subsumed in the religious mission,' state aid has the impermissible primary effect of advancing religion."[59]

His opinion rejecting the secular services program substituted a "religious atmosphere" test for the secular purpose-primary effect test of *Schempp*. Even though the services would be performed by public school personnel not under the control of religious authority,

They are performing important educational services in schools in which education is an integral part of the dominant sectarian mission and in which an atmosphere dedicated to the advancement of religious belief is constantly maintained. The potential for impermissible fostering of religion under these circumstances, although somewhat reduced, is nonetheless present.[60]

Finally, he added, the potential for divisive conflict is created by such aid requirements.

The dissenting opinions indicate the increasingly wide divisions within the Court. Mr. Justice Rehnquist, joined by Mr. Justice Burger, attacked the majority's distinction between textbooks on the one hand and instructional materials and equipment on the other as constitutionally insignificant. Concerning guidance counselors, for example, he observed:

[T]he Court's conclusion that the dangers presented by a state-subsidized guidance counselor are the same as those presented by a state-subsidized chemistry teacher is apparently no more than an *ex cathedra* pronouncement on the part of the Court, if one may use that term in a case such as this, since the District Court found the facts to be exactly the opposite—after consideration of stipulations of fact and an evidentiary hearing:

> The Commonwealth, recognizing the logistical realities, provided for traveling therapists rather than traveling pupils. There is no evidence whatsoever that the presence of the therapists in the schools will involve them in the religious missions of the schools. . . . The notion that by setting foot inside a sectarian school a professional therapist or counselor will succumb to sectarianization of his or her professional work is not supported by any evidence.[61]

Mr. Chief Justice Burger's dissent was, if anything, even more harsh:

> Indeed, I see . . . much potential for divisive political debate in opposition to the crabbed attitude the Court shows in this case.
>
> If the consequence of the Court's holding operated only to penalize *institutions* with a religious affiliation, the result would be grievous enough; nothing in the Religion Clauses of the First Amendment permits governmental power to discriminate against or affirmatively stifle religions or religious activity. . . . But this holding does more: it penalizes *children*— children who have the misfortune to have to cope with the learning process under extraordinarily heavy physical and psychological burdens, for the most part congenital. This penalty strikes them not because of any act of theirs but because of their parents' choice of religious exercise.[62]

In a 1976 case, *Roemer v. Board of Public Works*,[63] the Court continued its distinction between elementary and higher education, upholding a Maryland law providing annual grants of fifteen percent of the state's full-time pupil appropriation for students in the state college system "to private colleges, among them religiously affiliated institutions, subject only to the restrictions that the funds not be used for 'sectarian purposes.' "[64] The Court, speaking through Mr. Justice Blackmun, found a secular legislative purpose "supporting private higher education generally, as an economic alternative to a wholly public system."[65] The Court found the primary effect to be no different from that found in *Tilton* and *Hunt*. Mr. Justice Blackmun's analysis of the "entanglement" and "surveillance" problems is instructive:

We must assume that the colleges . . . will exercise their delegated control over use of the funds in compliance with the statutory, and therefore the constitutional, mandate. It is to be expected that they will give a wide berth to "specifically religious activity," and thus minimize constitutional questions.

Should such questions arise, the courts will consider them.[66]

In a statement quoted earlier, Mr. Justice Blackmun continued: "It has not been the Court's practice, in considering facial challenges to statutes of this kind, to strike them down in anticipation that particular applications may result in unconstitutional use of funds."[67] This is a different standard than that issued for primary and secondary schools. As for excessive entanglement, the justice observed that "the District Court found that in this case 'there is no necessity for state officials to investigate the conduct of particular classes of educational programs to determine whether a school is attempting to indoctrinate its students under the guise of secular education.' "[68] Additionally, as he noted,

[o]ccasional audits are possible here, but we must accept the District Court's finding that they would be "quick and nonjudgmental." They and the other contacts between the Council and the colleges are not likely to be any more entangling than the inspections and audits incident to the normal process of the colleges' accreditations by the State.[69]

In answering the "political divisiveness" argument, Mr. Justice Blackmun noted that the danger was lessened when the school was not an elementary or secondary school, but a college with a wider, more diverse constituency. Furthermore, there was a diminishing danger when the aid was extended to private colleges generally, more than two-thirds of which have no religious affiliation. This situation can be contrasted with *Nyquist*, where ninety-five percent of the aided schools were Roman Catholic. In addition, the substantial autonomy of the aided schools "was thought to mitigate political divisiveness, in that controversies surrounding the aid program are not likely to involve the Catholic Church itself, or even the religious character of the schools, but only their 'fiscal responsibility and educational requirements.' "[70]

The Court's 1977 decision in *Wolman v. Walter*[71] added no new principles for the handling of school aid cases, but perhaps no case better expresses the state into which constitutional adjudication has fallen. In 1976 the legislature of Ohio passed a statute authorizing six forms of aid to nonpublic schools.[72]

The statute was drawn with two objectives in mind—to aid private schools and to meet the constitutional standards established in the *Nyquist-Levitt-Meek-Roemer* line of cases. Despite Ohio's attempt to follow the lead of the Court, the justices were sharply divided in their opinions.[73] The Court not only found itself in the unenviable role of nit-picking, but had to rely on a variety of tests to come to a common judgment.

The justices' reasoning is instructive in this regard. Mr. Chief Justice Burger and Mr. Justice Stewart wrote no separate opinions. Mr. Justice Blackmun proposed the now familiar three-pronged test: "In order to pass muster, a statute must have a secular legislative purpose, must have a principal or primary effect that neither advances nor inhibits religion, and must not foster an excessive government entanglement with religion."[74] He found no trouble with the secular legislative purpose, and centered his argument on the latter two tests. Mr. Justice White based his vote on the reasoning in his *Nyquist* dissent, and Mr. Justice Rehnquist on his dissent in *Meek*. Mr. Justice Brennan argued solely on the basis of the potential for political division along religious lines, given the large sums of money at stake.[75] Mr. Justice Marshall supported the political divisiveness argument and added his own principle of a distinction between general welfare programs and educational assistance programs. The distinction, as he explained in a footnote, "is between programs that help the school educate a student and welfare programs that may have the effect of making a student more receptive to being educated."[76] He then proceeded to declare unconstitutional therapeutic services, i.e., academic guidance and counseling, which are designed to have precisely the welfare effects he stipulated!

Mr. Justice Powell accepted the basic reasoning of Mr. Justice Blackmun, but warned against any compulsion to find "analytical tidiness" in pursuit of blind constitutional absolutism.[77] Mr. Justice Stevens announced his return to Mr. Justice Black's original

Everson test that "[n]o tax in any amount, large or small, can be levied to support any religious activities or institutions, whatever they may be called, or whatever form they may adopt to teach or practice religion."[78] Not only did he ignore the fact that the secular aid was for students receiving secular aids and services, but he further blurred his absolutism by admitting that "[t]he State can plainly provide public health services to children attending nonpublic schools."[79] It is small wonder, granted this melting pot of constitutional theories, that Senator Moynihan said that *Wolman* "may be the most embarrassing decision in the modern history of the Court."[80]

In the summer of 1979 the Supreme Court affirmed without comment the ruling of the Third Circuit Court of Appeals on yet another school aid case.[81] The appeals court declared unconstitutional a New Jersey statute which provided that any taxpayer who had dependent children attending nonpublic elementary or secondary schools on a full-time basis might, for each child, take a tax credit of $1,000 against gross income. Because the opinion was upheld by the Supreme Court, was based primarily on a comparison of the *Walz* and *Nyquist* cases, and raised several interesting questions, it may be well to provide a short analysis.

The majority of the three judge-appeals court held the statute unconstitutional because the tax credit went only to parents of nonpublic school children and not to parents of public school children. The New Jersey legislature had attempted to make the grants part of a broader class, since similar $1,000 grants went to taxpayers who had dependents in college, taxpayers who were blind or disabled, married, or over sixty-five. But it left out that group which was most similar to the benefited group, parents with students in public school. The Court held that it was precisely this type of discrimination that was prohibited in *Nyquist*.

The appeals court also held that the exemption had a primary effect of advancing religion, since almost ninety-five percent of the nonpublic schools in New Jersey to which parents sent children were religiously affiliated. Quoting the district court decision, the appellate court held that the statute *rewarded* the enrollment of children in religiously affiliated schools, and was therefore unconstitutional. If New Jersey had had a graduated credit of up to

$1,000 based on actual expenditures, available to all parents with dependents in school, and if the recipient schools were required to submit separate budgets for secular and religious programs, with only expenditures for secular education to be used in calculating expenditures, the Court would have been more inclined to find the tax credit constitutional.

Mr. Justice Weis wrote an opinion which concurred with the holding for the sole reason that he believed the appellate court was bound by *Nyquist*. The rest of his opinion was a scathing critique of the Court's performance in this area. In response to the plaintiff's contention that this tax measure advanced religion, he observed,

> I have great difficulty . . . in understanding why the exclusion here [of $1,000 from gross income] is more of an aid to religion that a direct contribution to a church, synagogue, temple or mosque which is deductible under the Internal Revenue Code. . . . It is all the more puzzling because the benefits the state receives from the continued operation of a congregation are not as directly recognizable nor financially calculable as the education received by nonpublic school children.[82]

Looking at the Supreme Court's more general treatment in this area he concluded that

> [A]n analysis of the cases touching upon state assistance to nonpublic schools could proceed at length, but would merely illustrate the lack of a principled and logical thread. The reality is that the Supreme Court has marked out a series of boundaries and points of departure on an ad hoc basis.[83]

The unsettled status of the aid-to-private-schools issue is evident in the unending stream of cases to reach the Court. The latest case available when this book went to press was *Committee for Public Education and Religious Liberty v. Regan*.[84] By a 5-4 decision the Court upheld a New York statute directing payment to nonpublic K-12 schools for the costs of performing the secular, state-ordered tasks of administering state-prepared tests, record-keeping and reporting. Both the majority and minority agreed that the three-pronged test—secular legislative purpose, a principle or primary effect that neither advances nor inhibits religion, and no excessive governmental entanglement—provided the relevant constitutional principle. Not surprisingly, they disagreed on what the principle demanded. Justice White, writing for the majority, returned to his secular-sectarian distinction and found the reimbursements acceptable. Justice Blackmun, dissenting for himself and Justices Brennan and Marshall, returned to the direct-indirect distinction. He found this direct financial aid to religiously affiliated K-12 schools (reportedly an 8 to 10 million-dollar annual expenditure) to have the primary effect of advancing religion. Justice Stevens, dissenting for himself, continued to reinforce his image as the most absolutist member of the Court, bearing witness that the myth of separation is alive and well. "Rather than continuing the sisyphean task of trying to patch together the blurred, indistinct and variable barrier," he said, "I would resurrect the 'high and impregnable wall' between church and state constructed by the Framers of the First Amendment."[85]

The opinions in *Regan* confirm the conclusions the authors have reached through the detailed analysis of cases eschewed by Mr. Justice Weis. Because the Supreme Court has been unable to find and apply a consistent constitutional principle (and when agreeing on a principle, unable to agree on its application) it has found itself floundering in a quagmire of arbitrary distinctions, double standards, questionable historical interpretation, and educational nit-picking, only to reach unpredictable and inconsistent results. Consequently, it has not been able to develop any broad consensus in this area of constitutional law. Nor, despite the numerous cases it has addressed, has the Court developed that sense of settled law upon which sound policymaking depends. It may be well to conclude our discussion of the aid-to-private-schools cases with Justice White's concluding paragraph in *Regan:*

. . . Establishment Clause cases are not easy; they stir deep feelings; and we are divided among ourselves, perhaps reflecting the different views on this subject of the people of this country. What's certain is that our decisions have tended to avoid categorical imperatives and absolutist approaches at either end of the range of possible outcomes. This course sacrifices clarity and predictability for flexibility, but this promises to be the case until the continuing interaction between the Courts and the States —the former charged with interpreting and upholding the Constitution and the latter seeking to provide education for their youth—produces a single more encompassing construction of the Establishment Clause.[86]

As we will make clear in chapter 6, we believe that "single, more encompassing construction" to be fiscal neutrality. While the Court has not developed such a principle in school aid cases, it has come much closer in other Establishment Clause issues.

PROPERTY TAX EXEMPTIONS

The Court's single major case covering religious property tax exemptions began in interesting circumstances. Frederick Walz, a seclusive New York attorney, bought an abandoned piece of Staten Island property, about half the size of a tennis court, and initiated a law suit in which he claimed that the tax exemption given to New York City churches was an indirect subsidy of religion which he as a taxpayer was forced to make. This was, he contended, a serious violation of the Establishment Clause.

In *Walz v. Tax Commission* the court was not sympathetic.[87] By an 8-1 decision it supported the tax commission on three grounds. First, the tax exemption was not granted exclusively to churches, but to a broad class of eleemosynary organizations within which churches were treated equally with similar organizations. Second, taxing churches would involve assessments, collections, and foreclosures, bringing about excessive entanglement of churches and government. Finally, the unbroken historical practice of almost two hundred years showed not only a record of constitutional acceptance but that exemptions have not led to establishment.

Justice Burger's opinion was a major step toward the establishment of a neutralist interpretation of the religion clauses. One strength was the rejection of an absolute separation standard: "No perfect or absolute separation is really possible; the very existence of the Religion Clauses is an involvement of sorts—one which seeks to mark boundaries to avoid excessive entanglement."[88] Even more significant was his statement of what approached a fiscal neutrality position:

The Legislative purpose of the property tax exemption is neither the advancement nor the inhibition of religion; it is neither sponsorship nor hostility. . . . It has not singled out one particular church or religious group or even churches as such; rather it has granted exemption to all houses of religious worship within a broad class of property owned by nonprofit, quasi-public corporations which include hospitals, libraries, playgrounds, scientific, professional, historical, and patriotic groups.[89]

Justice Brennan's concurring opinion likewise contained strong neutralist elements. Quoting first from his *Schempp* opinion he observed that

[W]hat the Framers meant to foreclose, and what our decisions under the Establishment Clause have forbidden, are those involvements of religious with secular institutions which (a) serve the essentially religious activities of religious institutions; (b) employ the organs of government for essentially religious purposes; or (c) use essentially religious means to serve governmental ends, where secular means would suffice.[90]

After concluding that tax exemptions did not violate the intent of the Founding Fathers and that historical practice, while not conclusive, had considerable impact on "the interpretation of abstract constitutional language," Brennan turned to the two secular purposes of religious property tax exemptions. He stated that religious groups were exempted as part of a range of nonprofit groups which "contribute to the well-being of the community in a variety of *nonreligious* ways, and thereby bear burdens that would otherwise either have to be met by general taxation or be left undone, to the detriment of the community."[91] Secondly, he went on to affirm that religious organizations in their *religious* activities contributed "to the diversity of association, viewpoint, and enterprise essential to a vigorous pluralistic society."[92]

Of particular value in both opinions is the abandonment of a pretext of absolute separation, the affirmation that some government aid does go to religious organizations without violating the Constitution, and the treatment of religious organizations in the same manner as similarly situated groups. Yet, for the authors' perspective, the *Walz* opinions are seriously deficient in some respects.

To begin with, the authors believe that the *Walz* opinions leave the concept of "entanglement" inadequately defined. Indeed, Chief Justice Burger's discussion of degrees of involvement leaves the impression that the issue is one of quantity. In his words, ". . . the questions are whether the involvement is excessive, and whether it is a continuing one calling for official and continuing surveillance leading to an impermissible degree of entanglement."[93] Whether government aids or decides not to aid, taxes or decides not to tax, there is church-government involvement. The difference between involvement and entanglement is not one of quantity but of quality. Government requirements using published, objective standards equally applicable to all similar organizations, focused not on the distinctly religious aspects of the organizations but on the relevant secular aspects, are proper involvements and not entanglements. Tax foreclosures, tax liens, and the like present no more entanglement problems than do bankruptcy proceedings, financial fraud statutes, and the like. This is an uncomfortable principle for many who defend the churches' present privileged positions. Certainly the *Walz* court was not willing to go so far, preferring instead a more ambiguous test.

The authors feel that a second weakness of the case is the majority's failure to confront Justice Douglas's contention that there does exist a major distinction between churches and other non-profit, charitable institutions. Since this contention strikes at the heart of the fiscal neutrality position, it must be examined in some detail. "Government," writes Douglas,

could provide or finance operas, hospitals, historical societies, and all the rest because they represent social welfare programs within the reach of the police power. In contrast, government may not provide or finance worship because of the Establishment Clause any more than it may single out "atheistic" or "agnostic" centers or groups and create or finance them.[94]

Some paragraphs later Douglas concludes that

[T]he assumption is that the church is a purely private institution, promoting a sectarian cause. . . . Its sectarian faith sets it apart from all others and makes it difficult to equate its constituency with the general public. The extent that its facilities are open to all may only indicate the nature of its proselytism. Yet though a church covers up its religious symbols in welfare work, its welfare activities may merely be a phase of sectarian activity. I have said enough to indicate the nature of this tax exemption problem.[95]

The first problem with Douglas's assertion is that it is simply not true. Government does, in special circumstances, such as the military chaplaincy, directly finance religious worship, and has done so from the beginning of the Republic. It also provides, through the G. I. Bill, for the financing of religious studies for those veterans who choose to pursue them. But this is of minor importance compared to two other difficulties.

First, there is no constitutional assumption that a church is a "purely private" institution. Any church which holds property, builds buildings, enters into contracts, receives income and pays bills, attracts crowds, or engages in a hundred other activities that have a public impact, is not "purely private." Insofar as these activities are regulated by government, churches must be seen as participants in the public realm.

Second, much of what churches do is secular and similar to what nonreligious fraternal or charitable groups do. A sectarian faith does not set a church apart *in all regards*. Justice Douglas notwithstanding, there is the wide range of *secular* activities and functions that makes churches similar to other groups, and therefore eligible for similar treatment. The *motivation* for the existence and execution of secular activities is constitutionally irrelevant. Whether one wishes to make a profit, meet the needs of the poor and dispossessed, bear witness to Christian love, win sympathy for Israel, or win the votes of grateful constituents, is not legally significant.

Another weakness of the case is the majority's distinction between a subsidy and an exemption, an issue which will be discussed more fully in the next chapter.

OWNERSHIP OF RELIGIOUS PROPERTY

In chapter 1 we included a brief description of the early property conflicts, culminating in the neutralist *Watson v. Jones* doctrine.

In two later cases the Supreme Court confirmed the *Watson* doctrine and raised it to the level of constitutional principle. *Kedroff v. St. Nicholas Cathedral* grew out of the cold war between the U.S. and the U.S.S.R.[96] At issue was ownership and control of the Russian Orthodox Cathedral in New York. Despite both legislative and judicial efforts to free the cathedral from the control of the Communist-dominated Patriarchs of Moscow, in 1952 the Supreme Court insisted, this time on First Amendment grounds, that the Patriarchs were the legitimate hierarchical authority and could retain title to the property.

In 1969 the principle was affirmed once again in *Presbyterian Church in the United States v. Mary Elizabeth Blue Hull Memorial Presbyterian Church.*[97] In this case two Georgia churches attempted to withdraw from the General Assembly (and take the church property with them, of course) on the grounds that the latter had departed from doctrine in several regards. The Supreme Court of Georgia upheld the local churches only to be overturned by the United States Supreme Court. Writing for the majority, Justice Brennan ruled out any further attempts to apply the implied trust-departure from doctrine theory by state courts and suggested that states would do well to develop neutral principles of law. As he observed, almost in passing, ". . . there are neutral principles of law, *developed for use in all property disputes*, which can be applied without establishing churches to which property is awarded."[98]

The distinction between hierarchical and congregational churches was reaffirmed in a 1976 case, *Serbian Eastern Orthodox Diocese for the United States of America and Canada v. Milivojevich.*[99] Here the Court limited an Illinois court's ability to determine whether the internal decision of a governing church body had been made "arbitrarily" and in violation of its own rules. While the dissenters objected to the majority decision, both majority and minority accepted the same neutralist principle. As Justice Rehnquist observed,

> To make available the coercive powers of civil courts to rubber-stamp ecclesiastical decisions of hierarchical religious associations, when such deference is not accorded to similar acts of secular voluntary associations, would, in avoiding the Free Exercise problems petitioners envision, itself create far more serious problems under the Establishment Clause.[100]

The Georgia Supreme Court responded to the high court's decisions by developing another set of criteria. Because these criteria were explicitly called "neutral principles," they are of particular interest to us. In *Presbyterian Church v. Eastern Heights Church*, the Georgia court "examined the deeds to the properties, the state statutes dealing with implied trusts . . . and the Book of Church Order to determine whether there was any basis for a trust in favor of the general church."[101] Finding no such basis, the court awarded the property to the holders of the legal title, the local trustees.

In a second case the Georgia court applied the same principles to a United Methodist dispute. Although it could find nothing in the deeds or statutes, it did find an express trust provision that favored the general church in the United Methodist constitution, the Book of Discipline. On that basis it awarded legal title to the central church authority.[102]

The new Georgia rules were tested in the Supreme Court in the 1979 case, *Jones v. Wolf*.[103] A 5-4 majority upheld the Georgia procedure, but remanded to the Georgia court to determine whether the majority faction indeed represented the local church. Justice Blackmun's statement of the issue is particularly misleading:

The question for decision is whether civil courts, consistent with the First and Fourteenth Amendments to the Constitution, may resolve the dispute on the basis of "neutral principles of law," or whether they must defer to the resolution of an authoritative tribunal of the hierarchical church.[104]

Whatever else may be said, the Georgia court's claim to be applying neutral principles does not approach the type of neutralism espoused in this book. We shall explore that type more fully in chapter 6. The question we would have the Court ask is whether church property is being disposed of in a manner similar to the disposition of the property of other voluntary, charitable organizations. This was the Federal common-law principle laid down in *Watson* by Justice Miller:

Religious organizations come before us in the same attitude as other voluntary associations for benevolent or charitable purposes, and their rights of property, or contract, are equally under the protection of the law, and the actions of their members subject to its restraints.[105]

The neutrality of the Georgia arrangement remains to be seen. Will the courts apply the same review procedures to other similar groups? Although the Georgia case has departed from the line of cases following *Watson*, and been supported in the Supreme Court, it is not yet clear that the courts have given the wrong answer. Justice Blackmun, to our mind, asked the wrong questions.

EMPLOYMENT—RELATED ISSUES

CETA Workers

An issue now in the process of litigation is the use of Comprehensive Employment and Training Act (CETA) funds in church-run elementary and secondary schools.[106] CETA was developed during the "War on Poverty" of the 1960s, and church institutions participated from the beginning. The enabling legislation stipulated that "[P]articipants shall not be employed on the construction, operation or maintenance of so much of any facility as is used or will be used for sectarian instruction or as a place of worship."[107] Nor could CETA funds be used for religious or antireligious activities.

Federal District Court Justice Reynolds, acting on a petition by the Wisconsin Civil Liberties Union, ordered the Labor Department to terminate all existing CETA contracts with church-run schools and to bar all future contracts. Although there is no record of a single abuse in church-related schools since the beginning of the program, the CETA structure itself created excessive entanglement, reasoned the judge, since it allowed government agencies to supervise and audit employees in church schools. While he thought some jobs in church-run schools might be constitutionally permissible, he felt that others—such as teacher's aides—might create entanglement. In any event, he wrote,

In order to determine which CETA-funded employees were fulfilling constitutionally permissible functions at the schools and to insure that there was no ideological content to their positions, the defendant prime sponsors would have to predetermine the job content and thereafter to involve themselves significantly in the activities of the schools in order to properly supervise the activities of the employees. Such involvement, in turn, would lead to excessive government entanglement with religion.[108]

Judge Reynolds' opinion triggers several questions. Both public and private employers contract to provide CETA jobs. If *only* religious groups are singled out for nonparticipation, is this not discrimination solely on the basis of religious affiliation, that is, a religious test? If there is no record of abuse, (for example, using CETA workers for religious purposes), must church-run schools be presumed guilty and denied a chance to prove their innocence? Finally, any group which accepts CETA workers must agree to abide by the stated regulations and permit agency monitoring. Granted this voluntary agreement, can government monitoring realistically be called "entanglement"? Fiscal neutrality would require that the secular and sectarian components of the church-run schools be separated, and that in their secular activities the schools be treated according to the same regulations as other employers participating in the CETA program.

Unions in Religious Institutions

It is somewhat ironic that religious groups, which have long preached the right of working people to unionize, find many of their institutions fighting unionization of their own employees on the grounds of religious liberty. The Supreme Court's most current opinion in the matter is *National Labor Relations Board v. Catholic Bishop of Chicago.*[109] The NLRB had asserted jurisdiction over church-run schools in order to allow union elections and representation of lay teachers. The board distinguished between "completely religious" and "religiously associated" schools, claiming coverage only over the latter. Attorneys for the Archdiocese of Chicago argued that Congress never intended the National Labor Relations Act to cover religiously affiliated schools, and that any such coverage would infringe on First Amendment rights.

Chief Justice Burger delivered the opinion for a five-member majority. Essentially, the majority held that without an explicitly stated intention by Congress to include religiously associated schools, the Court would not uphold the jurisdiction of the NLRB. An examination of the National Labor Relations Act showed no such intention, and therefore the Board erred in asserting jurisdiction.[110]

The majority opinion was based on an interpretation of the

statute and did not reach or settle the constitutional question whether such jurisdiction, if it had been granted by Congress, would have violated the Free Exercise Clause of the First Amendment.

The minority opinion of Justice Brennan quickly pointed out that the majority invented a new rule of statutory construction to avoid tackling the constitutional question. The intent of the Act, claimed Brennan, was to cover all workers except those explicitly exempted, and employees in religiously affiliated schools were not exempted.[111]

An examination of the legislative history of the Act clearly shows that the dissenters were correct. At several points the exemptions simply implied by the majority were considered and rejected. The Wagner Act of 1935 did not exclude either religiously associated schools or any other private, nonprofit organization.[112] As a result, in administrative litigation, the NLRB held that "[N]either charitable institutions nor their employees are exempted from operation of the Act by its terms, although certain other employers and employees are exempted."[113] This interpretation was upheld by the Supreme Court on several occasions.[114] Other later attempts to create exemptions for religiously affiliated institutions were likewise rejected.[115]

What is important in the legislative history of the NLRA for our purposes is that the religiously affiliated institutions have been treated exactly as their nonsectarian counterparts, and Congress has resisted efforts to single them out for special treatment. What can be concluded from the Court's decision about the Act is that it did not deal with the constitutional issue of whether the NLRB may order religiously affiliated schools to hold union elections and accept unions if the majority of lay employees desire them. It avoided the issue by creating a new—although not imaginative—rule of statutory construction. The weakness of the argument and the closeness of the vote assure that the matter will come before the Court again. Legislative history suggests that religiously affiliated organizations ought to be treated as their nonsectarian counterparts are. Whether the Courts will follow this neutralist principle remains to be seen. In any event, until the constitutional issue is found, related issues such as religious conditions for employment, contract terms, and the possibility of entanglement cannot be satisfactorily resolved.

Unemployment Compensation Tax

In 1976 Congress triggered a new religion-government controversy when it amended the Federal Unemployment Tax Act to include coverage for elementary and secondary school teachers.[116] Secretary of Labor Ray Marshall ruled that the law should include church-related schools. On the other hand, Congress left intact a church-exclusion clause which exempted from coverage "employees of a church, convention or association of churches; or employees of an organization operated primarily for religious purposes and one operated, supervised, controlled or supported by a church."[117] A suit has been filed in the U.S. District Court in Louisville, Kentucky challenging the constitutionality of the Labor Department ruling. Basically the purpose of the law is to provide unemployment compensation for workers, including teachers, who have been fired from their positions. The tax, paid by the employer, is calculated as a percentage of an employee's salary, and may be paid either as a contribution—a quarterly tax payment of a percentage of lay employees' salaries—or as a reimbursement to the government when a claim is filed by a qualified former employee. Opponents of the tax argue that it infringes on religious liberty and religious control of their schools.

Undoubtedly Secretary Marshall's interpretation raises major church-government issues: the control of hiring and firing, the conditions of employment, entanglement, record-keeping, reporting and disclosure, government review of the fairness of employee dismissals, and, not least, the added cost of compliance.

Lower state courts to date have been more inclined to rule in favor of the church leaders' contention that the tax is unconstitutional, but the argument is not as one-sided as it might appear. For one thing, "college employees—including those at church-related schools—have been covered by the unemployment compensation law since the early 1970s."[118] The case for Catholic schools is further weakened by the fact that several dioceses, including that of Richmond, Virginia and several in New York state, have voluntarily accepted coverage of teachers by the Unemployment Tax Act. That fact at least casts a suspicious shadow over the claim of other dioceses of infringement on religious liberty. This is not so true for non-Catholic Christian schools which have never voluntarily complied.

Once again we anticipate that the Supreme Court will be called upon to settle the controversy. While it is uncertain how the Court will rule, several factors will have to be considered. First, all other nonprofit, voluntary and charitable organizations, including religiously affiliated colleges and hospitals, are covered by the Act. Such coverage has not led to excessive entanglement in religious questions, secular determination of religious doctrine, or the church-government controversy many of the current opponents fear. Does not exemption based solely on religious affiliation put churches in a uniquely privileged position? Second, current discussions have by and large avoided the other value involved: protection of workers from the arbitrary whims of employers. The Court must weigh employee interests in a reasonable security against the religious interests of employing institutions.

Finally, the need to comply with the Federal Unemployment Tax Act may in the long run be highly beneficial to religiously affiliated institutions if it encourages them to develop sound personnel policies and guidelines, establish supervisory and grievance procedures, and distinguish clearly between that employment within the institution which is religious in nature and that which is secular.

Employment-related issues have recently become a focal point in church-government controversy. That is all but inevitable given the pervasive government involvement in economic regulation and substantial employment by church-related institutions. But the controversies are not insoluble. We argue in this book for consistency in church-government relations. That consistency must exist between as well as within particular issues. We conclude in chapter 7 that public aid for the secular parts of religiously affiliated education is constitutionally permissible. We have intimated in this chapter that placement of CETA workers in religiously affiliated schools is also permissible. If that is the case, then the accompanying government regulation must also be accepted. Neither the courts nor the schools can have it both ways. If the secular and the religious are too intertwined for NLRB jurisdiction or Federal Unemployment Tax Act coverage, then they are too intertwined for aid. If the secular and the religious are separable enough for aid, then they are separable enough for NLRB jurisdiction and Tax Act coverage.

Public Ceremonies

We may conclude the chapter with an example that will probably never reach the Supreme Court: paying the bills for public religious ceremonies. Although the problem arises annually at Christmastime in one city or another across the nation, it was headline news during the October 1979 visit of Pope John Paul II to the United States at an estimated total cost of ten million dollars. The Pope visited six cities. In three, Boston, Philadelphia, and New York, city officials initially proposed to pay for all expenses, including the cost of constructing platforms for celebration of outdoor masses. In the remaining three, Chicago, Washington, D.C., and Des Moines, church officials planned to pay for construction of altars and related facilities.

Not surprisingly, controversy arose in those cities where officials planned to pick up all the expense. "Nobody has any problems putting up (public) money for clean-up, police overtime, police protection (and) traffic control," claimed Ed Doerr, a representative of Americans United for Separation of Church and State, "It is the use of tax money to build facilities expressly intended for religious rites that is wrong."[119] Not everyone agreed that that was the sole issue. Madelyn Murray O'Hair and her son brought suit in Washington, D.C. to block the papal mass on the Washington Monument Mall altogether. Such a mass on public land is unconstitutional, she contended, because it ". . . had no secular purpose, fosters government entanglement with religion, and has the principle effect of advancing religion through the use of U.S. Government property."[120]

At first glance the neutralist test—treat religious persons, activities, and institutions as one would treat similarly situated persons, activities, and institutions—would seem inappropriate, for who is similar to a Pope and what activity parallels a papal visit? The Pope is not only a religious leader, but also a major public figure similar to heads of state, astronauts, Olympic gold medal winners, and returning war heroes. Insofar as he is a public figure he is similar to others who hold rallies, draw crowds, lead parades, and receive tumultuous welcomes. Therefore we would agree with Mr. Doerr of Americans United that governments should pay for the strictly secular costs such as crowd control, protection, and cleanup, just as they do for other public figures, and church groups should pay for the religious rites, and the structures necessary to perform them. Contrary to Ms. O'Hair, we would argue that religious groups have just as much right to use public lands as other groups, and no more. The same principle would apply to nativity scenes, Hanukkah candles, and so forth.

CONCLUSION

In this chapter we have worked our way through legal issues in church-government relations by focusing primarily on case law. We have moved from the highly litigated area of aid to religiously affiliated schools through the taxation of religious property, ownership disputes, employment-related problems and public ceremonies. Even so, we have not covered all the possible areas of controversy. For example we have not delved into the expenditures for prison and military chaplaincy programs, exemption from income taxes for those with vows of poverty, or social security payments. We have discussed enough issues, however, to establish our main points.

It is clear that substantial sums of money are at stake in the litigated areas, whether it is money flowing from government in terms of support and tax expenditures, money flowing to government in terms of taxes, money flowing from one religious institution to another as a result of a court determination of ownership, or simply money flowing from religious institutions to their employees as a result of government-imposed regulations. We hope it is equally clear that the case law is often confusing, inconsistent, and in several cases, still very much in the process of development.

The viewpoint from which we have analyzed the issues is that of fiscal neutrality. As we will urge throughout the book, we believe fiscal neutrality provides the most consistent, just, and functional principle for determining sound public policy in church-government relations.

NOTES

1. We have made no attempt to be totally comprehensive in our analysis of Court cases. We have limited ourselves, with few exceptions, to Supreme Court opinions, and within that category to those in which a substantial or economic issue is involved.

2. 330 U.S. 1 (1947). *Everson* was the first case to apply the Establishment Clause to the states.

3. Id. at 15-16.

4. 392 U.S. 236 (1968).

5. 374 U.S. 203 (1963). Schempp declared unconstitutional the reading of Biblical verses and the recitation of the Lord's Prayer in public schools. It is notable for its incipient development and application of neutral principles to a church-state question. Since it is not a fiscal issue, we have not included it.

6. 392 U.S. at 243.

7. Id. at 243-44.

8. Id. at 245.

9. Id.

10. Id.

11. Id. at 249 (Harlan, J., concurring) (citing *Abington School Dist. v. Schempp*, 374 U.S. 203, 307 [1963]').

12. Id. at 253 (Black, J., dissenting). Just exactly *how* secular textbooks chosen by public school boards in subjects as math, modern languages and natural sciences, actively and directly assist the teaching and propagation of sectarian religion, Mr. Justice Black did not explain.

13. Id. at 256 (Douglas, J., dissenting).

14. Id. at 257-58 (Douglas, J., dissenting) (quoting the New York Court of Appeals holding in *Board of Education v. Allen*, 20 N.Y. 2d 109, 122, 288 N.E. 2d 791, 798, 281, N.Y.S. 2d 799, 809 [1967].

15. Id. at 266 (Douglas, J. dissenting). The assertions indicate, if not an emotional blindspot, perhaps a lack of information about parochial schools. One would expect that both a school board and, if necessary, a court, could easily formulate reliable standards to distinguish secular from sectarian books in the fields of math, modern languages, and natural sciences. If they cannot so distinguish, a whole new problem must be faced, that is, the use of the same textbooks in the public schools. Concerning nonsectarian books in religious schools, one begins to wonder if the justice ever examined the curriculum or library of a parochial school. The justice seemed to equate a parochial school with some sort of week-long Sunday school. In the former, the major part of the curriculum is devoted to *state-required* secular subjects and already utilizes secular textbooks, whereas the latter is dedicated almost exclusively to religious proselytizing.

16. 403 U.S. 602 (1971). *Lemon* involved a Pennsylvania statute and was consolidated with another case, *Robinson v. DiCenso*, 403 U.S. 602 (1971) (No. 70-570), involving a Rhode Island statute.

17. See the discussion of *Walz v. Tax Commission*, 397 U.S. 664 (1970) below. While this was a religious property tax case the "nonentanglement" test developed in *Walz* became an important standard for later school aid cases.

18. Id. at 609.

19. Id. at 614.

20. Id. at 618-19.

21. Id. at 619.

22. Id. at 668 (White, J., concurring in part and dissenting in part).

23. 403 U.S. 672 (1971).

24. 20 U.S.C. §§ 711-721 (1970) (repealed by Act of June 23, 1972), Pub. L. No. 92-318, § 161 (b) (2), 86 Stat. 303 (1972).

25. 403 U.S. at 681.

26. See 403 U.S. at 666 (White, J., concurring and dissenting in part).

27. If a religious test for public office was so unacceptable to the Founding Fathers that they wrote a prohibition into the Constitution, article VI, clause 3, one wonders how they could countenance a religious test as a criteria for sharing in public funds for secular education in church-affiliated schools!

28. 403 U.S. at 688.

29. Id. at 692 (Douglas, J., dissenting in part).

30. Donald Giannella, "Lemon and Tilton: The Bittersweet of Church-state Entanglement," 1971 *Supreme Court Review*: 173 (emphasis added).

31. Id.

32. 397 U.S. at 674.

33. *Abington School Dist. v. Schempp*, 374 U.S. 203, 225 (1963).

34. 426 U.S. 736 (1976).

35. Id. at 761.

36. Giannella, *supra* note 55, at 175.

37. *Hunt v. McNair*, 413 U.S. 734 (1973).

38. Virgil C. Blum, "Is the Supreme Court Anti-Catholic?" *Homiletic and Pastoral Review* 79 (May 1974): 7.

39. 413 U.S. 756 (1973). *Nyquist* was decided with a companion case, *Sloan v. Lemon*, 413 U.S. 825 (1973).

40. 413 U.S. at 774.

41. Id. at 777-78. The fact that 80-90 percent of the time and space allocation and 70-80 percent of the personnel utilization of the private school is routinely devoted to fulfilling state-mandated secular education requirements was apparently not part of the court record.

42. Id. at 780-83.

43. Id. at 791.

44. Id. at 794. Again, it is difficult to escape the conclusion that a religious test is being applied. If the benefited class had encompassed a broader range of religious groups, as in *Tilton*, or a more quaint group, as in *Yoder*, Mr. Justice Powell's argument would have been even weaker. In *Sloan* he made the same argument. (413 U.S. at 831.) Apparently he found unpersuasive the fact that "the benefited class" was already doubly taxed by having to pay for the public schools from which they did not benefit directly, as well as the tuitions at the religious schools where the majority of the expense went to meeting state-mandated requirements in secular subjects. Some commentators have found in *Sloan* a significant distinction between the indirect and insignificant benefit accruing to schools and the real effect of aiding all parents, which is precisely the effect of the tax credit concept. See also *Hearings on H.R. 9332 before the House Comm. on Ways and Means*, 95th Cong., 2d Sess. 116 (1977-1978) (statement of William B. Ball).

45. 413 U.S. at 803 (Burger, C.J., concurring in part and dissenting in part).

46. Id. at 804 (Burger, C.J., concurring in part and dissenting in part).

47. Id. at 806 (Rehnquist, J., dissenting in part).

48. Id. at 823 (White, J., dissenting).

49. Morgan, ''The Establishment Clause and Sectarian Schools: A Final Install-ment?,'' 1973 *SUP. CT. REV.*: 57.

50. Id. at 96.

51. Morgan proved somewhat prophetic. Immediately following *Nyquist* the Catholic League for Religious and Civil Rights was formed to provide a counter-balance to groups such as the Committee for Public Education and Religious Liberty (the appellant in *Nyquist*). A leading Catholic author in the field, Professor Virgil Blum, argued that the Court in the *Lemon-Nyquist* sequence showed itself to be imbued with an anti-Catholic bias. Particularly galling to Professor Blum was the Court's rejection of well-established rules of law in deciding constitutional questions that directly concern Catholics. The only solution he could urge was greater political activism by Catholics. Weber, ''Bishops in Politics: The Big Plunge,'' America 134 (1976): 220. This is not to argue that *Nyquist* was the sole cause for the spectacular growth in Catholic activism. *Roe v. Wade*, 410 U.S. 113 (1973), decided the same calendar year, was considered even more alarming by the Catholic leaders. In the meantime the Committee for Public Education and Religious Liberty, a collection of some 27 separationist and secularist groups, encouraged by its success in New York, was reorganized on a national level to pursue its separationist interest more effectively. The lesson in *Nyquist*, learned intuitively by the various interest groups, has been reinforced by more scholarly analysis: political militancy is effective in religion clause litigation. Frank J. Sorauf, *The Wall of Separation* (Princeton: Princeton University Press, 1976).

52. 413 U.S. 472 (1973).

53. Id. at 481-82.

54. Id. at 481.

55. Id. at 479.

56. Id. at 480.

57. 421 U.S. 349 (1975).

58. The Court, without a majority opinion, upheld a textbook statute similar to *Allen*. Id. at 373. Mr. Justice Brennan, joined by Messrs. Justices Douglas and Marshall, dissented, holding that the political divisive factor explored in *Lemon* must now be controlling. Id. at 374-75 (Brennan, J., dissenting).

59. 421 U.S. at 365-66 (quoting *Hunt v. McNair*, 413 U.S. 734, 743 [1973]).

60. Id. at 371-72.

61. Id. at 392 (Rehnquist, J., concurring in part and dissenting in part) (Quoting the district court opinion, 374 F. Supp. 639, 657 [E.D. Pa. 1972]).

62. Id. at 386 (Burger, C.J., concurring in part and dissenting in part).

63. 426 U.S. 736 (1976).

64. Id. at 739.

65. Id. at 754.

66. Id. at 760-61.

67. Id. at 761.

68. Id. at 762 (citations omitted).

69. Id. at 764 (citations omitted).

70. Id. at 765-66.

71. 433 U.S. 229 (1977).

72. Those forms authorized were: (1) purchasing secular textbooks approved by the superintendent of public instruction for use in the public schools for loan to the children; (2) supplying such standardized tests and scoring services as are being used in the public schools with nonpublic school personnel not being involved in the test drafting or scoring; (3) providing speech and hearing diagnostic services and diagnostic psychological services in the nonpublic schools, with the personnel performing the services being local board of education employees, physicians being hired on a contract basis, and treatment to be administered on nonpublic school premises; (4) supplying to students needing specialized attention therapeutic guidance and remedial services by employees of the local board of education or the State Department of Health, the services to be performed only in public schools, public centers, or in mobile units located off nonpublic school premises; (5) purchasing and loaning to pupils or their parents upon individual request instructional materials and instructional equipment of the kind used in public schools and that is incapable of diversion to religious use; and (6) providing field trip transportation and services such as are provided to public school students. Id. See 433 U.S. at 229-30.

73. Messrs. Justices Blackmun and Stewart upheld the constitutionality of textbooks, testing and scoring services, diagnostic and therapeutic services, but struck down instructional materials and field trips. Mr. Chief Justice Burger and Messrs. Justices Rehnquist and White upheld all six of the programs; Mr. Justice Brennan upheld only the textbook provision, but indicated he would uphold a more tightly drawn provision in that area, and Justice Stevens would strike down all the therapeutic and diagnostic services. The following chart illustrates the court voting on this issue.

	Bu	Re	Wh	Po	Bl	St	Stev	Ma	Br	
Textbooks	+	+	+	+	+	+	−	−	+	(7-2)
Testing & Scoring	+	+	+	+	+	+	−	−	−	(6-3)
Diagnostic Services	+	+	+	+	+	+	+	−	+	(8-1)
Therapeutic Services	+	+	+	+	+	+	+	−	−	(7-2)
Instructional Materials	+	+	+	−	−	−	−	−	−	(3-6)
Field Trips	+	+	+	+	−	−	−	−	−	(4-5)

74. 433 U.S. at 236.

75. Id. at 256 (Brennan, J., concurring and dissenting).

76. Id. at 259 n.4 (Marshall, J., concurring in part and dissenting in part).

77. Id. at 263 (Powell, J., concurring in part, concurring in the judgment in part, and dissenting in part).

78. Id. at 265 (Stevens, J., concurring in part and dissenting in part) (quoting *Everson v. Board of Ed.*, 330 U.S. 1, at 16 [1947]).

79. Id. at 266 (Stevens, J., concurring in part and dissenting in part).

80. Moynihan, *supra* Chpt. 1, note 47 at 36.

81. Public Funds for Public Schools of New Jersey v. Byrne, 390 F. 2d 514 (1979). 47 L.W. 3775 (1979). Cert. denied.

82. Id. at 521.

83. Id.

84. No. 79-1369 (20 February 1980).

85. Id. Slip op. at Stevens, dissenting pp. 1-2.

86. Id. Slip op. at 15.

87. 397 U.S. 664 (1970).

88. Id. at 670.

89. Id. at 672-73.

90. Id. at 680, quoting *Abington School District v. Schempp*, 374 U.S. 203 at 694 (1963).

91. Id. at 687 (emphasis added).

92. Id. at 689 (emphasis added).

93. Id. at 675.

94. Id. at 708-9.

95. Id. at 710.

96. *Kedroff v. St. Nicholas Cathedral*, 344 U.S. 94 (1952).

97. 393 U.S. 440 (1969).

98. 393 U.S. 440 at 449 (emphasis added).

99. 426 U.S. 696 (1976). See also *Md. and Va. Churches v. Sharpsburg Church*, 396 U.S. 367 (1970).

100. 426 U.S. 696 at 697 (1976).

101. 225 Ga. 259, 167 S.E. 2d 658 (1969).

102. *Carnes v. Smith*, 236 Ga. 30, 222 S.E. 2d 322 (1976), cert. denied, 429 U.S. 868 (1976).

103. No. 78-91 (2 July 1979).

104. Id. at 1.

105. *Watson v. Jones*, 13 Wall. 679 (1871).

106. *Decker v. U.S. Department of Labor*, 473 Fed. Supp. 770, (E.D. Wis. July 1979).

107. *The Record* (Louisville, Ky.), 9 August 1979, p. 12.

108. The irony has not gone unnoticed in the Catholic press. See George H. Higgins, "Unions and Catholic Institutions," *America* 143, no. 3 (26 January 1980), p. 54. Also, Steve Askin, "Higgins on church as 'boss,' " *National Catholic Reporter* 16, no. 17, (22 February 1980), p. 1.

109. 440 U.S. 490 (1979).

110. Id. at 506.

111. Id. at 511. Citing 29 U.S.C. #152, sec. 2(2).

112. 49 Stat. 449, sec. 2(2).

113. *Central Dispensary & Emergency Hospital*, 44 N.L.R.B. 533 at 540 (1942).

114. E.g., *Polish National Alliance v. NLRB*, 322 U.S. 643 (1944).

115. *NLRB v. Catholic Bishop of Chicago*, 440 U.S. 490 at 512-17 (1979).

116. As reported in *The Record* (Louisville, Ky.), 13 Dec. 1979, p. 4.

117. *The Record*, 23 August 1979, p. 6.

118. Ibid.

119. As reported in the *Courier-Journal* (Louisville, Ky.), 13 September 1979, p. A-16.

120. As reported in *The Louisville Times*, 18 September 1979, p. 1.

3

RELIGIOUS TAX EXEMPTIONS: THE CASE-KNIFE APPROACH

If there is a "wall of separation" between church and government, it is riddled with fiscal holes. The brief recitation of case law on church-government fiscal relations in chapter 2 makes it quite clear that the Supreme Court has permitted many forms of public aid to religious and religiously affiliated organizations. That such aid is now constitutional goes without question. As Justice Hughes said, ". . . the Constitution is what the judges say it is."[1]

The problem is that the Court apparently assumes that indirect aid is constitutional, but any public aid that can be traced directly to a religious organization is *ipso facto* in violation of the Establishment Clause. As a result, the Court has been forced to devise a patchwork of tests and distinctions that purport to keep government from giving aid to religious organizations. And yet, those tests and distinctions notwithstanding, hundreds of millions of dollars of economic benefits go from all levels of government to all types of religious and religiously affiliated organizations every year. It seems to be a classic example of what might be called the "case-knife mentality."

In *The Adventures of Huckleberry Finn*, Huck and Tom Sawyer are trying to dig Jim out of a shed where he is being kept. Huck suggests using some picks that are handy, but Tom refuses, saying that prisoners never have picks available. The only proper way to do the job is to use case knives. Huck says,

"Confound it, it's foolish, Tom."
"It don't make no difference how foolish it is, it's the *right* way—and

it's the regular way. And there ain't no *other* way, that ever *I* heard of, and I've read all the books that gives any information about these things. They always dig out with a case-knife."

Huck is finally persuaded and the digging begins. But after several hours of work with little more than blisters to show for their effort Huck complains that they'll never get the job done.

"Well, then, what are we going to do, Tom?"
"I'll tell you. It ain't right, and it ain't moral, and I wouldn't like it to get out; but there ain't only just the one way: we got to dig him out with the picks, and *let on* it's case-knives."
"*Now* you're talking!" I says; "your head gets leveler and leveler all the time, Tom Sawyer," I says. "Picks is the thing, moral or no moral."

After further discussion, Tom explains that

". . . [I]t might answer for *you* to dig Jim out with a pick, *without* any letting on, because you don't know no better. Gimme a case-knife."
He had his own by him, but I handed him mine. He flung it down, and says:
"Gimme a *case-knife.*"
I didn't know just what to do—but then I thought. I scratched around amongst the old tools, and got a pick-ax and gave it to him, and he took it and went to work, and never said a word. He was always just that particular. Full of principle.[2]

The Court can invoke lofty principles and use artificial distinctions to settle particular cases, but it cannot alter the realities of economic life. Taking the "case-knife" approach to church-government fiscal relations is bad public policy both because decision makers can never be certain what the rules are and because the practice breeds cynicism in a whole area of public law. Once conventional rules of understanding have been abandoned it is easier to create new rules than to cope with those that are inconvenient. Huck and Tom had been going in and out of the house on the lightning rod during their efforts to dig Jim out. After digging all night, Huck reports that:

When I got up-stairs I looked out at the window and see Tom doing his level best with the lightning-rod, but he couldn't cut it, his hands were so sore. At last he says:

"It ain't no use, it can't be done. What you reckon I better do? Can't you think of no way?"

"Yes," I says, "but I reckon it ain't regular. Come up the stairs, and let on it's a lightning-rod."

So he done it.[3]

If a pick is a case-knife, why can't a stairway be a lightning rod? And if one form of aid to religious organizations is declared not to be aid, then why can't some other form of aid be declared something other than aid as well? One can hardly be surprised that policymakers at all levels of government are finding it very difficult to determine what form of aid will pass constitutional muster or that the public abandons principles in favor of clichés. This is especially true of aid to sectarian elementary and secondary education. As chapter 2 showed, past decisions in this area focus more on particular funding schemes than on generally applicable principles. The result has been a burgeoning of litigation, to which there seems to be no end, as proponents and opponents press their claims and legislators try to mold policies to fit the constitutional contortions demanded by the Court.

Current policy justifications are conceptually deficient. The case-knife mentality is bad economics and must be recognized as such. Ignoring economic reality can only undermine the basis for public policy. Yet that is precisely what the Court does in stating its position on property tax exemptions.

In the *Walz* case the only justice in the 8-1 vote majority willing to concede that tax exemptions were the same as subsidies was Justice Harlan. He voted nonetheless to uphold the constitutionality of property tax exemptions because he agreed with the majority that exemptions provide less entanglement between church and government than any other alternative. This was the "entanglement" test which Chief Justice Burger formulated in writing the majority opinion and which came to form the third part of the current three-part test discussed in chapter 2. For our purposes here the most important part of the Court's reasoning was its argument that an exemption is not the same as a subsidy:

Obviously a direct money subsidy would be a relationship pregnant with involvement and, as with most governmental grant programs, could encompass sustained and detailed administrative relationships for enforcement of statutory or administrative standards, but not in this case. . . . The government does not transfer part of its revenue to churches but simply abstains from demanding that the church support the state. No one has ever suggested that tax exemption has converted libraries, art galleries, or hospitals into arms of the state or employees "on the public payroll."[4]

In supporting the Court's position on this issue, Dean Kelley delineates what he believes are the most important operational distinctions between a subsidy and a tax exemption.

1. In a tax exemption, *no money changes hands* between government and organization . . .
2. A tax exemption, in and of itself, *does not provide one cent* to an organization . . .
3. The *amount* of a subsidy is determined by the legislature or an administrator; there is no "amount" involved in a tax exemption because it is "open-ended" . . .
4. Consequently, there is *no periodic legislative or administrative struggle* to obtain, renew, maintain, or increase the amount, as would be the case with a subsidy. . .
5. A subsidy is not *voluntary* in the same sense that tax exempt contributions are . . .
6. A tax exemption does not convert the organization into an agency of "state action," whereas a subsidy—in certain circumstances—may.[5]

While this is the sort of reasoning the Court has found acceptable, these are largely distinctions without substance.

Taking the last of Kelley's points first, there is no reason why an organization needs to be converted into an "agency of 'state action' " just because it receives a government subsidy. Further, such a conversion need never have been intended. In the voluntary sector in particular (which obviously includes religion) government often encourages alternatives to agencies of state action. That encouragement can take the form of either a tax exemption or a check. The recipient organization benefits either way. The "certain circumstances" which turn an organization into an agency of state action are not necessarily the result of a subsidy.

With regard to the tax exemption being more voluntary than a subsidy, Kelley is only partially correct. When one is permitted to reduce one's tax liability by making a philanthropic contribution (for example, taking a federal income tax deduction for a contribution to a charitable organization), it is true that the individual determines with his or her contribution the size of the exemption and its beneficiaries. Obviously, the richer the contributor the more benefits he or she can control. This equity question will be discussed further in chapter 5 where federal income tax policies are examined. The difficulty with Kelley's distinction is that it does not stop at federal income tax deductions, but includes all tax exemptions. There is nothing voluntary about a so-called homestead exemption that allows a homeowner over sixty-five to exempt the first $8,900 of the value of his or her home from property taxation. If the homeowner qualifies he or she will get the exemption, just as a qualifying individual will receive Medicare benefits. In other words, for most exemptions the distinction Kelley attempts to make here is not a valid one.

The claim that tax exemptions are free from annual legislative battles has an element of truth, but again does not distinguish exemptions from subsidies. Some students of public policy are concerned about tax exemptions because they tend to be forgotten once they are written into law. Common Cause shows that a great many federal exemptions are largely ignored year after year.[6] That is not to say, however, that all of the exemptions escape scrutiny. Capital gains and investment tax credits both attracted considerable legislation and lobbying attention during the last three Congresses. So it is not true that all exemptions avoid the sort of legislative examination to which annual appropriations are subjected. On the other hand, exemptions are not the only forms of economic benefit that continue from year to year with little annual review. In addition to the fact that budgeting is essentially incremental, there are many entitlement programs which provide cash benefits that go unchallenged year after year. It is much more the nature of the benefit than the form (exemption or subsidy) that determines the political vulnerability of a given program.

In talking about exemptions being "open-ended" amounts, Kelley implies that this is a characteristic unique to exemptions. Of course that is not the case. With everything from social welfare programs—which provide benefits to all who qualify, to cost-plus defense department contracts, there are many open-ended governmental subsidy and cash expenditure programs. Exemptions are not distinctive in this respect either.

Kelley's first two points, that exemptions do not provide one cent and no money changes hands, bring us to the larger issue of a concept often labelled tax expenditures. The Congressional Budget and Impoundment Control Act of 1974 defines tax expenditures as,

> . . . those revenue losses attributable to provisions of the Federal tax laws which allow a special exclusion, exemption, or deduction from gross income or which provide a special credit, a preferential rate of tax, or a deferral or tax liability.[7]

The Act also requires the reporting of tax expenditures. What this means is that when the government passes a law giving a tax break to person X, reducing his tax liability $100, the government has just lost $100 in revenue. Person X is $100 richer and the government is $100 poorer than each would have been without the tax break. The same result could have been achieved by collecting the tax from person X and then returning it to him in the form of a $100 cash grant or subsidy. (For the sake of simplicity in this example we will make the unrealistic assumption of zero administrative costs.) In either case, with a $100 tax break or a $100 cash grant, person X comes out $100 ahead and the government $100 behind. The label "tax expenditure" comes from the notion that foregone taxes provide economic benefits which are essentially the same as governmental expenditures in the form of checks going to groups or individuals. The biggest difference is that tax expenditures never show up in the budget. Consequently, in the interest of more informed public policy, the 1974 Budget Control Act mandates the computation of tax expenditures. An example of those calculations is in Appendix Table 3-1.

These numbers may be criticized on two grounds. One criticism is the Kelley complaint that no money ever changes hands. A second is that the concept of tax expenditures is necessarily ill-defined. Since the second criticism is more fundamental it will be discussed first.

The problem with tax expenditures, charge their critics, is that all calculations depend on a starting point which is highly arbitrary and subject to considerable disagreement.[8] Actually computing a tax expenditure requires establishing what might be called a "normal'' tax revenue. The tax expenditure is then computed as the difference between the "normal" tax revenue and the lesser amount of revenue collected after some tax "break" has been allowed. For example:

$$R = (B) \times (r)$$
$$R' = (B) \times (r')$$
$$TE = (R) - (R')$$

where:

  B = the tax base (income, property, retail sales, etc.)
  r = the "normal" tax rate
  R = the "normal" tax revenue
  r' = the lower tax rate resulting from a tax "break"
  R' = the lower tax revenue caused by the tax "break"
  TE = the amount of the tax expenditure, i.e., the tax revenue foregone by the government because of the special tax treatment

    (*Note:* It is possible to change tax revenues by altering either the tax base or tax rate, or both)

If everyone agrees on what constitutes the "normal" tax revenue these computations are possible. However, if there is substantial disagreement about the "normal" base or rate the calculations can never get past the first step. And that, say tax expenditure critics, is the basic problem.

   If the tax rate has changed every year for the past five years, which rate is to be used for calculating the tax expenditures? And what if the tax base has also been changing, for example, by varying the definition of taxable income? In fact, what is to be done about tax bases as a general principle? Critics contend that the tax expenditure concept inevitably leads to the conclusion that everything is subject to taxation, because by definition, anything not taxed is benefiting from a tax expenditure. Philosophically this produces a very unhealthy view of government *vis à vis* its citizens. And as a practical matter the assumption that anything not taxed is benefiting from a tax expenditure can lead to all manner of absurd examples.

Supporters of tax expenditure calculations respond by saying that some difficult computations at the margin are not enough to eliminate the usefulness of the concept. If there were a tax of 20¢ per $100 of assessed valuation of real property in city A, and if all property owners were required to pay the tax except those whose last names begin with G or W, then it seems fair to say that property owners with names beginning with G and W are getting a special tax break. It also seems fair to say that we can compute what that tax break is costing city A this year by determining what those property owners would have paid in property tax had they not received special tax treatment. The individuals getting the tax break might prefer not to have the information gathered and spread abroad for fear that public indignation would force termination of their special treatment, but it is possible to argue that policymakers cannot be considered to be completely informed until they have information about tax expenditures as well as budgetary expenditures. And finally, it seems fair to say that property owners G and W enjoy an economic benefit because of their special treatment. The contention that tax expenditures convey no economic benefit because no money changes hands is just economic foolishness. A property owner who does not have to pay $100 in property taxes has $100 more than he would have had without the special treatment. With that money he can now buy whatever he wishes rather than all the dreary things local governments pay for.[9] Conventional wisdom dictates that in an election year it is popular to vote for tax cuts. Voters like tax cuts because they think they get an economic benefit from the money which can be kept for private consumption rather than turned over to the government for public spending. They may not be economists but average citizens *do* know when they are coming out ahead on tax cuts.

Tax laws at all levels of government are full of exceptions and special dispensations for this classification and that, all put there in response to demands from groups who believed they deserved special treatment and had something to gain by getting it. Critics of the concept of tax expenditures would have us believe that all these groups have been wrong, that special treatment and economic benefits from tax exemptions are illusions. It is a position that stretches credulity beyond what even social scientists are allowed.

In most cases it is possible to identify special tax treatment (for the purposes of this inquiry, for religious or religiously affiliated organizations) and it is at least conceptually possible to calculate what it costs the government to provide that economic benefit to the organization. Pretending, as the Supreme Court does, that a tax exemption produces no direct economic benefit to the group or individual involved, is just bad economics. As Richard Morgan says,

. . . no one has yet convincingly distinguished for constitutional purposes, a governmental subsidy from a tax exemption. . . . On reflection it seems passing strange that American opinion should assume at one and the same time, that government may not contribute to the maintenance of religious institutions and that exemption of such institutions from the normal taxes paid by individuals, businesses, and so on, is perfectly permissable. This is, in the words of one commentator, "[O]ne of the most pervasive and firmly established anomalies in American law."[10]

Brookings Institution Senior Fellow Henry Aaron accurately observes that,

There is no logical distinction whatsoever between credits, deductions, and matching grants. If you name me a deduction, I can give you a matching grant, or credit; it will not take any fancy computer to calculate an equivalent formula or a genius to understand it. In some cases deductions may be simpler, in others credits or matching grants, but you name the distribution you want and I can give it to you through any one of the three devices. For this reason, it really surpasses my understanding as an economist how the lawyers and courts in general can sustain distinctions among these various tax devices, calling some constitutional and others unconstitutional.[11]

One of the empirical problems to be discussed later involves the difficulty of determining how much economic benefit an organization enjoys when it acts as the conduit for public money. When the form of the assistance is a budgetary allocation, the Supreme Court takes a very careful look at the program—even though the economic benefit to the religious organization may be indirect and not very substantial. However, when the form of the assistance is a tax expenditure the Court chooses to ignore the economic benefit bestowed, even though the benefit goes directly to the organization and is often quite substantial. Providing students with textbooks helps the sectarian school they attend, if only because it reduces the total cost of attending that school. If the students previously bought their own textbooks, it is not easy to impute a precise dollar benefit enjoyed by the school itself. In contrast, if the school's property is exempt from property tax there is no question that the school itself benefits from a tax expenditure. The irony is that what is in fact the most direct government aid to religious and religiously affiliated organizations has been largely ignored by the Court because it refuses to admit that tax expenditures are aid at all.

This state of affairs raises an issue on which there is disagreement. Do religious organizations have a uniquely strong claim to property tax exemptions? A standard accommodationist argument is that religious organizations provide valuable services and improve the moral tone of the community, making it a better place to live.[12] For these benefits received, the community has a *quid pro quo* obligation to religious organizations to provide some benefit in return—and the property tax exemption is the traditionally accepted form. Actually, this form is probably better than more exact alternatives because it is very difficult to determine a church's "fair share" for services like fire and police protection. One would need to determine how much a church "ought" to owe in property taxes and then subtract the value of benefits provided to the community free of charge to determine whether any property tax liability remains. Far easier, accommodationists contend, is to assume that the city is in the church's debt for what the church does to improve the community and just forget about paying property taxes.[13]

There are flaws in this argument if one takes it seriously. First, in *Walz* the Court property rejected the *quid pro quo* contention, recognizing that not all religious organizations contribute equally to the well-being of the larger community. Attempting in any serious way to base exemptions on benefits received from the exempted organization would lead to very unequal treatment of different churches (even within the same denomination) and present local and state authorities with impossible administrative difficulties. It is hard enough for assessors to fix a price on a piece of real estate. How could they reasonably be expected to place a dollar value on the moral character a given church has contributed to the community? Even if the concept of a "fair share" is confined to marginal costs to the community—the costs of the additional services the community must provide because there is now a church there rather than an empty lot—computations are far from easy.[14]

In addition to these practical shortcomings, this accommodationist argument has a philosophical failing related to basic principles of public finance. Readers interested in more detailed expositions of public finance theory can turn to many excellent works.[15] It is enough for our purposes here to discuss briefly the concepts of divisible benefits and free riders.

The benefits that come from some goods and services can be divided. That is, people who do not pay for the good or service can be excluded from enjoying the benefits of that good or service. If you do not pay for a pizza you do not get to eat it; if you do not pay for admission to the theater you do not get to see the motion picture. (This naturally assumes that you obey the law and do not steal the pizza or sneak into the show.) With other goods and services, the benefits are not so easily divided and those who pay cannot exclude those who do not pay from enjoying the benefits. If there is a swamp between your house and your neighbor's and your neighbor pays to have the swamp drained, there is no way your neighbor can keep you from enjoying the benefit of fewer mosquitos even though you did not contribute toward the cost of draining the swamp.

The size of the collectivity involved may well have an effect on the willingness of individuals to contribute voluntarily for the provision of goods and services with nondivisible benefits.[16] However, it is quite clearly in the individual's economic self-interest not to volunteer to pay if he or she knows the service will be provided whether the contribution is made or not. National defense is an example frequently used. You know the United States will have planes, guns, and ships whether you pay your federal taxes or not. So your economic incentive is not to pay—to be what is called a free rider. Of course if everyone is a free rider then there is no money for national defense or other goods and services with nondivisible benefits. And that is unacceptable because it has been determined as a matter of public policy that there should be money spent for national defense. It might also have been determined as a matter of local public policy to drain the swamp next to your house. If you were asked to contribute voluntarily for these worthy causes you might give something, but it would probably not be as much as you will give when you get a tax bill and are required to pay it or suffer unpleasant consequences. If the government were run on donations, how many of us would voluntarily give as much as we paid in taxes last year? Taxes, then, are one way the public forces individuals to pay for goods and services they want but will not pay for voluntarily because the benefits are nondivisible.[17]

The essential shortcoming of the accommodationists' position on religious property tax exemption is that they want to be free riders. They are willing to pay for goods and services that have divisible benefits. In the private sector it goes without saying that plumbers will be paid for fixing leaky church pipes and stationery stores will be paid for paper delivered. Similarly, accommodationists are willing to pay for water the churches receive from a public utility. However, a line is drawn for goods and services with nondivisible benefits provided by the public sector. Paying for water is acceptable, but paying for police services is not. While this desire to be a free rider whenever possible is a perfectly understandable position, it leaves the accommodationists on shaky ground. If churches can pay for one good or service provided by the public sector, why not all of them? The fact that the benefits of one service are more divisible than those of another does not change the civic or economic obligation of the members *vis à vis* the commonweal.

Accommodationists argue that requiring church members to pay property taxes on their homes and on the church to which they belong amounts to double taxation; it is a penalty for being church members. What this argument ignores is that the church property receives benefits from the public sector quite apart from any benefits received or costs borne by church members as homeowners. If the church catches fire it is the church building, not church members' homes, that requires the services of firefighters. This is basically just a variation of the free rider problem. Accommodationists want to make untenable distinctions between the public and private sectors. They are willing to buy fire insurance on the church even though the church members already have fire insurance on their own homes. Those are seen as two separate benefits. However, when it comes to paying for public fire protection for the church and for members' homes it is viewed as double taxation. In other words, where the benefits are clearly divisible (there is no insurance coverage if the premium is not paid) accommodationists are willing to pay—largely because there is no choice. Where benefits are nondivisible the accommodationists do not want to pay, hoping to be free riders.

The point here is not to urge the repeal of religious property tax exemptions, but rather to expose flaws in court distinctions and accommodationists' arguments. There is no economic, philosophical, or constitutional necessity for religious organizations to be granted unique exemptions from property taxes. Indeed, if at some future date more extensive use is made of user charges at the local level religious organizations will likely find themselves paying more to the public sector. For example, a city could mandate fire inspections and require that property owners pay a fee for the inspection—much like automobile safety inspections. Religious organizations might be expected to pay the fee like all other property owners.[18] This is, as we shall discuss in chapter 6, a viable alternative.

Finally, religious property tax exemptions are granted by every state in the union. Survey data indicate that there is general public support for religious property exemptions.[19] It seems a very remote political possibility that these exemptions will be eliminated. We do not argue that they should be. Our difficulty is with the rationales underlying such exemptions. For many years before the *Walz* case there were complaints that religious property exemptions violated the Establishment Clause because the exemptions subsidized religious organizations. In their rebuttal of these complaints accommodationists mustered arguments about the value of contributions religious organizations make to the community. However, it is quite clear that there is no satisfactory way to quantify such contributions and translate them into dollars. In short, the accommodationists' justification for religious property exemptions cannot be supported empirically. Vagueness is their strength.

The accommodationists have a further problem because even though they enjoy general public support, their cause is more self-serving than grounded in sound theory. Everyone wants to be a free rider if at all possible. No one wants to pay more taxes than necessary, and religious organizations are no exception. When the claim is extended still further, to assert that religious organizations have a unique right to property tax exemptions, we have gone beyond what the Court has ever held.

The Supreme Court's attempt to cope with the issue has done little to improve the situation. The Court was probably right to say that deciding whether to provide property tax exemptions is a legislative question; it is the province of the representative branch to determine whether certain types of property shall be exempt from taxation. Unfortunately, the Court went on to justify this position by saying that a tax exemption is not a subsidy. While the Court can alter the law, it cannot alter economic reality. And in this case economic reality is that tax exemptions are tax expenditures, and tax expenditures *do* provide economic benefits to beneficiaries that are virtually indistinguishable from a subsidy or budgetary expenditure. This is an important point because when the Court adopts what we have called a case-knife mentality, it makes it virtually impossible for public officials, and indeed for the Court itself, to formulate consistent policy. One need look no further than the *Wolman* case to see how thoroughly the Court has managed to confuse even itself. When the Court makes distinctions between direct and indirect aid or between subsidies and exemptions, it is calling a pick a case-knife. If a pick is a case knife does a jackhammer qualify too or do we have to take into account size and means of power for establishing what is a case-knife? What a tangled web we must weave to perpetuate the fiction.

The point is that when the Court began adopting a case-knife mentality because that seemed easier and less disruptive at the time, it was, to use another metaphor, sowing the wind. We are now reaping the whirlwind of confusion that has grown from that dissimulation. Policy on church-government fiscal relations is not consistent and certainly is not predictable. Equity and effectiveness also suffer. And none of this is necessary. If policy is based on fundamental precepts that are clear, and by all reasonable measures correct, the Court, religious groups, and public policymakers will be better served. Let us admit that churches are aided by government (and have been since the beginning of the Republic) and develop a constitutional theory that (1) recognizes this reality and (2) provides a foundation for rational rules surrounding that aid.

The gravamen of this chapter should be so clear by now that a detailed review of the cases discussed in chapter 2 is not necessary. The public sector provides aid in a variety of forms to religious and religiously affiliated organizations. Attempts to make distinctions between exemptions and subsidies, and between direct and indirect aid, are misguided. They ignore economic benefits bestowed by the public sector on religious organizations and may be fully justified, but neither existing case law nor accommodationist pleas for special treatment make good economic sense. Instead, policy needs to be based on an objective understanding of what exists. And of course doing that requires having good information. Unfortunately, there are many problems with the available information, as we will see in the next chapter.

NOTES

1. Mark Twain, *The Adventures of Huckleberry Finn* (New York: Washington Square Press, 1960).

2. Ibid.

3. Ibid.

4. 397 U.S. 644 at 694.

5. Dean Kelley, *Why Churches Should Not Pay Taxes* (New York: Harper and Row, 1977), p. 33.

6. Common Cause, *Gimme Shelters: A Common Cause Study of the Review of Tax Expenditures by the Congressional Tax Committee* (Washington, D.C.: Common Cause, 1978).

7. 31 U.S.C. 1302 (a) (3).

8. For example, see Boris I. Bittker, "Churches, Taxes and the Constitution," *Yale Law Journal* 78 (1969): 1285 and Tax Institute of America, *Tax Impacts on Philanthropy* (Princeton: Tax Institute of America, 1972).

9. It is sometimes said that one cannot buy a chalice with a tax exemption. That is wrong. The money that is not paid in taxes is a saving that can inceed be used to buy a chalice.

10. Richard E. Morgan, *The Supreme Court and Religion* (New York: The Free Press, 1972), pp. 103-04.

11. Henry Aaron, "Federal Encouragement of Private Giving," in *Tax Impacts on Philanthropy*, Tax Institute of America. (Princeton: Tax Institute of America, 1972), p. 211.

12. Bittker and Kelley develop this argument at some length. An example of an abbreviated list of these benefits is: "there must be some justification for permitting the tax exemption to continue. The defenses usually expounded to mitigate the economic tax loss resulting from the tax exemptions are: 1) to reward the private institutions for rendering socially desirable services; 2) to compensate the private institutions for rendering services (e.g., education) which, but for the performance by the private institution, would have to be performed by government; 3) to encourage religious teaching because such teaching improves the moral tone of the community; 4) to promote or encourage the particular activity or function conducted by the institution; 5) to encourage their unique contributions to the pluralism of American society by promoting diversity of viewpoint, enterprise, and association." *De Paul Law Review* XX (1971): 263.

13. It is probably worth noting that this accommodationist argument actually supports a neutralist position because religious organizations are not the only groups contributing the welfare of the community. The logical conclusion is that all nonprofit groups should be exempted from property taxes. As we will see in chapter 7, that seems generally to be the case, but without regard for the level of economic benefits the organization provides in services or receives in tax expenditures from the property tax exemption.

14. Robert A. Leone and John R. Meyer, "Tax Exemption and Local Property Tax," in *Local Public Finance and the Fiscal Squeeze: A Case Study*, ed. John R. Meyer and John M. Quigley (Cambridge, Mass: Ballinger, 1977), pp. 41-67.

15. See, for example, Richard A. Musgrave and Peggy B. Musgrave, *Public Finance in Theory and Practice* (New York: McGraw-Hill, 1973). See also Jesse Burkhead and Jerry Miner, *Public Expenditure* (Chicago: Aldine-Atherton, 1971).

16. Mancur Olson, *The Logic of Collective Action: Public Goods and the Theory of Groups* (Cambridge, Mass: Harvard University Press, 1973).

17. Consideration of merit goods and other aspects of collective supply and demand are omitted simply to make the explanation here as uncomplicated as possible for readers unfamiliar with the concepts being discussed.

18. Some observers advocate a much more extensive use of service charges to reduce the size of tax expenditures, e.g., National Tax Association - Tax Institute of America, Report on the Property Taxation Committee, "The Erosion of the Ad Valorem Real Estate Tax Base," *Tax Policy* 40 (1973). One step beyond would be payments in lieu of taxes. For example, see Alfred Balk, *The Religious Business* (Richmond, Va.: John Knox Press, 1968), p. 119. On the other hand, if some classes of property owners, such as nonprofit organizations, were exempted from the fee, religious organizations should be included in the list; exempting only religious organizations would violate the neutralist requirement for equal protection.

19. D. A. Gilbert and Paul J. Weber, "Political Implications of Public Opinion on Religious Property Tax Exemptions," *Assessors Journal* 13 (June 1978): 113-22.

4

AID TO RELIGION:
WHO GETS WHAT?

Once we have established that the public sector does indeed provide aid to religious and religiously affiliated organizations, it seems logical to ask how much money is involved. Normally that question is of greatest interest to separatists, who are anxious to demonstrate the prodigal and flagrant way in which the First Amendment is being violated. While that bias must be recognized in much of what is written on this topic, there is another more objective reason for seeking to put a dollar amount of public aid to religious and religiously affiliated organizations: the need for policymakers to predict and assess the results of their policies. Incomplete or inaccurate data make it difficult to formulate policy that will actually do what is intended, and make it even more difficult to know what has happened once a policy is implemented. Charging ahead without any feedback is rather like driving a car with one's eyes closed—some very unpleasant jolts may be expected.

We have seen in preceding chapters that bad case law produced the need for justifications that are themselves based on faculty economic reasoning. Taken together, bad law and bad economics have helped produce bad data. For example, if a tax expenditure is not aid, then why bother to compute its magnitude? For that matter, why impute a dollar value for any form of indirect aid? Where data are collected, they are very often not disaggregated in a way that permits identifying what portion goes to sectarian and what portion goes to nonsectarian institutions. This chapter will illustrate these sorts of data problems by examining religious property tax exemptions, federal income tax policies, and aid to education at elementary and secondary (K-12) and higher education levels. In the cases of property tax exemptions and aid to K-12 education the discussion will focus primarily on the paucity of data. For federal income tax and higher education the investigation will go beyond any previous work and make some estimates of the level of aid involved.

PROPERTY TAX

Before the *Walz* decision, many students of church-government relations were uneasy about the exemption of churches from property taxation. Arvo Van Alstyne's 1959 comment expressed this uneasiness: "One of the most pervasive and firmly established anomalies in American law is the permissibility of subsidization of religious institutions through tax exemption in a legal order constitutionally committed to separation of church and state."[1] Some separationists saw church property tax exemptions as a clear violation of the Establishment Clause, and therefore unconstitutional. Others saw it as a logical conclusion of the separationist doctrine. Accommodationists, on the other hand, viewed the exemptions as an appropriate deference to religion within the free exercise requirements of the First Amendment. In any case, everyone agreed, the Supreme Court had not ruled on the issue and the practice was widespread and well established.

The history of religious property tax exemptions is extensively discussed elsewhere[2] and need not be recapitulated here. Suffice it to say that religious property tax exemptions have been traced from the Egyptian pharoahs through the Roman Empire and Europe to the very earliest days of European settlement in this country. Today religious property tax exemptions exist in all fifty states and the District of Columbia. In sixteen states the state constitution makes religious property tax exemptions mandatory;[3] in fifteen others the constitutional language is permissive;[4] three states have a mixture of permissive and mandatory constitutional provisions.[5] The remaining sixteen states have either general authorizations for granting property tax exemptions or case law to support such powers.

The precise nature of the exemption varies a great deal from state to state. Some states require that a property be used for religious purposes, such as worship, in order to qualify for exemption, whereas in others, property is exempted if it is owned by a religious group. Still other states have both use and ownership tests for exemption. Places of worship are generally exempt. For other kinds of property, however, provisions differ from state to state. Van Altstyne's detailed review cites several different types of church property:[6] church land; tangible personal property of churches; church endowments and intangibles; living quarters for clergy and church personnel; church cemeteries; church-affiliated schools and colleges; hospitals, reformatories; poor houses; recreational facilities; asylums; homes for the aged; missionary societies; and others.[7] His general conclusion is that,

[D]espite frequently reiterated judicial apologetics as to the rule of "strict construction" which attends tax exemption laws, perusal of the decisions creates a definite impression that the explicit statutory language in which the exemption is framed normally has a great deal more to do with the result in contested cases (almost invariably cases in which judicial relief is sought following administrative denial of exemption) than general rubrics. . . . [And] some of the apparent lack of uniformity appears to be in reality merely the fortuitous consequence of inadvertent differences in draftsmanship, of possibly intuitive preferences for particular phraseology based upon largely inarticulated and inadequately considered premises.[8]

One reason for so much confusion about the justification for religious property tax exemptions is that legislative intent is not always clear when tax expenditures are enacted. The reason for granting the benefit need never be stated. A specified class of entities is simply not subject to the tax in question. That leaves observers with the task of inferring the legislative intent for themselves, and this leaves room for a wide range of misinterpretation. All that can be said with assurance is that the legislative body intended to provide some economic benefits as a general encouragement to the activities affected.

In the case of property tax exemptions for religious organizations, legislative intent is both varied and cloudy.[9] Because it is not altogether clear exactly what the policy is supposed to produce, it is very difficult to assess the effectiveness of this public policy. We know that proportionately more benefits go to religious organizations that own more real property than to those owning less, because if those with more property were required to pay property taxes their tax bill would be greater.[10]

To calculate the property tax revenues foregone because of exemptions granted to religious organizations, one needs to know the assessed value of exempted property. For assessors busy trying to maintain accurate assessments on taxable property, there is little to be gained by spending time and effort assessing or reassessing property that will not be taxed. Quigley and Stinson were able to identify only ten states that require the assessing of religious property.[11] Even in those states the assessment may not be accurate. As indicated in table 4-1, the ratio of assessed value to actual market value varies widely from state to state and within states. When the assessments that affect actual government revenues are themselves unreliable, it is reasonable to expect that the assessments made simply for reporting purposes are still less reliable. Beyond that, even when a good faith effort is made to assess religious property, there are many technical difficulties. How much is a church worth? What would it bring if it were sold? For some churches the structure may represent the greatest value. For others, particularly those located in central business districts, the property is valuable because of the site, not the building. Where land is more important, a market value might be ascertained. However, when improvements on the land must be taken into account, assessing is more difficult. Churches are not sold very often and they do not lend themselves to many alternate functions. It is hard to say what you can get for a used church.

Since so little information is collected about the value of religious property and what data we do have may not be completely accurate, estimates of the aggregate value of religious property tax exemptions can be nothing more than guesses.[12] The estimates most often cited are those assembled by Larson and Lowell for fourteen selected cities. The title of their book quite clearly reveals their point of view on the subject: *The Religious Empire: The Growth and Danger of Tax-Exempt Property in the United States.*[13] Or, as one of their earlier collaborations was titled, *Praise the Lord for*

Table 4-1

State Variations in Assessing Religious Property

STATES	RATIO OF ACTUAL ASSESSMENT TO LEGAL STANDARD	COEFFICIENT OF INTERAREA DISPERSION[1] (PERCENT)
Arizona	59.4	9
California	80.0	8
Colorado	69.0	10
Connecticut	n.c.[2]	16
Maryland	47.8	5
Minnesota	28.3	14
New Jersey	n.c.	21
New York	25.8	32
Ohio	73.8	8
Pennsylvania	26.6	26

Sources: Column One: Advisory Commission on Intergovernmental Relations, *The Property Tax in a Changing Environment*, M-83 (Washington, D.C.: Government Printing Office, 1974), p. 7.

Column Two: U.S. Department of Commerce, Bureau of the Census, *1972 Census of Governments*, vol. 2, *Taxable Property Values and Assessment —Sales Price Ratios*, pt. 2, "Assessment-Sales Price Ratios and Tax Rates," p. 57.

[1]The coefficient of interarea dispersion is defined as the mean of deviations (disregarding sign) from the median among the (assessment) ratios divided by the median ratio, with result expressed as a percentage. In other words, it is a measure of how much variation there is in assessment. The higher the number, the more the variation. Nearly half of the single family non-farm house assessments surveyed had coefficients less than 20%.

[2]n.c. = not computed

Tax Exemption.[14] With their bias so clear, it is interesting to note in table 4-2 that even Larson and Lowell's numbers show religious property constituting only 5.2 percent of the total tax base for all fourteen cities. Table 4-3 makes this a bit clearer by breaking the dollar amounts into percentages. The percentage of the total property tax base exempt in the religious category ranges from a high of 7.7 percent in St. Paul to a low of 2.5 percent in Cleveland. Adding

Table 4-2

An Analysis of Property in Fourteen Cities
(in thousands of dollars)

CITY	ALL	TAXABLE	EXEMPT	PUBLIC	PRIVATE
Boston	$ 8,500,000	$3,500,000	$5,000,000	$3,800,000	$1,200,000
Providence	1,970,000	1,446,200	523,800	225,500	298,300
Hartford	2,200,000	1,500,000	700,000	427,000	273,000
Baltimore	6,000,000	4,240,000	1,760,000	1,145,000	615,000
Washington	17,400,000	8,330,000	9,070,000	7,650,000	1,420,000
Richmond	2,524,795	1,963,958	560,836	414,484	146,351
Pittsburgh	4,165,000	2,858,000	1,307,000	696,000	611,000
Buffalo	3,200,000	2,000,000	1,200,000	735,000	465,000
Cleveland	6,400,000	4,500,000	1,900,000	1,200,000	700,000
St. Louis	5,400,000	3,470,000	1,930,000	1,400,000	530,000
St. Paul	4,850,436	3,529,174	1,321,262	822,072	499,190
Minneapolis	4,963,374	3,581,786	1,381,588	880,363	501,224
Denver	5,444,865	4,343,136	1,101,730	700,000	401,700
Portland, Ore.	7,843,069	6,601,804	1,241,265	938,526	302,739
Totals	80,861,539	51,864,058	28,997,479	21,033,945	7,963,534
Ratios					
Of All	100.0%	64.1%	35.9%	26.0%	9.8%
In Category		64.1%	35.9%	72.5%	27.5%

CITY	SECULAR	RELIGIOUS	PROTESTANT	CATHOLIC	JEWISH
Boston	$ 720,000	$ 480,000	$ 175,000	$ 245,000	$ 60,000
Providence	203,740	94,540	15,730	65,560	17,250
Hartford	139,000	134,000	76,000	57,140	860
Baltimore	225,000	390,000	181,000	161,200	47,500
Washington	726,000	694,000	334,000	342,000	18,000
Richmond	26,521	119,830	110,729	7,515	1,586
Pittsburgh	385,000	253,000	94,220	127,500	31,300
Buffalo	270,000	195,000	61,500	124,500	9,000
Cleveland	340,000	360,000	155,000	175,000	30,000
St. Louis	165,000	365,000	168,000	180,000	17,000
St. Paul	124,513	374,679	209,490	156,488	8,701
Minneapolis	232,017	269,217	184,758	73,145	11,314
Denver	127,000	274,700	161,000	90,000	23,700
Portland, Ore.	112,592	190,147	140,712	41,149	8,286
Totals	3,769,402	4,194,123	2,067,419	1,842,197	284,497
Ratios					
Of All	4.6%	5.2%	2.6%	2.3%	.3%
In Category	47.3%	52.7%	26.0%	23.1%	3.6%
Of Religious			49.3%	43.9%	6.8%

Source: Martin A. Larson and Stanley C. Lowell, *The Religious Empire* (Washington, D.C.: Robert B. Luce, 1976).

religious property to the tax rolls would increase general revenues generated by cities from their own sources by the amounts shown in the last column of table 4-3. The percentage added ranges from 0.5 percent in Cleveland to 4.9 percent in Hartford. The conclusion is quite clear: taxing religious property is not the answer to central city fiscal woes. Nonetheless, exempt properties do present a problem for central cities, as table 4-3 shows. What one needs to keep in mind, however, is that the type of exempt property having the most detrimental effect on central city tax bases is not religious but governmental (see table 4-2). Quigley and Schmenner found a decrease in the proportion of private sector and local government exempt property between 1909 and 1969, while the proportion of state government exempt property doubled and the federal government's proportion tripled.[15] We cannot put a dollar value on the tax expenditure of religious property tax exemptions, but we can say that it is a rather small and decreasing portion of the total cost of property tax exemptions.

FEDERAL INCOME TAX

The contributions and other income that religious organizations receive are largely exempt from taxation. In addition, individuals making contributions to religious organizations may usually deduct the amount of the contribution from the gross income on which they must pay federal income taxes. These two quite distinct public policies are often confused when people talk about an organization being in danger of losing its exemption, when in fact what will happen (for instance, for political activity) is that contributors will no longer be able to deduct their contributions to that organization.[16] The prospect strikes fear in the heart of organizational officials, not because their organization might be paying income taxes, but because contributions will probably dry up.

Losing a deduction could be expected to affect an individual's willingness to contribute to a religious, charitable, or other 501 (c) (3) organization (for which contributions are tax deductible)—only if deductions are itemized. For taxpayers who have relatively little income and take the standard deduction, not being able to deduct

Table 4-3

The Relative Significance of Religious Property Tax Exemptions on Fourteen Central Cities

	Percent of Total Property That is Tax Exempt	Percent of Tax Exempt Property That is Religious Property	Religious Exempt Property as a Percent Of Total Property	Additional Revenue From Taxing Religious Property As a Percent of City's Total General Revenues From its Own Sources[1]
Boston	59.4%	9.8%	5.8%	4.7%
Providence	26.5	17.7	4.7	4.1
Hartford	30.8	18.8	5.8	4.9
Baltimore	29.5	22.0	6.5	3.5
Washington, D.C.	52.1	7.7	4.0	.9
Richmond	22.2	21.2	4.7	2.0
Pittsburgh	31.4	19.1	6.0	3.4
Buffalo	37.3	16.1	6.0	4.5
Cleveland	29.1	8.6	2.5	.5
St. Louis	34.9	18.9	6.6	1.3
St. Paul	27.2	28.3	7.7	3.8
Minneapolis	31.9	16.9	5.4	3.1
Denver	20.2	24.8	5.0	1.2
Portland, Oregon	15.8	15.2	2.4	1.1

Sources: Larson and Lowell, *The Religious Empire,* and computations from U.S. Department of Commerce, Bureau of the Census, *City Government Finances,* Washington, D.C.: Government Printing Office, 1976.

[1]The percentage is computed from census data: percentage = $\dfrac{(Tp)(Er)}{Rt}$

Tp = total property tax revenues from own sources

Er = percent property tax base exempt for religious purposes

Rt = total general revenue from own sources

what they contribute to United Way or what they drop in the offering plate on Sunday means nothing. In contrast, taxpayers with high incomes and high marginal tax rates will be very much aware of deductions that can reduce total tax liability, and changes in deductions may affect their giving.

Table 4-4 is a simplified illustration of how the deduction works. If a married couple with $50,000 in income has a marginal tax rate of fifty percent, they will pay $25,000 in taxes and have $25,000 left to spend (column I). If they choose to give $1,000 to a church and the contribution is not deductible, the money has to come out of disposable income after taxes are paid; what they have left then is $24,000. However, if the $1,000 contribution is deductible, it comes off the top (column II), reducing their adjusted gross—or taxable—income to $49,000 and their tax bill to $24,500. Being able to deduct their contribution puts an extra $500 in the couple's pocket.[17] That $500 is a tax expenditure. All $1,000 goes to the church, but it costs the contributor only $500. The other $500 comes from the federal government.

We cannot say exactly how much deductions for contributions to religious organizations cost the federal govenment in tax expenditures. Pursuant to the Congressional Budget and Impoundment Control Act of 1974, the Treasury Department and Joint Committee on Internal Revenue Taxation estimate tax expenditures for "major functional categories." Unfortunately, religious contributions are not estimated separately; they are included in the category "charitable contributions other than health and education." Determining the portion of the $3,935,000,000 tax expenditure estimated for that category that can be attributed to religious giving is not easy because other sources of information report giving, not tax expenditures. There is an important difference between giving and tax expenditures. The contribution is the amount of money actually given. The tax expenditure is the value of the taxes lost because of the deduction taken for the contribution. The two cannot be used interchangeably because not all contributions are itemized as deductions.

In the case of giving to religious organizations this is important, because it has been established that lower-income classes concen-

Table 4-4

The Effect of Deductibility on
Charitable Contributions*

		(I) WITHOUT A DEDUCTION	(II) WITH A $1,000 DEDUCTION
Taxable Income	(A)	$50,000	$49,000
Marginal Tax Rate	(B)	50%	50%
Taxes (AxB)	(C)	$25,000	$24,500
Disposable Income (A-C)	(D)	$25,000	$24,500
Contribution	(E)	$ 1,000	—
Final Disposable Income (D-E)	(F)	$24,000	$24,500

*This simplified example compiled by the authors ignores all other deductions and exemptions and applies the full marginal rate for a married couple filing a joint return on $50,000 of salary income. The intention is to illustrate how a deduction creates a tax expenditure.

trate their philanthropic giving on religion, as shown in table 4-5. For many of these families the deductibility of religious contributions means very little because they use the standard deduction. Normal increases or decreases in their religious giving will not affect their tax liability and their contributions will not be counted as tax expenditures. As a result, multiplying the percentage of philanthropic giving going to religion (in fiscal year 1977 it was 47 percent)[18] against total tax expenditure estimates for philanthropic giving (in fiscal year 1977 it was $5,250 million)[19] will produce a total of $2,467.5 million and will overestimate the religious tax expenditure. Religious contributions may be 47 percent of the total given, but some unknown portion of that total has not been claimed as a deduction. Certainly the tax expenditure for contributions to religious organizations is not more than $2,467.5 million, and is probably less than $2,000 million.

A closer estimate can be derived by applying the income class percentages in table 4-5 to tax expenditure estimates for philanthropic giving disaggregated by income class. The results are shown in table 4-6. What the separation into income classes does is reduce

Table 4-5

**The Distribution of Giving to Major Donee Areas,
by Income, 1972**

ADJUSTED GROSS INCOME	PERCENT OF TOTAL GIVING OF EACH INCOME GROUP GOING TO:		
	Religion	Federated Drives*	Special Areas**
Under $10,000	70%	13%	17%
$10,000 to $20,000	66	15	19
$20,000 to $50,000	51	17	32
$50,000 to $200,000	27	17	56
$200,000 and over	7	9	84

Source: Commission on Private Philanthropy and Public Needs, *Giving in America: Toward a Stronger Voluntary Sector* (n.p.: Commission on Private Philanthropy and Public Needs, 1975).

  *Includes United Funds, Community Chests, etc.
  **Includes educational institutions, museums, hospitals

the skewing of upper-income giving, which goes in relatively smaller proportions to religion. While lower than the $2,467.5 million estimate which came from a grosser level of analysis, this $1,975.12 million estimate is probably still too high—the percentages attributed to the two lowest-income classes no doubt being greater for contributions than deductions, and hence overstated.

In summary, it must be concluded that data are simply not collected in a way that permits accurate calculation of the revenue lost by the federal government because of income tax deductions for religious contributions. However, these estimates indicate that the total is very likely less than $2 billion a year.

AID TO HIGHER EDUCATION

Chapter 2 explained that *Tilton v. Richardson* has permitted substantial numbers of dollars to flow into sectarian institutions of higher education. As a point of information it would be interesting

Table 4-6

Estimates of Tax Expenditures from Deductions of Contributions to Religious Organizations Disaggregated by Income Class

Income Class	Estimated Tax Expenditure for Charitable Contributions (in millions)	Percent of Charitable Contributions Given to Religious Organizations	Tax Expenditure for Religious Giving Deductions (in millions)
Under $10,000	$ 68	70%	$ 47.6
$10-$20,000	678	66	447.48
$20-$50,000	1,954	51	996.54
$50-$200,000	1,525	27	411.75
Over $200,000	1,025	7	71.75
Total	$5,250		$1,975.12

Sources: Column one: Edmund S. Muskie, "Muskie Says Benefits of Many Tax Breaks Go Mostly to the Wealthy," *Muskie News,* Press Release, 13 February 1978.

Column two: Commission on Private Philanthropy and Public Needs, *Giving in America: Toward a Stronger Voluntary Sector* (n.p.: Commission on Private Philanthropy and Public Needs, 1975).

Column three: Computed from columns one and two.

to know how many public sector dollars are going to these colleges and universities. However, that is very difficult to determine because most fiscal data are simply disaggregated into categories of public and private. While that division serves many analytical purposes, it is not very helpful for studying aid to religiously affiliated schools; making no differentiation between Stanford and Concordia Lutheran Junior College creates too many problems. Aggregate estimates of public aid to private schools are interesting,[20] but not very useful for our purposes here because there is no way to know what proportions are going to religiously affiliated institutions.

Clearly, what needs to be done is to identify religiously affiliated institutions of higher education and find out how much public sector money they receive.[21] Unfortunately, not all enumerators agree. The most comprehensive list was developed by Pattillo and Mackenzie, using returns from a survey of "1,189 private institutions of higher learning listed in the *Education Directory*, 1962-63 (except theological schools, Bible colleges and other institutions devoted exclusively to the preparation of persons for church vocations)."[22] Although there is a risk that their list is somewhat dated, they have identified and substantiated a religious affiliation for more colleges and universities than any other source, including the *Directory of Higher Education.*

Using the Pattillo and Mackenzie list of schools, it is possible (although tedious) to go through the list of 2,517 institutions that the National Science Foundation reports received aid from selected federal agencies. Institution names are not always the same on the NSF printout as they are in the Pattillo and Mackenzie or other listings, so there is some possibility of error in the matching process. Still, the amounts involved for single institutions are generally small enough that the total would hardly be affected. As Appendix A shows, the total federal obligations to religiously affiliated institutions of higher education (including seminaries and the like) approaches a half billion dollars per year. This does not include aid which can yield indirect benefits to the institution, such as veteran's benefits for individuals attending religiously affiliated institutions. Nor does it include direct economic benefits in the form of exemption from taxes on such assets as real property or tuition paid by the military for students on ROTC or even active status. State aid is also not included.[23] Nonetheless, Susan Nelson's general conclusion about private higher education clearly applies to the sectarian sector as well.

The private sector is not an "independent" sector, at least financially. Existing public policies play a crucial role in the financing of private higher education. Though many schools may still receive little benefit from government programs, the principle of public contributions, direct or indirect, to private colleges and universities is firmly established.[24]

We cannot estimate with assurance the total dollar value of these economic benefits going from the public sector to religiously af-

Table 4-7

**Attitudes of Opinion Leaders in Thirty-Two States toward Private Higher Education,
as Judged by Executive Directors of State Associations
of Private Colleges and Universities, 1975**

	Favorable	Neutral	Unfavorable	No Response or Not Applicable	Total
Political Leaders:					
Governor	25	5	2	0	32
Governor's staff	21	8	2	1	32
Legislature	24	5	3	0	32
Legislative education committees	24	6	2	0	32
Legislative committee staffs	20	7	1	4	32
Coordinating agency staff	20	6	2	4	32
Coordinating agency board	20	5	2	5	32
Major media	19	8	2	3	32
Educational Leaders:					
State universities	14	13	3	2	32
State colleges	8	11	11	2	32
Community colleges	6	13	8	5	32
Other public post-secondary education	6	11	3	12	32
Proprietory schools	10	14	2	6	32
Public secondary schools	15	6	6	5	32
Private secondary schools	23	2	0	7	32
Secondary school counselors	15	9	2	6	32
Overall Political Climate	24	6	2	0	32

Source: Howard R. Bowen and W. John Minter, *Private Higher Education* (Washington, D.C.: Association of American Colleges, 1975), p. 40.

filiated colleges and universities, but we can say the total is substantial, and the aid seems likely to continue. For instance, if the political judgments of executive directors of state associations of private colleges and universities reported in table 4-7 are correct, state aid will continue to flow to private institutions. Eulau et al. find that the inclination to assist private higher education is greatest in states where private schools educate a relatively large proportion of the state's college students.[25] Nelson's correlations agree.

The factors that seem most related to state aid are (1) an explicit desire to help a private sector where it is an important force in the life of the state, (2) a high budget priority afforded higher education in general, and (3) a lack of commitment to low tuition at public institutions. It is particularly noteworthy that the level of state subsidy to public higher education is independent of aid to the private sector.[26]

Some skeptics might disagree with Nelson's last statement, contending that when money goes to private colleges and universities there is that much less available for the public institutions. To test this notion Nelson examined higher education expenditures in eleven states. She found that

> [T]he regression analysis indicates that only in New York is the trade-off hypothesis clearly valid. In three states—California, South Carolina, and Ohio—there is strong evidence that the opposite is true—that state aid to public and private higher education move together. Alabama and Minnesota show neither a trade-off nor a positive relation, while the findings for the other five states are simply inconclusive.[27]

No matter what condition obtains in a particular state, whether a high or low level of state funding for private higher education, drastic changes seem unlikely. What we have found is that a large amount of federal funding goes to church-affiliated colleges and universities under a variety of direct and indirect aid programs. Exact figures are impossible to obtain. In 1975 aid approached half a billion dollars. We can assume that in the years since then it has increased.

PRIMARY AND SECONDARY EDUCATION

Discussions about public aid to nonpublic primary and secondary (K-12) schools generally focus on budgetary allocations. As chapters 1 and 2 pointed out, the Supreme Court has been almost exclusively preoccupied with aid that would show up in a public sector budget—buying textbooks, providing transportation, and the like. On one level it can be conceded that these are appropriate concerns because many programs and many dollars are involved.

Exactly how many public sector dollars find their way to sectarian K-12 schools is difficult to pin down for a number of reasons. Programs and funding levels at federal, state, and local levels change from year to year. In addition, the confusion that arises from not being sure what the Court will and will not allow means that programs get implemented in the hope that they will pass constitutional tests, only to disappear when the Court strikes them down. The result is that dollar amounts going to sectarian K-12 schools in one year cannot necessarily be expected to follow a straight-line projection into following years. Further, there are problems caused by the way data are collected and aggregated. For some programs there is no thorough and systematic reporting of funds going to nonpublic schools.[28] In other instances the method of reporting or accounting for funds may mask or distort the extent of economic benefits conferred by the public sector or received by nonpublic schools. "In-kind" assistance such as dual enrollment, shared facilities, service programs, and pupil transportation may not involve an actual transfer of funds. The benefit will therefore not show up in the nonpublic school budget and the total costs involved may or may not be reflected in the public sector budget.[29]

Finally, the data are most often simply divided into public and nonpublic classifications. For K-12 education this is not as big a problem as it is for higher education, because approximately eighty-nine percent of nonpublic K-12 schools are church-related. However, as tables 4-8 and 4-9 show, the split between church- and nonchurch-related private schools varies considerably from state to state, especially for grades 9 through 12. In Illinois, Pennsylvania, and Wisconsin, nonpublic K-12 education is largely sectarian; in Florida and Texas the nonpublic school enrollment is divided quite evenly between sectarian and nonsectarian schools; and in Mississippi and Virginia there is greater enrollment in nonsectarian than sectarian private schools. It may be of use for rough approximations to assume that slightly less than 90 percent of funds listed as going to nonpublic schools is actually finding its way to sectarian institutions, but it overlooks many variations from state to state. It also ignores the nature of the program involved. A program sending large numbers of dollars to an inner city parochial school with many minority students may provide no aid at all to a suburban prep school or military academy. This point is illustrated rather well in Table 4-10. Sectarian K-12 schools participate in federal programs designed to help the needy at a much higher rate than do nonsectarian schools. Whether this difference in participation rates is due to differences in educational philosophy, financial need, types of students, or some combination of these, the fact is that at least some federal money going to nonpublic K-12 schools flows at quite different rates to sectarian and nonsectarian schools.

Table 4-8

Percentage Distribution of Enrollment in Elementary and Secondary Schools by Control and by State: Spring 1970

STATE	KINDERGARTEN THROUGH GRADE 8				GRADES 9 THROUGH 12			
	Total	Public schools	Nonpublic schools Church-related	Non-church-related	Total	Public schools	Nonpublic schools Church-related	Non-church-related
1	2	3	4	5	6	7	8	9
United States	100.0	88.1	9.7	2.2	100.0	90.2	6.8	3.0
Alabama	100.0	93.0	2.3	4.6	100.0	96.6	1.3	2.0
Alaska	100.0	97.5	1.1	1.4	100.0	95.6	2.0	2.4
Arizona	100.0	91.4	5.6	3.0	100.0	93.7	4.0	2.3
Arkansas	100.0	95.5	2.0	2.5	100.0	97.1	1.3	1.6
California	100.0	91.5	6.8	1.7	100.0	92.9	5.0	2.1
Colorado	100.0	92.7	5.9	1.4	100.0	93.4	4.2	2.3
Connecticut	100.0	86.7	11.6	1.7	100.0	83.5	9.2	7.3
Delaware	100.0	86.7	10.0	3.4	100.0	88.6	5.7	5.7
District of Columbia	100.0	89.7	6.3	4.0	100.0	85.3	6.6	8.0
Florida	100.0	89.5	5.5	5.0	100.0	93.3	3.5	3.2
Georgia	100.0	94.5	1.4	4.1	100.0	96.3	1.0	2.7
Hawaii	100.0	89.2	5.4	5.5	100.0	87.2	3.7	9.1
Idaho	100.0	93.9	2.9	3.2	100.0	97.4	1.6	1.0
Illinois	100.0	82.9	15.9	1.2	100.0	85.3	12.1	2.6
Indiana	100.0	89.8	9.1	1.1	100.0	92.7	5.6	1.7

(continued)

Table 4-8 (continued)

STATE	KINDERGARTEN THROUGH GRADE 8				GRADES 9 THROUGH 12			
	Total	Public schools	Nonpublic schools		Total	Public schools	Nonpublic schools	
			Church-related	Non-church-related			Church-related	Non-church-related
1	2	3	4	5	6	7	8	9
Iowa	100.0	89.7	9.7	.6	100.0	90.7	7.7	1.6
Kansas	100.0	92.5	6.7	.7	100.0	93.4	4.7	1.9
Kentucky	100.0	89.6	8.4	2.0	100.0	91.0	6.2	2.8
Louisiana	100.0	84.2	10.9	4.9	100.0	87.4	8.3	4.3
Maine	100.0	94.1	5.2	.7	100.0	94.0	2.3	3.7
Maryland	100.0	87.0	10.4	2.7	100.0	88.0	7.2	4.8
Massachusetts	100.0	83.1	13.7	3.1	100.0	83.2	11.0	5.7
Michigan	100.0	87.4	11.8	.8	100.0	89.0	9.2	1.7
Minnesota	100.0	86.9	12.4	.7	100.0	91.5	6.7	1.8
Mississippi	100.0	92.2	2.0	5.7	100.0	94.6	1.1	4.3
Missouri	100.0	86.8	11.9	1.3	100.0	88.3	8.2	3.5
Montana	100.0	92.4	5.0	2.6	100.0	93.2	5.1	1.7
Nebraska	100.0	86.1	13.4	.4	100.0	88.1	10.3	1.6
Nevada	100.0	96.7	2.9	.4	100.0	95.8	2.8	1.4
New Hampshire	100.0	82.9	13.4	3.7	100.0	86.9	8.0	5.1
New Jersey	100.0	81.7	16.8	1.5	100.0	84.0	11.7	4.2
New Mexico	100.0	93.5	3.6	2.9	100.0	96.2	1.2	2.6
New York	100.0	81.1	16.8	2.0	100.0	83.3	12.0	4.7
North Carolina	100.0	95.2	1.3	3.5	100.0	97.6	.5	2.0
North Dakota	100.0	91.3	7.0	1.7	100.0	93.6	5.4	1.0
Ohio	100.0	86.5	12.5	1.0	100.0	88.2	9.3	2.5
Oklahoma	100.0	97.1	1.7	1.2	100.0	97.2	1.3	1.5

Oregon	100.0	91.6	5.3	3.1	100.0	94.7	3.8	1.6
Pennsylvania	100.0	80.4	17.7	1.8	100.0	83.7	12.6	3.7
Rhode Island	100.0	79.8	17.7	2.5	100.0	84.0	10.6	5.4
South Carolina	100.0	94.2	1.5	4.3	100.0	96.8	1.0	2.2
South Dakota	100.0	93.2	5.8	.9	100.0	94.5	4.1	1.4
Tennessee	100.0	94.4	2.2	3.5	100.0	95.3	1.7	3.0
Texas	100.0	92.9	3.7	3.5	100.0	95.9	2.0	2.0
Utah	100.0	98.1	1.5	.4	100.0	97.6	1.2	1.2
Vermont	100.0	89.9	7.2	2.9	100.0	88.8	6.2	4.9
Virginia	100.0	92.5	2.9	4.6	100.0	94.9	1.7	3.4
Washington	100.0	93.7	4.9	1.4	100.0	94.4	3.5	2.1
West Virginia	100.0	95.4	2.9	1.7	100.0	95.8	2.5	1.7
Wisconsin	100.0	80.1	19.3	.6	100.0	89.4	8.8	1.8
Wyoming	100.0	96.1	3.0	.9	100.0	97.6	1.1	1.3

Source: U.S. Department of Health, Education, and Welfare, Education Division, *Digest of Education Statistics 1976 Edition*, by W. Vance Grant and C. George Lind, National Center for Education Statistics, NCES 77-401 (Washington, D.C.: Government Printing Office, 1977), p. 45.

Table 4-9

Enrollment in Elementary and Secondary Schools,

STATE	KINDERGARTEN THROUGH GRADE 12							KINDERGARTEN	
	Total	Public schools	Nonpublic schools		Total	Public schools	Nonpublic	
			Church-related	Non-church-related			Church-related	
1	2	3	4	5	6	7	8
United States	50,715,261	44,983,062	4,499,857	1,232,342	3,024,398	2,544,400	130,600
Alabama	865,168	813,803	17,782	33,583	30,489	12,668	2,147
Alaska	83,990	81,518	1,079	1,393	6,606	6,333	37
Arizona	462,980	476,018	23,810	13,157	22,896	14,021	2,039
Arkansas	457,090	433,839	8,017	10,734	11,714	4,860	635
California	4,925,470	4,526,521	308,338	90,611	353,916	333,498	7,704
Colorado	574,037	533,554	31,096	9,387	39,638	37,147	548
Connecticut	765,637	656,676	83,789	25,167	57,193	54,767	1,692
Delaware	144,702	126,177	12,764	5,761	9,241	7,459	287
District of Columbia	162,893	144,305	10,453	8,135	10,219	9,121	302
Florida	1,552,537	1,406,486	77,179	69,872	85,823	50,179	6,358
Georgia	1,133,339	1,076,262	15,129	41,948	45,711	22,313	2,344
Hawaii	199,748	176,983	9,770	12,995	14,615	12,980	560
Idaho	190,183	180,095	4,735	4,753	7,919	3,998	240
Illinois	2,790,061	2,331,644	414,460	43,957	188,593	170,240	12,017
Indiana	1,329,368	1,204,626	108,136	16,606	88,430	80,969	2,157
Iowa	718,299	646,327	65,439	6,533	52,224	50,849	961
Kansas	550,294	510,694	33,805	5,795	35,962	34,813	700
Kentucky	765,203	688,743	59,626	16,834	18,441	10,026	1,006
Louisiana	985,160	837,682	100,819	46,659	43,894	25,772	6,340
Maine	252,340	237,388	11,067	3,885	18,179	17,606	346
Maryland	1,012,474	883,295	96,439	32,740	65,445	56,532	2,453
Massachusetts	1,381,151	1,148,438	178,995	53,718	85,194	63,628	4,522
Michigan	2,415,258	2,122,968	266,622	25,668	175,055	168,627	4,580
Minnesota	1,026,670	906,388	109,904	10,378	70,140	66,833	1,975
Mississippi	594,610	552,064	10,718	31,828	23,800	14,878	1,792
Missouri	1,134,652	989,702	123,614	21,336	74,926	68,655	3,612
Montana	187,224	173,470	9,434	4,320	8,093	5,322	269
Nebraska	378,851	328,441	47,462	2,948	27,230	26,150	969
Nevada	122,328	117,964	3,517	847	8,545	8,370	70
New Hampshire	177,517	149,026	21,235	7,256	9,501	5,986	293

	GRADES 1 THROUGH 8				GRADES 9 THROUGH 12			
schools	Total	Public schools	Nonpublic schools		Total	Public schools	Nonpublic schools	
Non-church-related			Church-related	Non-church-related			Church-related	Non-church-related
9	10	11	12	13	14	15	16	17
340,389	33,210,219	29,375,178	3,371,239	463,802	14,480,634	13,063,465	989,018	428,451
15,674	590,713	565,354	12,400	12,959	243,966	235,781	3,235	4,950
236	57,990	56,651	652	687	19,394	18,534	390	470
5,938	311,421	290,590	16,571	4,260	128,663	120,507	5,200	2,956
5,719	310,315	302,159	5,705	2,451	130,561	126,820	1,677	2,064
12,714	3,135,376	2,858,575	229,407	47,394	1,436,178	1,334,448	71,227	30,503
1,948	369,576	342,428	23,546	3,602	164,823	153,984	7,002	3,837
1,234	491,412	421,199	62,164	8,049	217,027	181,210	19,933	15,884
1,495	96,125	83,849	10,241	2,035	39,336	34,869	2,236	2,231
796	111,497	100,050	7,420	4,027	41,177	35,134	2,731	3,312
29,286	1,029,887	947,887	55,558	26,442	436,827	407,420	15,263	14,144
21,054	779,467	757,173	9,580	12,714	308,161	296,776	3,205	8,180
1,075	127,678	113,908	7,084	6,686	57,455	50,095	2,126	5,234
3,681	122,840	118,831	3,533	476	59,424	57,866	962	596
6,336	1,818,374	1,493,160	307,732	17,482	783,094	688,244	94,711	20,139
5,304	869,209	779,037	85,176	4,996	371,729	344,620	20,803	6,306
414	454,978	404,074	48,149	2,755	211,097	191,404	16,329	3,364
449	348,942	321,383	25,275	2,284	165,390	154,408	7,830	3,062
7,409	532,061	483,303	45,283	3,475	214,701	195,414	13,337	5,950
11,782	677,917	581,759	72,622	23,536	263,349	230,151	21,857	11,341
227	162,664	152,550	9,104	1,010	71,497	67,232	1,617	2,648
6,460	671,946	584,684	74,137	13,125	275,083	242,079	19,849	13,155
17,044	898,132	753,666	130,605	13,861	397,825	331,144	43,868	22,813
1,848	1,542,776	1,333,380	197,731	11,665	697,427	620,961	64,311	12,155
1,332	652,543	561,493	87,592	3,458	303,987	278,062	20,337	5,588
7,130	412,702	387,696	7,130	17,876	158,108	149,490	1,796	6,822
2,659	750,112	647,599	94,544	7,969	309,614	273,448	25,458	10,708
2,502	123,209	116,006	6,328	875	55,922	52,142	2,837	943
111	240,706	204,625	35,046	1,035	110,915	97,666	11,447	1,802
105	81,045	78,228	2,527	290	32,738	31,366	920	452
3,222	119,552	100,935	17,057	1,560	48,464	42,105	3,885	2,474

(continued)

Table 4-9 (continued)

STATE	KINDERGARTEN THROUGH GRADE 12				KINDERGARTEN		
	Total	Public schools	Nonpublic schools		Total	Public schools	Nonpublic
			Church-related	Non-church-related			Church-related
1	2	3	4	5	6	7	8
New Jersey	1,768,886	1,456,665	272,117	40,104	126,243	114,014	8,929
New Mexico	294,927	277,954	8,687	8,286	11,173	6,805	500
New York	4,280,362	3,498,963	662,258	119,141	295,980	264,880	21,423
North Carolina	1,227,202	1,176,681	12,991	37,530	39,557	17,667	3,123
North Dakota	165,940	152,675	10,780	2,485	6,801	5,130	162
Ohio	2,746,111	2,387,776	319,290	39,045	180,977	170,431	4,346
Oklahoma	615,149	597,564	9,549	8,036	34,362	31,251	396
Oregon	515,102	476,637	24,852	13,613	23,737	14,398	890
Pennsylvania	2,854,337	2,322,115	464,706	67,516	174,152	156,783	7,612
Rhode Island	220,742	178,765	34,750	7,227	14,686	12,477	790
South Carolina	673,072	638,993	9,290	24,789	23,575	10,934	1,847
South Dakota	183,072	171,415	9,698	1,959	11,375	11,022	126
Tennessee	919,183	869,714	18,722	30,747	33,542	19,328	1,519
Texas	2,820,732	2,643,322	90,659	86,751	125,009	63,470	11,995
Utah	309,555	303,271	4,341	1,943	21,334	20,884	276
Vermont	111,967	100,289	7,765	3,913	6,094	4,497	293
Virginia	1,134,726	1,057,063	29,602	48,061	48,581	28,785	2,578
Washington	865,429	812,584	38,867	13,978	57,574	54,022	548
West Virginia	402,286	384,429	11,127	6,730	8,218	4,484	232
Wisconsin	1,184,416	980,668	192,437	11,311	86,903	83,107	3,051
Wyoming	87,826	84,812	2,130	878	5,393	5,045	9

Source: U.S. Department of Health, Education, and Welfare, Education Division, *Digest for Education Statistics,* NCES 77-401 (Washington, D.C.: Government Printing

GRADES 1 THROUGH 8					GRADES 9 THROUGH 12			
schools			Nonpublic schools				Nonpublic schools	
Non-church-related	Total	Public schools	Church-related	Non-church-related	Total	Public schools	Church-related	Non-church-related
9	10	11	12	13	14	15	16	17
3,300	1,144,313	923,952	204,669	15,692	498,330	418,689	58,519	21,112
3,868	200,071	190,635	7,167	2,269	83,683	80,514	1,020	2,149
9,677	2,754,382	2,209,351	493,403	51,628	1,230,000	1,024,732	147,432	57,836
18,767	831,569	811,616	8,183	11,770	356,076	347,398	1,685	6,993
1,509	108,062	99,723	7,873	466	51,077	47,822	2,745	510
6,200	1,780,234	1,525,440	241,698	13,096	784,900	691,905	73,246	19,749
2,715	398,441	389,002	6,772	2,667	182,346	177,311	2,381	2,654
8,449	330,856	310,279	17,940	2,637	160,509	151,980	6,022	2,527
9,757	1,826,141	1,450,793	349,343	26,005	854,044	714,539	107,751	31,754
1,419	145,199	115,153	27,496	2,550	60,857	51,135	6,464	3,258
10,794	460,341	444,905	5,635	9,801	189,156	183,154	1,808	4,194
227	115,683	107,451	7,258	974	56,014	52,942	2,314	758
12,695	624,640	601,662	12,716	10,262	261,001	248,724	4,487	7,790
49,544	1,920,220	1,835,913	62,799	21,508	775,503	743,939	15,865	15,699
174	194,035	190,456	2,894	685	94,186	91,931	1,171	1,084
1,304	73,812	67,308	5,477	1,027	32,061	28,484	1,995	1,582
17,218	776,013	733,981	21,628	20,404	310,132	294,297	5,396	10,439
3,004	552,068	516,993	29,447	5,628	255,787	241,569	8,872	5,346
3,502	273,782	264,669	7,921	1,192	120,286	115,276	2,974	2,036
745	752,490	589,023	159,168	4,299	345,023	308,538	30,218	6,267
339	56,702	54,641	1,853	208	26,731	25,176	274	331

of Education Statistics 1976 Edition, by W. Vance Grant and C. George Lind, National Center Office, 1977), p. 44.

Even with all these caveats in mind, available information permits two broad generalizations: a wide array of programs is funneling money into sectarian K-12 schools and many dollars are involved. For the reasons mentioned above, it is difficult to determine precisely how many dollars of public aid go to sectarian K-12 schools. Daniel Sullivan's estimate is roughly $650 million for nonpublic schools, including sectarian and nonsectarian. What is most interesting to note about his estimates in table 4-11 is that economic benefits coming through tax deductions and exemptions exceed those coming from direct expenditures—at the federal level, at the local level, and for total aid.

Sullivan's estimates reinforce two points made in chapter 3. The Court has been very concerned about budgetary allocations for nonpublic K-12 education, when it may well be that a larger total economic benefit is being enjoyed from tax expenditures. Moreover, the economic benefits that come from tax expenditures clearly inure to the educational institution. With direct or budgetary expenditures that is not necessarily the case. When a school is exempted from a tax on its property, the economic benefit clearly goes to the institution. However, if parents are responsible for transporting their children to a nonpublic school and the state begins providing free school bus transportation, the institution receives only an indirect economic benefit. Consequently, even if all the difficulties in determining the level of public aid to sectarian K-12 schools mentioned earlier were overcome, there would still remain the problem of computing the total economic benefit enjoyed by the schools themselves.

The Court alleges that for the aid to be permissible the school can get no economic benefit whatever. However, that is simply not the current state of affairs. The data already presented make it abundantly clear that sectarian K-12 schools receive substantial economic benefit from the public sector. On the other hand, totaling up every form of aid that goes to nonpublic K-12 schools, and implying that all such money is providing a direct economic benefit to religious instruction or the propagation of religion, is also misleading. The public sector provides a considerable amount of dollars of direct and indirect economic benefit to sectarian K-12 schools.

Table 4-10

School Participation Rates in Selected Federal Assistance Programs, by Affiliation: United States, October 1, 1976

AFFILIATION	NUMBER OF SCHOOLS	PROGRAM PARTICIPATION							
		One or more		ESEA		Food and milk			
		Number	Percent	Number	Percent	Number	Percent		
All schools	14,757	12,083	81.9	11,154	75.6	8,564	58.0
Nonaffiliated	2,210	1,129	51.1	900	40.7	588	26.6
Affiliated	12,547	10,954	87.3	10,254	81.7	7,976	63.6
Baptist	310	49	15.8	36	11.6	19	6.1
Calvinist	182	167	91.8	159	87.4	158	86.8
*Catholic	8,986	8,846	98.4	8,567	95.3	6,313	70.3
Episcopal	304	187	61.5	156	51.3	105	34.5
Jewish	264	240	90.9	210	79.5	187	70.8
Lutheran	1,366	1,055	77.2	850	62.2	920	67.3
**S. D. A.	517	111	21.5	41	7.9	90	17.4
Other	618	299	48.4	235	38.0	184	29.8

Source: National Center for Education Statistics, *Nonpublic School Statistics, 1976-77, Advance Report* (Washington, D.C.: U.S. Department of Health, Education, and Welfare, 1977), p. 4.

*Roman Catholic (not including Eastern Orthodox)

**Seventh Day Adventist

Table 4-11

**Public Aid to Nonpublic Schools and Total Income of
Nonpublic Schools, Fiscal Year 1971**

TYPE OF AID AND INCOME ITEM	AMOUNT (MILLIONS)	PERCENTAGE OF TOTAL
Federal Aid		
Direct Expenditures	99.4	4.0
Income Tax Deductions	126.3	5.1
Total	225.7	9.2
State Aid		
Direct Expenditures	207.7	8.5
Income Tax Deductions	6.3	0.3
Total	214.0	8.7
Local Aid		
Direct Expenditures	2.1	0.1
Property Tax Exemptions	207.4	8.4
Total	209.5	8.5
Total Public Aid		
Direct Expenditures	309.2	12.6
Tax Deductions/Exemptions	340.0	13.8
Total	649.2	26.4
Total Income Plus Nonreported Public Aid and Subsidies	2,455.7	100.0

Sources: Direct expenditures from *Public Aid to Nonpublic Education*, a study prepared by the staff of the President's Commission on School Finance (Wash-
ingon, D.C., 1971). Local expenditures are estimated as 1 percent of state
expenditures. State income tax is estimated as 5 percent of federal income
tax.

From: Daniel J. Sullivan, *Public Aid to Nonpublic Schools* (Lexington,
Mass.: D.C. Heath, 1974), p. 93.

Exactly how much economic benefit is involved cannot be determined. The data are too sketchy and the calculations necessary would be very complex, requiring many restrictive assumptions.

CONCLUSION

This discussion of data problems has been more suggestive than exhaustive. The objectives have been to illustrate the types of data deficiencies that one encounters in trying to determine the level of public aid to religious and religiously affiliated organizations and to provide monetary approximations where possible. To summarize:

1. In some instances the data are simply not collected. The value of religious property tax exemptions is a good example.
2. Where data are collected, they are hardly ever put together in a way that facilitates understanding church-government fiscal relations.
3. Data are often aggregated in ways that make it difficult to know what portion is sectarian and what portion is nonsectarian. Higher education and federal income tax information are examples of this problem.
4. Gross estimates are often subject to considerable error because practices may vary considerably. These differences may be within the public sector, for example, varying state or local government practices, or within the private sector, for example, varying proportions of sectarian and nonsectarian involvement.
5. Imputing dollar values to some economic benefits is often difficult. This is especially true for K-12 education.
6. Determining the ultimate beneficiary of public aid is not always easy. Again, K-12 education is a good example.

12 education is a good example.

Two general conclusions can be drawn from the analysis here. First, the difficulties with data vary with the policy area; it is possible to make better cost estimates for some policies than others. Second, none of the cost estimates are as comprehensive or accurate as they might be. Although it is clear that a substantial amount of money is involved, one simply cannot say with precision how many dollars worth of aid goes every year from the public sector to religious and religiously affiliated organizations. But does it matter? We believe it would not if courts and other policymakers were to adopt a more realistic theory of church-government relations.

There is a difference between knowing the size of the tax expenditure for property tax exemptions in general, and knowing the tax expenditure for religious property tax exemptions in particular. The interests of policymaking and implementation can be well served by good information about property tax exemptions. More particular information about religious and religiously affiliated organizations is necessary *only* if these organizations are to be treated differently from other organizations subject to the policy.

We will argue in chapter 6 that religious and religiously affiliated organizations ought not to be singled out for special advantage or disadvantage. If all similarly situated organizations actually were treated the same way, the need to collect information about the amount of money going to religious and religiously affiliated organizations would be substantially reduced. The emphasis could then be on generating data most useful for formulating, monitoring, and improving the policy as a whole. With data collection, as with case law and its justification, the desire to segregate religious organizations from other similar organizations has created a welter of public policy problems.

NOTES

1. Arvo Van Altstyne, "Tax Exemption of Church Property," *Ohio State Law Journal* 20 (1959): 461.

2. Chester Antieau, Phillip Mark Carroll, and Thomas Carroll Burke, *Religion Under the State Constitutions* (Brooklyn: Central Book, 1965).

3. The constitutional language is mandatory in: ALA. CONST. art. IV, § 91; ALASKA CONST. art. 9, § 4; ARK. CONST. art. 16, § 5; KAN. CONST. art. 11, § 1; KY. CONST. § 170; LA. CONST. art. X, § 4; MINN. CONST. art. IX, § 1; N.J. CONST. art. 8, § 1, par. 2; N.M. CONST. art. VIII, § 3; N.Y. CONST. art. XVI, § ; N.D. CONST. art. XI, § 176; OKLA. CONST. art. X, § 6; S.C. CONST. art. X, § 4; S.D. CONST. art. XI, § 6; UTAH CONST. art. XIII, § 2; VA. CONST. art. XIII, § 183.

4. In the following constitutions the language is permissive: ARIZ. CONST. art. 9, § 2; FLA. CONST. art. IX, § 1, GA. CONST. art. VII, § 2-5404; ILL. CONST. art. IX, § 3; IND. CONST. art. 10, § 1; MO. CONST. art. X, § 6; MONT. CONST. art. XII, § 2; NEB. CONST. art. VIII, § 2; NEV. CONST. art. 8, § 1; TENN. CONST. art. II, § 28, TEX. CONST. art. VIII, § 2; W.VA. CONST. art. X, § 1.

5. Even in those states where no express authority to exempt is conferred upon the legislature, statutory exemptions are uniformly sustained as a general exercise of comprehensive legislative power. See, e.g., *Trustees of Griswold College v. State*, 46 Iowa 275 (1877); Opinion of the Justices, 141 Me. 442, 42 A.2d 47 (1945); *Mayor*

etc. of Baltimore v. Minister of Trustees of Starr Methodist Protestant Church, 106 Md. 281, 67 Atl. 261 (1907). Van Altstyne, p. 462.

6. See also "Constitutionality of State Property Tax Exemptions for Religious Property," *Northwestern University Law Review* 66 (March-April 1971): 118-145.

7. Van Altsyne, "Tax Exemption of Church Property."

8. Id., pp. 465, 503-04.

9. See Antieau et al.

10. Tax Institute of America, *Tax Incentives* (Lexington, Mass.: Heath Lexington Books, 1971), pp. 215-16. "Unidentified Speaker: 'Then, another query was whether the present system is not really discriminatory as between various types of religious activity, where you have at the one extreme the storefront church in Harlem that has no tax exemption benefit at all, because it occupies rented premises, through the heavily occupied Catholic church that serves a very large population through using its facilities very intensively, to the suburban Protestant church that typically is active between eleven o'clock and twelve o'clock on Sunday and virtually deserted the rest of the week.' Mr. Balk: 'Yes, this is what I meant by society's encouraging inadvertently certain activities that may not be to its benefit. We are not necessarily encouraging holiness or helping the poor or advancing missionary work overseas by the way the property tax exemptions are constituted for churches. We are encouraging big buildings, and churchmen are worried about that.' "

11. John M. Quigley and Debra Stinson, *Levels of Property Tax Exemption*, Exchange Bibliography, no. 840 (Monticello, Illinois: Council of Planning Librarians, July 1975).

12. For example, Martin A. Larson and Stanley C. Lowell, *The Churches: Their Riches, Revenues and Immunities* (Washington, D.C.: Robert B. Luce, 1969).

13. Martin A. Larson and Stanley C. Lowell, *The Religious Empire: The Growth and Danger of Tax Exempt Property in the United States* (Washington, D.C.: Robert B. Luce, 1976).

14. Larson and Lowell, *Praise the Lord for Tax Exemption* (Washington, D.C.: Robert B. Luce, 1969).

15. John M. Quigley and Robert W. Schmenner, "Property Tax Exemption and Public Policy," *Public Policy* 23 (Summer 1975): 269-71.

16. These provisions are discussed in more detail in chapter 7.

17. Individuals may deduct allowed charitable contributions up to fifty percent of adjusted gross income, or thirty percent of adjusted gross income in the case of gifts of appreciated property. For corporations the limit, with some adjustments, is five percent of taxable income.

18. Commission on Private Philanthropy and Public Needs, *Giving in America: Toward a Stronger Voluntary Sector* (n.p.-Commission on Private Philanthropy and Public Needs, 1975). The American Association of Fund-Raising Counsels reports that in 1979 43.3 billion dollars were given to charity. Of this 20.1 billion went to religion, 6 billion to education, 6 billion to health and hospitals, 2.7 billion to arts and humanities, and 1.2 billion to civic and public causes.

19. Edmund S. Muskie, "Muskie Says Benefits of Many Tax Breaks Go Mostly to the Wealthy," *Muskie News*, Press Release, 13 February 1978.

20. Susan Nelson, "Financial Trends and Issues," in *Public Policy and Private Higher Education*, ed. David Breneman and Chester E. Finn, Jr. (Washington, D.C.: The Brookings Institution, 1972), p. 104.

21. The problems of determining religious affiliation will be discussed in chapter 5.

22. Manning M. Pattillo, Jr. and Donald M. MacKenzie, *Church-Sponsored Higher Education in the United States* (Washington, D.C.: American Council on Education, 1966), p. 32.

23. Similar comprehensive figures for state aid were not located.

24. Susan Nelson, "Financial Trends and Issues," p. 105.

25. Heinz Eulau, Harold Quinley, and David D. Henry, *State Officials and Higher Education*, A general report prepared for the Carnegie Commission on Higher Education (New York: McGraw-Hill, 1970).

26. Nelson, pp. 93-94.

27. Ibid., p. 95.

28. U.S. Congress, Senate, Committee on Finance, Thomas Vitullo-Martin, *Testimony on Tuition Tax Credit Bill, Hearings Before a Subcommittee on Taxation and Debt Management of the Senate-Finance Committee on S-2142*, 95th Cong., 2d sess.

29. Daniel J. Sullivan, *Public Aid to Nonpublic Schools* (Lexington, Mass.: D.C. Heath, 1974), p. 94.

5

DISTINCTION
WITHOUT MERIT

Makers of public policy have found it very difficult to develop a good working definition for religious organizations. The problem is a serious one if the policy objective is to set religious organizations apart for special treatment because the definition controls eligibility, and therefore the flow of benefits received from, or denied by, the public sector. However, a fiscal neutrality approach to church-government relations seeks to ensure equal treatment for members of classes of charitable and nonprofit organizations. Since fiscal neutrality would impose the same burdens and provide the same benefits for religious and all similarly situated organizations (see chapter 6), there would be very few instances in which it would be necessary to define religious organizations as a special category.

This chapter will discuss some of the problems that have been created by attempts to define religious organizations for purposes of fiscal public policy. It is a very difficult task, so it is not surprising that the result has been a confusing amalgam of policies that sometimes work to the advantage, and sometimes to the disadvantage, of religious organizations. Setting religious organizations apart for special treatment is not only fraught with technical difficulties, but also poses serious problems of equity that violate the equal protection tenets of neutrality, and, we think, of the Constitution!

Charles Whelan identifies more than fifteen different ways federal law describes individuals and entities in some way connected with religion.[1] One result is that, ". . . as the matter now stands, 'church' may mean one thing to the Treasury Department in Sections 511-14 and another in Section 170."[2] These and other problems are thoroughly and cogently discussed by Whelan and need not be repeated here. Suffice it to say that the wide variety of forms and functions adopted by religious organizations in this country make it very difficult to develop a single definition sufficient for all purposes.

The Internal Revenue Service uses a working definition of "church" that seems reasonable enough as far as it goes:

(1) a distinct legal existence, (2) a recognized creed and form of worship, (3) a definite and distinct ecclesiastical government, (4) a formal code of doctrine and discipline, (5) a distinct religious history, (6) a membership not associated with any church or denomination, (7) a complete organization of ordained ministers ministering to their congregations and selected after completing prescribed courses of study, (8) a literature of its own, (9) established places of worship, (10) regular congregations, (11) regular religious services, (12) Sunday schools for the religious instruction of the young, and (13) schools for the preparation of its ministers.[3]

Whelan's observation is that,

[O]bviously, these criteria are well constructed to exclude "instant churches," itinerate evangelist, religious orders and ecumenical organizations. Equally obviously, however, they go far beyond the traditional and empirical criteria of creed, cult, congregation, clergy and continuity.[4]

Current policy, in other words, favors "main line" religious institutions and consequently is not providing equal protection to all sectarian institutions or to sectarian *vis à vis* nonsectarian institutions. How has this come to pass? Whelan suggests four considerations that seem to have been important to Congress in formulating policy:

(1) preservation of the fiscal separation of church and state;
(2) accommodation of the Code, where possible without significant net expense to the government, to individuals in special religious situations and to religious organizations with a distinctive economic system;
(3) continuation of the tradition, so far as the basic tax exemption is

concerned, of classifying religious organizations in common with exempt nondenominational and secular institutions;

(4) innovation, so far as certain corollaries of tax exempt status are concerned, by creating new classifications that will equalize the tax status of church-related institutions that serve the general public (e.g., hospitals) with the tax status of their secular counterparts but that will not eliminate all distinctions between churches and exempt secular organizations.

The first of these considerations may or may not have been important in the actual deliberations of Congress. The second and the third demonstrably were. It is the fourth consideration, however, that seems to have been the foundation of most of the church distinctions that Congress has introduced into the Code through the 1950 amendments, the Tax Reform Act of 1969, the Employee Retirement Income Security Act of 1974, and the Tax Reform Act of 1976.[5]

The heart of the problem, therefore, is that Congress, Treasury, and Internal Revenue Service have been trying to create a separate classification for religion. Their efforts have floundered for two reasons. One is the variety of religious structures and functions already mentioned. A second reason is that for purposes of fiscal public policy, what distinguishes religious organizations from non-religious organizations is often not as significant as the characteristics they share. As chapter 3 emphasized, religious organizations serve many of the same social functions as nonreligious organizations. It is this larger class of mediating structures between the public and private sectors that public policy is seeking to encourage.

From a fiscal neutrality perspective, attempting to use religion as a distinct classification is both unnecessary and unwise. Defining "charity" as an operational or workable concept has been an evolutionary process.[4] As chapter 1 noted, the roles of both the public and private sectors have changed considerably over time. Accordingly, the definition of what constitutes a charitable organization has gradually been altered and refined. In every instance, however, the generic definition or description of a charitable organization has included religious organizations. For our purposes here, that means that while it may not always be easy to decide whether some unusual operation can properly be classified as charitable, there has never been any question about the fact that religious organizations fall clearly within the boundaries of any reasonable definition.[7] Consequently, public policymakers need not squander their limited resources trying to define religion or to determine whether religious organizations fall within the broader class of charitable or mediating institutions. It should be sufficient, Dean Kelley argues, that a group *claims* to be a church, *"offers some explanation of* the ultimate meaning of life," and has a *"body of adherents* with sufficient *continuity* to be identifiable over time and in sufficient *numbers* to support it by their voluntary contributions."[8] In answer to charges that this approach may lead to abuses, Kelley responds by saying that,

Charlatanry in religion is neither as prevalent nor as pernicious as some magistrates seem to feel. People are entitled to let themselves be fooled if they want to. The authors of the First Amendment were willing to take a calculated risk of tolerating occasional religious charlatans rather than giving the government the responsibility of investigating, supervising, and —in consequence—sponsoring and controlling, the practitioners of religion. It should not be the responsibility of government to inspect and certify religions as it does meat. Consumers of religion will need to be their own guardians to a greater degree than in other areas of consumership not protected by the First Amendment: that is the meaning of *freedom*, and particularly *religious* freedom.[9]

Viewed as a fiscal issue, the point is that the marginal costs that might be imposed by occasional deception are so small compared to the values of the religious liberty protected, that the expense is very worthwhile. Giving religion a wide berth in this respect provides a clear protection of religious freedom. It is unfair for the public sector to declare that a given group is not truly a religious organization because it is suspected that sometime in the future the group may engaged in "improper" activities. The clear effect is to discriminate between religious organizations by finding some "guilty" before the fact. It would be preferable to accept their claim to be a religious organization and then subject them to neutral enforcement of the law. Problems arise today because that does not pen. For example, *The Wall Street Journal* reports that

[U]nscrupulous financial advisers are tempted into the church-bond business partly because, like other dealers bringing out new bond issues, they receive their commissions off the top—from the first bonds sold—and

then they can run for it. They benefit, too, from a lack of state and federal
attention to church finances. Civil authorities have been reluctant to
burden churches with costly bond-registration procedures or to take
actions that seem to breach the wall between church and state.[10]

The fiscal neutrality position is that governmental action should be
reserved for activities and circumstances in which there is a need for
supervision and control—and then government should act. As *The
Wall Street Journal* goes on to point out,

> Most [state] securities commissioners say they would like to see the regis-
> tration exemptions abolished and guidelines strengthened. Wallace Rogers,
> a securities investigator in Georgia, which had a rash of church bankruptcies
> several years ago, says the problem has "virtually disappeared" since a new
> state law forced churches and other nonprofit organizations to register
> bond issues.[11]

The application of a more strictly neutral public policy produced
sounder bond issues, which ultimately benefited investors, civil and
ecclesiastical authorities alike.[12]

Returning to the Internal Revenue Code, we see other concessions to religion that have serious equity deficiencies. If a "minister
of the gospel" receives a housing allowance as part of his or her
compensation, the portion actually used to provide a home can be
excluded from gross income under the provisions of section 107 of
the Internal Revenue Code. If a parsonage is furnished, the rental
value of the home is excluded from gross income. These benefits
are not available to anyone else. An employee of a religious organization was denied section 107 benefits available to co-workers
simply because they were ordained and he was not.[13] The effect of
section 107 is clearly a violation of fiscal neutrality.

> Section 107 grants economic benefits to qualifying ministers that are
> unavailable to other taxpayers. Rather than constituting an incidental bene-
> fit to religion, the parsonage exclusion singles out a narrow class for special
> tax treatment. By limiting the exclusion to a class of taxpayers who are
> eligible solely on the basis of religious qualifications, Congress has made a
> law respecting an establishment of religion in violation of the first amend-
> ment. Congress would not be displaying an improper hostility toward
> religion by terminating the parsonage exclusion, since ministers still might

qualify for an exclusion under section 119. Ministers who fail to qualify under section 119 would not be subject to unfair discrimination but rather would be liable for taxes in accordance with the same rules that apply to taxpayers generally.[14]

Another example of special deference granted to religion is section 6033 of the Internal Revenue Code, which specifies the obligations of exempt organizations to file annual financial returns with the Internal Revenue Service. The Tax Reform Act of 1969 expanded reporting requirements considerably, leaving religious or religiously affiliated organizations part of a very select group not compelled to file a Form 990 return.[15] When the Treasury Department attempted to amend section 6033 provisions dealing with "integrated auxiliaries," a storm of protest arose.[16] A wide variety of churches objected to what they perceived as a threat to their educational, charitable, and social activities. The fear was not that these activities would be outlawed or taxed from existence, but that they would be required to file a Form 990, reporting where such operations got their money and how they spent it. In drafting the final regulations the Treasury Department made some concessions to church objections, but stated that "[T]he fundamental vice remains: the regulations exclude the traditional educational, charitable and welfare activities of the churches from the tax concept of 'church activities.'"[17] The result is that churches get special treatment by not having to file a Form 990. Still, they object to the regulations because some of the operations for which the churches are responsible must file a Form 990. The position of the churches is essentially that

[B]esides implying a narrow and unhistorical definition of churches and posing a threat to multi-corporate churches the final regulations create an extremely difficult interpretational problem by requiring that the "principal activity" of an integrated auxiliary be "exclusively religious."[18]

The churches' conclusion is that if integrated auxiliaries cannot be separated properly from worshipping congregations, they should all be classified together and none should be required to file a Form 990. Of course, one could agree that attempts to distinguish integrated auxiliaries are misguided, but then go on to conclude that auxiliaries and churches alike should *all* file 990 forms.

Considering how strenuously church officials objected to the prospect of filing Form 990 for schools, hospitals, orphanages, and the like, it would be an understatement to say that they would not sit quietly by if serious consideration were being given to requiring churches themselves to file 990 forms. Standard arguments would be trotted out, as they have in the past: having to file a 990 form would infringe on religious practice and free speech guarantees granted by the First Amendment; it would be expensive; and it would be time-consuming. The arguments are specious. Completing a Form 990 once a year has little more impact on religious beliefs and practices than complying with a local building code. Philosophically, this is the same slippery slope encountered with property tax exemptions. Churches are willing to comply with a building code because they receive a direct benefit—the roof does not collapse in the middle of a service. However, if some expense and disclosure can be avoided by not filing an informational tax return, then the "separation of church and state" is solemnly invoked. Special treatment is not requested as a favor, but demanded as a right. In chapter 6 we will point out that there are few instances in which the free exercise of religion is so directly incumbered that it is appropriate to use religion as a basis for granting special fiscal treatment. Certainly the filing of informational tax returns and the inclusion of a housing allowance in gross income are not examples of threats to religious liberty.[19]

On the other side of the special treatment coin, religious organizations find themselves largely set apart by section 501 (c) (3) and 501(h) restrictions on political activity. Before the Tax Reform Act of 1976, organizations included in 501(c) (3) risked losing their exempt status if they devoted a "substantial part" of their activities to "carrying on propaganda, or otherwise attempting, to influence legislation." This restriction was attacked on a number of grounds.[20] "Substantial part" was never defined, and it was left to the Internal Revenue Service to establish rather arbitrarily that fifteen percent be the cutoff. The effect then is to permit larger organizations to do more lobbying than small organizations; fifteen percent of a one million-dollar budget will go a lot further than fifteen percent of a ten thousand-dollar budget. In the religious sector this benefits "main line" churches at the expense of smaller and perhaps less conventional, more radical, and more controversial churches. Other shortcomings in 501(c)(3) are its restriction of free speech and its failure to provide equal protection by being underinclusive. Business leagues, veterans' organizations, labor organizations and others are not required to restrict their political activity in return for their exempt status. That is not true for 501(c)(3) organizations.

When Congress attempted to clarify the "substantial part" language of 501(c)(3), its efforts were generally supported by 501(c)(3) organizations, with the exception of churches. The result is that section 501(h) added by the Tax Reform Act of 1976 "excludes from the new rules all churches and conventions or associations of churches, their integrated auxiliaries and all members of an 'affiliated group of organizations' if one of the members of the group is a church, a convention, or association of churches, or an integrated auxiliary thereof."[21] Special treatment in this case works to restrict the activities, and perhaps even the constitutional rights, of religious organizations. Applying a fiscal neutrality policy in this instance and including religious organizations in 501(h) would expand religious liberty and activity.

The difficulties that are encountered in trying to specify what is meant by "religious affiliation" can be illustrated by looking at what it means for a college or university to be religiously affiliated. Needless to say, that relationship can take many different forms. Historically, it is important to remember that

> [T]he American college was founded to meet the "spiritual necessities" of a new continent. It was designed primarily as a "nursery of ministers," and was fostered as a "child of the church." The movement for the founding of colleges in America before the Civil War was identified with the rise and growth of religious denominations in this country. . . .[22]

Of the 207 permanent colleges founded in this country before the Civil War, 180 or eighty-seven percent had a religious affiliation (see table 5-1). There have sometimes been attempts to make less of these early church ties, but as Tewksbury points out, doing so usually requires a misreading of history.

Table 5-1

**Permanent Colleges and Universities Founded
before the Civil War, Arranged according to
Denominational and Other Association**

S.N.	DENOMINATIONAL AND OTHER ASSOCIATION	TOTAL PERMANENT COLLEGES
1	Presbyterian	49
2	Methodist	34
3	Baptist	25
4	Congregational	21
5	Catholic	14
6	Episcopal	11
7	Lutheran	6
8	Disciples	5
9	German Reformed	4
10	Universalist	4
11	Friends	2
12	Unitarian	2
13	Christian	1
14	Dutch Reformed	1
15	United Brethren	1
16	Semi-State*	3
17	Municipal**	3
18	State	21
	Total Colleges Listed	207

Source: Donald G. Tewksbury, *The Founding of American Colleges and Universities Before the Civil War* (New York: Arno Press, 1969), p. 90.

*Tulane (La.), Mississippi (Miss.), and Centenary (La.).
**College of Charleston (S.C.), University of Lousville (Ky.), and College of the City of New York (N.Y.).

The statement that Harvard was founded in order to "advance learning and perpetuate it to Posterity" has often been quoted to indicate that Harvard was established in the interests of general learning, but it is to be noted that the remainder of the quotation reads as follows: "dreading to leave an illiterate ministry to the churches when our present ministers shall lie in the Dust." President Josiah Quincy stated, moreover, in no uncertain terms that Harvard had fulfilled the design of its founder in that during the years from 1636 to 1692 the college had been "conducted as a theological institution."[23]

A natural response to Tewksbury is that even though Harvard once had strong sectarian ties, that is no longer the case. The same applies to many other colleges and universities. The origin of an institution is not enough to determine whether a functional religious affiliation exists. Therefore, an operational definition of religious affiliation needs to include the many dimensions a relationship might take. Pattillo and Mackenzie suggest six:

1. Board of control includes members of church and/or members nominated and/or elected by church body.
2. Ownership of the institution by the religious body.
3. Financial support by the religious body.
4. Acceptance by the institution of denominational standards or use of the denominational name.
5. Institutional statement of purpose linked to a particular denomination or reflecting religious orientation.
6. Church membership a factor in selection of faculty and administrative personnel.[24]

Drawing on the position of the American Civil Liberties Union, Swomley has developed a list of four criteria for determining when a college or university is not religiously affiliated:

a. No administrator, faculty member or student is required to be an adherent of any religious faith;
b. No administrator, student or faculty member is required to attend religious services or participate in religious programs of any kind or pass any religious test; nor be subject to disciplinary measures based on religious criteria;

c. The institution is not under the direction or control of any religious body or ecclesiastical official;

d. It is not designed primarily to provide or promote religion or religious activity.[25]

Items "c" and "d" in Swomley's list seem largely to be elaborations of number 5 in Pattillo and Mackenzie's criteria. Swomley's item "a" extends Pattillo and Mackenzie's number 6 to include students. Swomley's item "b" is an entirely new addition to the Pattillo and Mackenzie list. Taken together, these two lists constitute a rather comprehensive operational definition of religious affiliation for institutions of higher education.

An operational definition of this complexity will obviously produce a continuum of relationships. For some institutions all of these ties with religious groups will exist. For other institutions, there will be no relations at all. Those two types will set the extremes on the continuum, and will clearly be either religiously affiliated or not. But what of the others that fall in between? Is one of these relationships sufficient to constitute "religious affiliation"? Pattillo and Mackenzie argue that it is. They deemed institutions to have relationships with religious bodies in significant degree if these institutions checked one or more items in response to their survey. Nonetheless, they warn against assuming that religious affiliation is easily described in terms of either-or. "It leads," they say, "to easy generalizations which sometimes obscure more than they illuminate. The relationships between colleges and universities and religious organizations are much too complex to be shown adequately on a one-dimensional graph."[26] This good advice is often ignored. Primary and secondary schools, as well as institutions of higher education, are generally viewed as either religiously affiliated or not. The extent and nature of the relationship tends to be overlooked. In many instances this does not create a problem because the relationships between the educational institution and the religious group are, in fact, quite extensive. As table 5-2 shows, Pattillo and Mackenzie found that more than seventy percent of the institutions they identified as having some connection with religious groups had at least five types of relationships according to

Table 5-2

**Number of Different Elements of Relationship
to Religious Bodies Reported by Individual Institutions***

NUMBER OF ELEMENTS OF RELATIONSHIP	FREQUENCY NUMBER	PERCENT
1	9	1.1
2	25	3.1
3	76	9.3
4	131	16.0
5	253	31.0
6	323	39.5
Total	817	100.0

Source: Manning M. Pattillo, Jr. and Donald M. Mackenzie, *Church-Sponsored Higher Education in the United States* (Washington, D.C.: American Council on Education, 1966), p. 32.

*The information summarized in this table was obtained from a questionnaire which was sent to the presidents of all 1,189 private institutions of higher learning listed in the *Education Directory, 1962-1963* (except theological schools, Bible colleges, and other institutions devoted exclusively to the preparation of persons for church vocations).

their criteria. Still, tables 5-3 and 5-4 indicate that some types of relationships were much more common than others, and that differences in frequencies often separate along denominational lines.

Without belaboring the point, it can simply be said that ignoring the many variations that can exist within the rubric "religious affiliation" does not improve the ease or quality of public policy decision making for educational institutions at the fringe. Even Pattillo and Mackenzie did not know what to do with eighteen institutions "having a clear religious orientation but no relationship to a particular church."[27]

Table 5-3

Number of Institutions Reporting Each Element of Relationship

ELEMENT OF RELATIONSHIP	FREQUENCY	
	N	%
1. Composition of board of control	687	84.1
a. Church membership required	574	70.3
b. Board members nominated/elected by church	438	53.6
2. Institution owned by church (or religious order or congregation)	573	70.1
3. Institution receives financial support from official church sources	766	93.7
a. For educational and general budget	602	73.7
b. In form of contributed services (Roman Catholic)	242	29.6
c. For capital purposes	364	44.6
4. Institution affiliated with church college organization/subscribes to set of standards	631	77.2
a. Institution affiliated with denominational organization of colleges	529	64.7
b. Institution subscribes to standards or policy set by church for colleges	393	48.1
5. Institutional statement of purpose reflects religious orientation	782	95.7
6. Preference given church members in faculty and staff selection	575	70.4

Source: Manning M. Pattillo, Jr. and Donald M. Mackenzie, *Church-Sponsored Higher Education in the United States* (Washington, D.C.: American Council on Education, 1966), p. 34.

The issue is raised here because it is ignored by the Supreme Court. In the case of primary and secondary education the Court apparently assumes that any relationship at all between a religious group and an educational institution constitutes religious affiliation. With higher education the Court sidesteps the problem by arguing, as we saw in chapter 2, that college students are somehow less impressionable than primary and secondary students. There is no evidence produced to support that contention; it is simply taken as self-evident that students with a high school diploma have devel-

Table 5-4

Number of Institutions in Seven Groups Reporting Each Kind of Relationship to Religious Body

KIND OF RELATIONSHIP	FREQUENCY BY CHURCH GROUP													
	Catholic		Non-Catholic		Baptist		Lutheran		Methodist		Presbyterian		Newer Groups	
	N	%	N	%	N	%	N	%	N	%	N	%	N	%
1. Composition of board of control	276	81.4	411	86.0	70	89.7	43	97.7	111	88.8	58	84.1	17	100.0
a. Church membership required	269	79.4	305	63.8	59	75.6	38	86.4	71	56.8	34	49.3	16	94.1
b. Board members nominated/elected by church	115	33.9	323	67.6	55	70.5	35	79.5	95	76.0	48	69.6	7	41.2
2. Institution owned by church (or religious order or congregation)	321	94.7	252	52.7	49	62.8	35	79.5	71	56.8	29	42.0	7	41.2
3. Institution receives financial support from official church sources	329	97.0	437	91.4	75	96.2	43	97.7	123	98.4	66	95.7	8	47.1
a. Support for educational and general budget	181	53.4	421	88.1	73	93.6	41	93.2	120	96.0	64	92.8	8	47.1
b. Support in form of contributed services	242	71.4	0	0.0	0	0.0	0	0.0	0	0.0	0	0.0	0	0.0
c. Support for capital purposes	59	17.4	305	63.8	55	70.5	33	75.0	85	68.0	36	52.2	7	41.2
5. Institution affiliated with church college organization/subscribes to set of standards	233	68.7	398	83.3	67	85.9	38	86.4	112	89.6	62	89.8	7	41.2
a. Institution affiliated with denominational organization of colleges	191	56.3	338	70.7	63	79.5	23	52.3	101	80.8	53	76.8	2	11.8
b. Institution subscribes to standards or policy set by church for colleges	143	42.2	250	52.3	35	44.9	27	61.4	64	51.2	55	79.7	5	29.4
5. Institutional statement of purpose reflects religious orientation	325	95.9	457	95.6	76	97.4	43	97.7	118	94.4	68	98.6	17	100.0
6. Preference given church members in faculty and staff selection	252	74.3	323	67.6	65	83.3	38	86.4	77	61.6	45	65.2	14	82.4

Source: Manning M. Pattillo, Jr. and Donald M. Mackenzie, Church-Sponsored Higher Education in the United States (Washington, D.C.: American Council on Education, 1966), p. 35.

oped a substantial capacity for the critical evaluation of philosophical and theological questions.[28] Some students may be able to do that in the ninth grade and others will lamentably go all the way through college without making much progress in that area. In casting about for a way to justify aid to sectarian higher education the Court has made a distinction without substance.

The neutralist perspective would do away with the fiction of student malleability and make all the policies for education consistent. The Court's conclusions about permissible aid to higher education are consistent with the neutralist perspective. The problem is that the Court is right for the wrong reasons. Adopting the neutralist perspective for aid to educational institutions will produce more coherent and defensible public policies. Public aid should go equally to nonpublic colleges and universities, regardless of degree of religious affiliation, as long as the aid is for a valid secular purpose. For example, public aid should not be used to build a chapel or support a minister on either a public or private college campus.

A fiscal neutrality approach to public aid for private higher education does not necessarily favor one form of assistance over another. Whether the aid is a budgetary allocation or tax expenditure, whether designated recipients are students, faculty members, or institutions is less important—from the neutralist perspective—than the policy objective of equal treatment for all private colleges and universities, regardless of religious affiliation. The result produced by *Tilton v. Richardson* is a long step in this direction.

CONCLUSION

Two points emerge from the discussion of religious affiliation that are central themes for this chapter. First, attempting to make clear distinctions between sectarian and nonsectarian is complicated by the tremendous variety of complex relationships that have evolved in this country's religious community. Second, ignoring distinctions between the sectarian and nonsectarian for most fiscal public policies produces a far more equitable result for all the similarly situated organizations. The key question is: in what ways are they different? Where sectarian and nonsectarian organizations are alike, for instance, in not operating for the economic benefit of their members, or in accounting for their funds, a fiscal neutrality approach requires that the two be treated equally.

As we have seen from illustrations in this chapter, the application of fiscal neutrality would both confer benefits and impose requirements on religious organizations that they do not have under existing policy. Equal protection necessitates redressing inequities wherever they exist. The changes, whether they seem to work to the advantage or disadvantage of religious organizations, are justified in the name of equity. The fact that religious organizations might be expected to favor some of the changes dictated by fiscal neutrality and oppose others is probably an indication that the approach is sufficiently evenhanded to make accommodationists and separationists happy and unhappy at the same time. When both sides believe they win some and lose some from fiscal neutrality, policy must be headed in the right direction.

One final note may be appropriate at this point. There is widespread belief that granting religious organizations special status discriminates against atheist groups. In fact such groups are granted tax-exempt status.[29] This is appropriate since they are similar to other nonprofit literary, scientific, educational, and religious groups. A neutralist theory of the First Amendment would be a further step toward destroying any belief that atheists are, or should be, discriminated against.

NOTES

1. Charles Whelan, "Church in the Internal Revenue Code: The Definitional Problems," Fordham Law Review 45 (1977): 887-89.

2. Ibid., p. 917.

3. Ibid., p. 925.

4. Ibid., p. 925.

5. Ibid., p. 922.

6. John P. Persons, John J. Osborn, and Charles F. Feldman, "Criteria for Exemption Under Section 501(c)(3)," The Commission on Private Philanthropy and Public Needs, Research Papers vol. 4: Taxes (n.p.: Department of the Treasury, 1977), pp. 1902-2043.

7. Laurens Williams and Donald V. Moorehead, "An Analysis of the Federal Tax Distinctions Between Public and Private Charitable Organizations," The Commission on Private Philanthropy and Public Needs, Research Papers, vol. 4: Taxes, pp. 2099-2129. Williams and Moorehead suggest four ways to distinguish charitable

organizations: (1) type of organization; (2) public support; (3) functional test; (4) public control. By any of these tests religious organizations are easily included.

8. Dean M. Kelley, "Operational Consequences of Church State Choices." *Social Problems* (January-February 1967): 60-61 (emphasis in original).

9. Ibid., pp. 64-65 (emphasis in original).

10. John Koten, "Faith Under Test: Some Charity Bonds Plunge Into Default; Investor Losses Mount," *The Wall Street Journal*, 27 February 1978, p. 1.

11. Ibid.

12. Closer government supervision might help avoid the fate such as that of the New Testament Baptist Church, which had to go into receivership. "Church officials say and court records show that the church floated one bond issue after another to finance the earlier bonds. About 18 months after the pastor had departed, his successor and a remaining deacon agreed that there was no hope. They asked for legal help and started the process that led to court. Because the church's records are a shambles, it may never be known how many people invested in the bonds that added up to more than $700,000, about three times the value of the church's assets, $262,000. And it may be years before investors know who will get some money back and who will get none." Dennis Cusick, "Misplaced Faith?," *The Louisville Times*, 15 June 1979, p. 1.

13. *Kirk v. Commissioner*, 425 F.2d 492 (D.C. Cir.), *cert. denied*, 400 U.S. 853 (1970). Roger H. Taft, "Tax Benefits for the Clergy: The Unconstitutionality of Section 107." *Georgetown Law Journal* 62 (1974): 1270.

14. Roger H. Taft, "Tax Benefits for the Clergy," p. 1272.

15. A. Who Must File Form 990—An annual return on this form is required of organizations (including foreign organizations and cooperative service organizations described in sections 501 (e) and (f) exempt from tax under section 501(a) of the Code except:

(1) A *church*, an interchurch organization of local units of a church, a convention or association of churches, or an integrated auxiliary of a church (such as a men's or women's organization, religious school, mission society, or youth group).

(2) A school below college level affiliated with a *church* or operated by a religious order, even though it is not an integrated auxiliary of a church.

(3) A mission society sponsored by or affiliated with one or more churches or church denominations, more than one-half of the activities of which society are conducted in, or directed at persons in, foreign countries.

(4) An *exclusively religious* activity of any *religious order*.

(5) For tax years ending on or after December 31, 1976, an organization (other than a private foundation as described in 8 below) that normally has gross receipts in each taxable year of not more than $10,000.

(6) A state institution, whose income is excluded from gross income under section 115.

(7) An organization described in section 501(c)(1). Section 501(c)(1) organizations are corporations organized under an Act of Congress if: (a) such cor-

porations are instrumentalities of the United States, and (b) such corporations are exempt from Federal income taxes (under Acts as amended and supplemented).

(8) A private foundation exempt under section 501(c)(3) and described in section 509(a). (Required to file Form 990-PF, Return of Private Foundation Exempt from Income Tax.)

(9) A stock bonus, pension, or profit-sharing trust which qualified under section 401. (See Form 5500, Annual Return/Report for Employee Benefit Plan.)

(10) A *religious* or apostolic organization described in section 501(d). (Required to file Form 1065, U.S. Partnership Return of Income.) Emphasis added.

16. Whelan, "Church," p. 893.

17. Ibid., p. 898.

18. Ibid., p. 899.

19. We have already challenged the utility of the entanglement test developed in *Waltz* and therefore do not consider it here as a major objection to filing 990 forms, for example. The argument would be that failure to provide all or part of the information required by the 990 forms would leave the organization subject to investigations and penalties which in themselves would be excessive entanglements of the federal government in church affairs. The response is that government involvement of this sort is no more "entangling" than the enforcing of health codes.

20. John Michael Clear, "Political Speech of Charitable Organizations Under the Internal Revenue Code," *University of Chicago Law Review* 41 (1973): 352-76.

21. Whelan, "Church," p. 919.

22. Donald G. Tewksbury, *The Founding of American Colleges and Universities Before the Civil War* (New York: Arno Press, 1969) p. 55.

23. Ibid., p. 81.

24. Manning M. Pattillo, Jr. and Donald M. Mackenzie, *Church-Sponsored Higher Education in the United States* (Washington, D.C.: American Council on Education, 1966) p. 230.

25. John M. Swomley, Jr., *Religion, the State and the Schools* (New York: Pegasus, 1968), p. 146.

26. Pattillo and Mackenzie, *Church-Sponsored*, p. 30.

27. Ibid., p. 20.

28. It might be argued that this states the case unfairly, but certainly it is a logical inference to be drawn from the Court's reasoning.

29. See the literature of the American Atheists, Box 8223, Lexington, Kentucky 40533.

6

THE THEORY OF FISCAL NEUTRALITY

Having completed a critique of case law, economic theorizing, and the state of current information, we are now in a position to present an alternative theory of the First Amendment religion clauses. We begin with a proposal developed nearly two decades ago by Philip Kurland of the University of Chicago Law School:

> [T]he thesis proposed here as the proper construction of the religion clauses of the first amendment is that the freedom and separation clauses should be read as a single precept that government cannot utilize religion as a standard for action or inaction because these clauses prohibit classication in terms of religion either to confer a benefit or to impose a burden. [1]

This simple thesis warrants some clarification and development. First, the purposes of the religion clauses can be summed up as freedom, separation, *and equality.* Freedom, as understood here, includes toleration and protection of all beliefs and practices compatible with preserving peace and order. Separation is necessary not only to assure toleration and protection of dissenters but to provide religious freedom on a more profound level for all beliefs and practices—a freedom which both keeps government out of religious affairs (Roger Williams's vision) and religion out of governmental affairs (Jefferson's vision), but in a manner consistent with current social, economic, and technological realities. The separation envisioned is neither absolutist nor accommodationist. It is strictly neutralist and is directed at assuring complete religious voluntarism and equality in the government's treatment of religious and non-religious interests and individuals.

While the application of the clauses in conjunction is difficult, it is both possible and necessary. It can be done by reading the clauses as an equal protection doctrine,

[F]or if the command is that inhibitions not be placed by the state on religious activity, it is equally forbidden the state to confer favors upon religious activity. These commands would be impossible of effectuation unless they are read together as creating a doctrine more akin to the reading of the equal protection clause than to the due process clause, i.e., they must be read to mean that religion may not be used as a basis for classification for purposes of government action, whether that action be the conferring of rights or privileges or the imposition of duties or obligations.[2]

Neither the Free Exercise nor the Establishment Clause is seen as absolute; that is, not every action is protected from government regulation because one who performs it claims it is a religious action, and not every aid is prohibited to religion in every circumstance. Once this lack of absoluteness is admitted, interpreting the clauses becomes a matter of drawing lines between what is permissible and what is not. Fiscal neutrality draws the line on equal protection grounds.

Acceptance of fiscal neutrality is not a denial that religion can be used as a class for purpose of identification of a compelling personal interest or recognition of a significant social unit. It would be incongruous, to say the least, to hold that the Constitution could recognize the existence of religion, but that the government based on that Constitution could not. A religious classification is used by pollsters, for example, as a valid, differentiating social indicator. Such use, even by a governmental agency, would not be a violation of the fiscal neutrality principle, but simply a recognition of an objective fact of personal value preference or of social organization. Examples of such use would include acknowledgment of the presence of a church, assembly hall, or synagogue when planning road construction or placing traffic control signs. At the same time, identification and recognition of personal interests and social organizations do not depend on, or lead to, a legal definition of religion. They do imply that in relevant secular aspects, individual religious interests and social groups are similar to other interests and groups, not because of their content, but because of the compelling function of religion in an individual's life (that is, it is a fundamental interest) and financial, legal, and other public and secular aspects of a religion's social organization, such as its charitable, fraternal or non-profit nature, its regular tendency to draw large crowds into certain areas, its use of the mails, and its investment policies.[3] Put in other words, fiscal neutrality implies that there is seldom a *legally significant* characteristic of religion so unique that it is not shared by nonreligious individuals and groups.

We may turn now to a justification for the use of a fiscal neutrality principle, and a discussion of the principle as a legal concept. The historical account of the First Amendment's creation in chapter 1 relates the struggle of the Founding Fathers to articulate a coherent principle. Later commentators have focused on either "separation" or "accommodation" of church and government as a proper statement of that principle. As a result, they have not paid proper attention to the struggle to protect both free exercise and equality for religious individuals and groups. We believe fiscal neutrality to be not only wholly compatible with the intent of the Founding Fathers, but an accurate reflection of the values they were striving to preserve. The task we have set ourselves is to remain faithful to the fundamental values and purposes which the Founding Fathers hoped to see endure through changing circumstances, what Harry Jones has called "the historic purpose of the First Amendment,"[4] and to explicate the relevant circumstances of contemporary society within which the fundamental values and purposes must be preserved, especially those which have changed from the time of the Founding Fathers.

There are four major developments which have radically changed the circumstances within which church-government problems must be faced. First, the Founding Fathers envisioned a strong central government of limited and separated powers. They acknowledged the significant role of religion in the social order, but clearly intended to separate it from the important role of government. "They expected religion to play a part in the established social order, but also expected the state to play a minimal role in forming that order. In their view the state was to maintain the public peace and security so that individuals and groups would be free to shape their own destinies."[5]

The primary reality which other interpretations of the First Amendment have not adequately integrated is the tremendously expanded role of government. The kinds of action considered to be within the proper scope of government have broadened considerably since the First Amendment was formulated. The state has assumed the far more active and positive role of allocating resources through extensive taxation, insurance, contracting, and welfare policies, and actively structuring the social order through wide-ranging economic and social regulation. Yet to speak of a pervasive, positive government is not to speak of a fully collective or totalitarian government. An enormous amount of government business, and therefore its influencing and structuring of the social order, is conducted through contracts for goods, services, and research with private businesses and individuals, including charitable and nonprofit organizations. Government contracts with private suppliers each year amount to several billion dollars. Research and building grants, in addition to payments for services, go each year to private foundations, universities, and hospitals, many of them church-related. The critical question, then, of how government ought to treat religious groups and interests, has become a fundamentally different one from that confronting our predecessors. The Founding Fathers could consider religious liberty as freedom *from* governmental power. The current problem is to protect religious liberty *in the midst of* governmental power. "To withhold studiously from religious groups all benefits flowing from governmental structuring of the social order will not only result in deprivations not demanded by the purposes of nonestablishment but in some cases will actually frustrate them."[6] It is not too much to say that depriving religious interests and groups of the benefits of a society organized by positive government on a level of equality with similar groups is a violation of the religious liberty guarantee. It is precisely a deprivation based on the expression of religious convictions.

A similar problem exists with regard to the Establishment Clause. Donald Giannella observes that:

If religious groups are to enjoy political equality in the sense that they will be able to participate in and have access to the benefits emanating from governmental programs structuring our social order on equal terms with other private groups, a shift from an obsolete no-aid theory of nonestablishment to one of strict neutrality is appropriate.[7]

The contemporary problem, then, is one of religious liberty in the face of pervasive government: the freedom of groups and individuals from governmental discrimination on the basis of religious convictions, and the freedom of government and the public from religious establishment. How can the problem be resolved? In their original, classic work on equal protection, Joseph Tussman and Jacobus TenBroeck pointed the way:

But whatever our past or present preferences, it is certain that a concern with equality will be increasingly thrust on us. We have tended to identify liberty with the absence of government; we have sought it in the interstices of the law. What happens, then, when government becomes more ubiquitous? Whenever an area of activity is brought within the control or regulation of government, to that extent equality supplants liberty as the dominant ideal and constitutional demand. . . . [t]he course of events has radically altered the social context of the First Amendment and made necessary positive administrative action to promote and secure these rights. To think primarily in terms of protection against encroachment by public authority is now to commit the sin of irrelevance.[8]

The second major development radically altering the import of the First Amendment religion clauses has been the application of major segments of the Bill of Rights to the states through the due process clause of the Fourteenth Amendment.[9] Perhaps in no other area is the application so jarring, for in no other area was there such a clear intent of the Founding Fathers to separate federal from state jurisdictions. The evidence is conclusive that unless such a separation had been made at the time, the First Amendment could never have won acceptance in the state ratifying conventions,[10] or in the First Congress, as the failure of Madison's attempt to restrict the states clearly demonstrates. The problem now is not simply what Congress may or may not do, but what individual state legislatures, agencies, and local government units may or may not do in a vast variety of local circumstances. The same standards of religious liberty and nonestablishment must now apply universally.

The third development, less revolutionary than the previous two, but still significant, is a change in perception of the issue as well as a change in the issue itself. That is, the constitutional issue in religious liberty and nonestablishment cases must be perceived not simply as a matter of the invasion of a right or the abuse of a power by government, but as both a *clash of rights* and a *clash of interpretation of rights* in which the courts must act as mediators.[11] Several examples will suffice to illustrate the former type of clash. *Sherbert v. Verner*[12] may be seen as a clash between the right of a person to observe a religious holiday and the right of taxpayers to be protected from possible unemployment relief chiselers. *Wisconsin v. Yoder*[13] may be seen as a clash between the rights of parents to control the education of their children and the rights of children to an adequate education or the rights of a state to set standards for an educated citizenry. *United States v. Seeger*[14] may be seen as a clash between the right of conscientious objection and the country's right to demand military service of its citizens. *Walz v. Tax Commission*[15] may be viewed as a clash between the right of a taxpayer to a fair tax and the right of religious groups not to be burdened by taxes. The Court has traditionally solved the problem of clashing rights in other First Amendment areas through a process of comparison and balancing.[16] Such balancing is not incompatible with fiscal neutrality.[17]

Richard E. Morgan's work, *The Politics of Religious Conflict*,[18] documents the second type of clash, that between various interpretations of rights; Morgan views the growing number of religiously motivated professional litigating and lobbying groups and sees them as the primary initiators of religio-political conflict. In a more recent book, *The Wall of Separation*, Frank Sorauf has documented several instances of separationist groups actively searching for plaintiffs in order to bring test cases to court.[19] As Sidney Mead has pointed out elsewhere, the corporate differences of religious institutions

. . . can, and often have resulted in justifiable issues subject to adjudication in the civil courts and having far-reaching consequences. For example, the progressive elimination of religious exercises in the public schools in the forms of Bible reading and prayers was not the result of initiative on the part of the civil authorities, but rather, the result of the initiative of religious groups that rightly questioned the legality of using the civil power to impose the forms of a particular "sect" on all the persons in a public institution of the pluralistic society.[20]

What is needed in this situation of clashing rights and clashing interpretations is not simply to demand limits on government invasion of rights or extension of benefits on a case by case basis premised on one or another policy preference, but to develop known, general, neutral standards by which to resolve clashing rights or clashing interpretations when courts must mediate. One problem with the simple case by case approach without fundamental guiding principles is that issues mutate and are never well resolved. Another problem is that case by case adjudication without standards tends to be, in fact and perception, arbitrary, biased, and capricious, or based on inappropriate criteria, such as the popularity of a religious organization or the novelty of its practices. At the same time, simple appeals to "separation" or "free exercise" smack of jingoism and are not adequate guides for resolving the issue of clashing public and private rights in specific cases.

The fourth contemporary circumstance that has radically influenced our understanding of the church-state problem is an increased consciousness of the range and importance of the *secular* functioning of religious individuals and organizations.[21] Since the government has expanded into the social services field, much of what was once considered church-related activity (if for no other reason than because church-related groups performed them) is now by common understanding considered secular even when performed by church-related groups. This is not to deny that motives may be secular in some cases and religious in others, or that religious and secular functions may at times be so intertwined as to be inseparable. However, much heretofore "religious" activity is now routinely seen as secular, and is therefore the object of governmental regulation and subsidy, as for example the care of unwed mothers and arranging for adoptions.

On the other hand, the desire of religious organizations to participate in the benefits of technological breakthroughs such as radio and television, and commercial advances such as mass fund raising and investment opportunities, has led to an expansion of religion into what was previously considered secular activity.

Activities that must now be considered secular but in which religious groups participate include using government services such as police and fire protection and public mails and roads; having a relationship to the record-keeping, inspecting, incorporating, and taxing agencies of government; maintaining health care facilities such as hospitals, old age homes, and homes for troubled children; educating children in secular subjects; owning property for religious and secular purposes; using public communications media; direct lobbying activity; and functioning as religiously motivated or identified persons in secular positions (nuns teaching in public schools, ministers and priests sitting in Congress, ministers directing HEW programs). Needless to say, the problem of secular functioning is complicated by the fact that different religious organizations participate in different ways and to greater and lesser extents in secular affairs.

The contemporary problems can be better solved if the religion clauses are read in the light of a thrust toward equality. It is the contention of the authors that both liberty and justice are better served if the religion clauses are read as being controlled by the equal protection clause of the Fourteenth Amendment. We believe that *it is necessary to move from a view that liberty is found in the interstices of law to a view that liberty is found in the equal application of law.* Liberty is one of the goals of a democratic society. As the areas left free of government regulation and beyond government support or mediation become fewer and smaller, liberty must be grounded in equality. With a reliance on the equal protection clause the area of religious liberty can be expanded without detriment to other liberties or to government's secular functioning.

The Court, in the *Cantwell* and *Everson* cases, has already held that both the religious liberty and the nonestablishment clauses apply to the states under the due process clause of the Fourteenth Amendment.[22] This limited application, that is, without a similar application under the equal protection clause, may indicate an earlier emphasis on liberty at the expense of equality. It is becoming increasingly clear, at least in the area of religion, that liberty is best preserved by a balancing concern for equality, and that religious liberty and establishment problems can best be handled primarily as equal protection problems are handled, in other words, in terms of valid and suspect classifications.

From this perspective, the fiscal neutrality thesis may be restated as follows: religion may not be used as a basis for classification for purposes of governmental action, whether to confer rights or privileges or to impose duties or burdens. When, however, such a prohibition would result in an inequitable infringement on religious liberty, a religious classification may be made and treated as a suspect classification subject to strict scrutiny by the courts. Stated another way, if religion may not be used as a basis for classification to bestow a benefit or impose a burden, it still may be used as a basis for classification to *prevent* a burden on religious liberty or a privilege amounting to establishment.[23] Seen in this light, fiscal neutrality not only protects liberty but is imbued with an appropriate flexibility as well.

To understand this, we must turn to two legal concepts closely related to equal protection: classification and suspect status. To define a legal class "is simply to designate a quality or characteristic or trait or relation, or any combination of these, the possession of which, by an individual, determines his membership in or inclusion within the class."[24] In its concern for equality, the Constitution requires that those who are similarly situated be treated similarly, and the degree to which a law does this is the measure of its reasonableness. A common formula for valid classification is that "it includes all and only those persons who are similarly situated with respect to the purpose of the law."[25]

The concepts of neutrality and suspect classification provide a clear, consistent standard for legislative and administrative decision makers. They also provide a known standard of review. The judicial task, when a statute or ruling is challenged, remains to retain a proper respect for the legislative branch and state lawmaking bodies, and to safeguard constitutional values. To these ends it must discover the purpose of the legislation by looking at the words, the evil sought to be remedied or benefit bestowed, prior law, accompanying legislation, enacted statements of purpose, formal public pronouncements, and internal legislative history.[26]

Legislation in pursuit of a proper secular purpose may fail to accomplish that purpose by either being underinclusive or over-inclusive. An underinclusive class is one which imposes a burden or extends a benefit to some persons similarly situated, but not to all. An example would be to give draft exemptions to Jehovah's Witnesses and Friends, but not to Methodists. An overinclusive classi-fication is one which imposes a burden or extends a benefit upon a wider range than necessary for the purpose of the legislation. An example would be a statute forbidding the serving of alcoholic beverages—including sacramental wine—to minors.

The Court has never explicitly stated that any classification is intrinsically and for all purposes unconstitutional, but several categories approach the status of forbidden classifications: race, color, and creed (article VI, paragraph three of the Constitution, barring religious tests, says, in effect, that religious classifications cannot be employed). Rather than utilize forbidden classifications the Court utilizes a milder form, "suspect classifications," in which there is "a presumption of unconstitutionality against a law employing certain classifying traits."[27]

When probable purpose is found, the Court may ask these ques-tions: is the most probable purpose permissible, and is there a reasonable relationship of the classification to the most probable purpose, or is it arbitrary and/or insidious? An impermissible purpose is one for which an otherwise valid classification is related rationally to a discriminatory objective—in the present context, either to burden or benefit religion unequally. This would be true whether religion itself is used as the basis for classification or another classification is used for the same purpose. For example, an Internal Revenue Service ruling that newspapers owned or sub-stantially controlled by nonprofit tax exempt organizations may not endorse particular candidates for public office is an unfair burden falling primarily on religious publications, even though religion is never explicitly mentioned.

If religion is considered a suspect classification, it follows that a statute utilizing religion is automatically suspect, will demand a very heavy burden of justification, and will be subject to the most rigid scrutiny. Further, more than just a rational connection to a legitimate public purpose will be required. To explore a parallel area, in the area of racial classification the Court apparently has not adopted a per se rule, but tends to weigh values such as public interest versus private detriments, benefits versus risk, actual costs versus rights infringed, and long-term interests and detriments versus short-term.[28] In some instances it will permit benign racial classifications in order to overcome the effects of past discrimination. In other instances it will allow delayed implementation, in order to make the process of implementation more orderly.[29]

Some observers worry that to forbid specific classification to religious entities and activities would deny religious liberty the status of a substantive, independent liberty and would act to the detriment of religion. This is not a correct understanding of the concept as developed here. Three interrelated factors are relevant. First, very much of religious activity and all of religious thought are fully protected in the speech, press, and assembly clauses of the First Amendment, as well as by the due process and equal protection clauses of the Fourteenth Amendment. Double protection serves no additional function. Second, unlike the speech, press, and assembly clauses, the religion clauses are twofold, prohibiting the establishment of religion as well as guaranteeing its free exercise. The recognition of an independent liberty must be such that it offends neither one nor the other. Classification in terms of religion may tend to discriminate either by favoring religious interests at the expense of other similarly situated interests, or by burdening religious interests in such a way as to have a "chilling effect" on religious liberty. The most equitable solution to this dilemma is to treat religious groups and interests like similar groups and interests. For example, religious groups seeking to sell bonds should conform to the same legal standards as other nonprofit groups such as the American Red Cross, the American Legion, the March of Dimes, and the American Cancer Society. A religious order seeking funds to support missionary efforts should conform to the same fundraising rules and regulations as other groups. A religious school seeking funds for the secular education it provides should conform to the same testing, accreditation, and attendance standards as public schools.

To some this will seem exceedingly harsh. It need not be. Precisely because religious liberty is an independent, substantive right, it functions as an indicator of the need for broader classification and more widely available liberties. That is, within a broader classification the thrust must be toward greater liberty for similarly situated groups rather than toward equal restriction.

Religious liberty is a protected legal right, but not a uniquely privileged right, that is, it gives no rights on the basis of religious commitment that do not extend equally to similarly situated interests. In that sense it is a qualified legal right—qualified by the Establishment Clause.[30] This is not, to repeat, a denial of an independent right. As Kenneth C. Davis has written in a somewhat different context,

That the right is . . . qualified makes it no less a right. Other rights are qualified too, including the right to life and an owner's right to his property. A young man having a right to live may be drafted and ordered into enemy fire at the discretion of an officer. A farmer who owns his farm may lose part of it at the discretion of the highway engineer.[31]

In brief, as independent and substantive as it is, the right to free exercise of religion is both limited by the Establishment Clause and subject to balancing against other independent and substantive rights.

Third, laws must classify and the very idea of classification is discrimination. Laws impose a burden or extend a benefit to those within a designated class and deny it to those outside the class. The state cannot function without classifying its citizens for some purposes, of course, and the tests of valid classifiation are whether the purpose is a legitimate one, and whether all those persons—and only those—who are similarly situated are included in the class. The point to be made here is that for most legitimate purposes, classification in terms of religion is not reasonable, and that in most cases, either broader or narrower classification will provide full protection for religious liberty as well as for the liberty of those who are similarly situated.

Nor is the broader/narrower classification doctrine a technical subterfuge. It is rather a *broadening* of the liberty claimed by religious interests to other interests similarly situated. It can be considered a subterfuge only if it is assumed that religious groups have no equal rights to advocate specific governmental policies, and that legislatures have no right to legislate such policies in an equitable manner—just as they would respond to any interested group. Of course this is not the case. There does remain the troublesome problem of false classification, of course, which, while purporting to relate to other matters, would actually be classification in terms of religion. This is not a problem limited to the religion clauses, and the only remedy is careful scrutiny of the legislation.[32]

Granted the "fiscal neutrality, no classification" doctrine as a general principle, there could conceivably remain instances where classification precisely in terms of religion may be necessary to protect liberty and equality. This would be the case whenever increased governmental regulation places such direct or indirect burdens on the free exercise of religion as to destroy or severely damage it, or when increased government benefits are extended for legitimate secular purposes to voluntary associations and it would be both fair and efficient to include religious associations on an equal basis. When this is the situation, religious classification must be treated like race and sex, as a suspect classification subject to rigorous scrutiny by the courts.

The suspect classification concept is not used in this instance to overcome past discrimination or to extend special benefits, but to preserve neutrality. The question immediately arises: what are the principles that justify such a classification and define its limits? Giannella has offered two such principles which may be adapted. The first is the principle of free exercise neutrality that "permits and sometimes requires the state to make special provision for religious interests in order to relieve them from both direct and indirect burdens placed on the free exercise of religion by increased governmental regulation."[33] Such a provision is consonant with the "protected civil right" nature of religious liberty, but in accordance with the general neutralist position, must be extended to other similar groups and cannot be utilized uniquely to relieve religious organizations of the common burdens of existence in a political society.

The second principle is that of political neutrality. Its aim is not to remove governmental burdens on the practice of religion, but rather

. . . to assure that the establishment clause does not force the categorical exclusion of religious activities and associations from a scheme of governmental regulations whose secular purposes justify their inclusion. The principle of political neutrality recognizes that religious associations operate in the temporal realm and accordingly can be legitimately included among the beneficiaries of the prevailing order established and sustained by the state. If religious groups are to be effectively organized bodies rather than loose associations of mendicants, they must be able to own property, enter into contracts, hire employees, and engage in a host of activities with secular dimensions and consequences. In short, making religious voluntarism a reality requires that religious associations be treated with political equality, and accorded civil opportunities for self-development on a par with other voluntary associations.[34]

We consider Giannella's principles to be clarifications of fiscal neutrality as developed above, rather than modifications.

CONCLUSION

In chapter 6 we have set out the basic contours of a neutralist interpretation of the religion clauses of the First Amendment. Beginning with the original Kurland proposal, the theory has been advanced in several ways. It relies more heavily on equal protection doctrine, substituting suspect classifications where Kurland flatly forbad classification at all; it recognizes an independent, substantive right to religious liberty, demanding only that privileges granted to or burdens imposed on religious individuals or groups be equally granted or imposed on similarly situated individuals and groups. Where there must be exceptions for uniquely religious activities, these are allowed only to preserve neutrality and are justified and limited in two subclassifications, free exercise neutrality and political neutrality.

Neutrality as we have presented it has a number of values. It remains faithful to the underlying purposes of the writers of the First Amendment while at the same time it takes into account the changes in American society and law that have radically altered the environment within which the First Amendment values must be preserved; it provides a rule of law, a clear, general principle based on the text of the Constitution, for legislators and the public prior to legislation and litigation, thereby allowing the Court to perform a properly judicial mode of review, rather than establishing arbitrary policy; it provides an ideal consonant with the rest of the First

Amendment, that of equal liberty, and takes advantage of the recent developments in equal protection;[35] it allows adequate flexibility under well-developed standards which encourage judicial craftsmanship; it generates questions of religious liberty and establishment in a form appropriate for judicial resolution; it results in broadening the area of personal freedom by allowing to other individuals and groups the same liberty considered appropriate for religious individuals and groups. At the same time, it provides strict standards for the acceptability of any aids to religion. Finally, while it does not eliminate the need for the Court to define religion, it radically narrows the range of problems in which such a definition is necessary, and puts the burden of definition where it is most appropriate—on the one who claims a religious exemption or privilege.[36]

It is our conclusion that the neutrality doctrine provides the most appropriate interpretation of the religion clauses of the First Amendment and provides the basis for sound public policy in this controversial area.

NOTES

1. Phillip B. Kurland, *Religion and the Law* (Chicago: Aldine Press, 1963), p. 18.

2. Ibid.

3. For a discussion of one secular pursuit (investment policy) of one church group, see James Gollin, "There's an Unholy Mess in the Churchly Economy," *Fortune*, May 1976, p. 223.

4. Harry W. Jones, "Church-State Relations: Our Constitutional Heritage," in H. Stahler, ed., *Religion and Contemporary Society* 156 (1963):173.

5. Donald Giannella, "Religious Liberty, Nonestablishment and Doctrinal Development, Part II: The Nonestablishment Principle," *Harvard Law Review* 81 (1968): 514.

6. Ibid. at 515.

7. Ibid.

8. Joseph Tussman and Jacobus TenBroeck, "Equal Protection of the Laws," *California Law Review* 37 (1939): 380.

9. For an excellent historical summary of this development, see Henry J. Abraham, *Freedom and the Court*, 2d ed. (New York: Oxford University Press, 1973), Chapter III.

10. Mark deWolf Howe, "The Constitutional Question," in *Religion and the Free Society*, Fund for the Republic, 49 (1958): 51-52.

11. *West Virginia State Board of Education v. Barnette*, 319 U.S. 624 at 630 (1943).

12. *Sherbert v. Verner*, 374 U.S. 398 (1963). The plaintiff, a Seventh-Day Adventist, lost her job when the mill in which she worked changed to a six-day work week. Unable to find other suitable work, she applied for unemployment benefits. The state of South Carolina refused to pay since work was available if she would work on Saturday. The Supreme Court decided for Mrs. Sherbert.

13. *Wisconsin v. Yoder*, 406 U.S. 205 (1972). The Old Order Amish refused to send their children to school until age 16 as Wisconsin law demanded. The Supreme Court held the state must make an exception for the Amish.

14. *United States v. Seeger*, 380 U.S. 163 (1965). Seeger refused to be inducted into the armed forces since he was opposed to participation in war under any circumstances. The Court upheld his right to conscientious objector status even though he refused to claim a belief in a personal God.

15. *Walz v. Tax Commission*, 397 U.S. 664 (1970).

16. See *Cohen v. California*, 403 U.S. 15 at 22-23 (1971); *Street v. New York*, 394 U.S. 576 at 591-93 (1969); *NAACP v. Alabama*, 357 U.S. 449 at 460-66 (1961); *American Communications Association v. Doud*, 330 U.S. 382 at 394 (1950); For a more theoretical discussion, see Laurent B. Frantz, "The First Amendment in the Balance," *Yale Law Journal* 71 (1962):1424; Wallace Mendelson, "The First Amendment and the Judicial Process: A Reply to Mr. Frantz," *Vanderbilt Law Review* 17 (1964): 481-82; also Thomas Emerson, "Toward a General Theory of the First Amendment," *Yale Law Journal* 72 (1963): 912-914.

17. However, see Alan Schwartz, "No Imposition of Religion: The Establishment Clause Value," *Yale Law Journal* 77 (1968): 701-04. For a somewhat more developed conception of balancing in the area of religious liberty, see Morris J. Clark, "Guidelines of the Free Exercise Clause," *Harvard Law Review* 83 (1969): 327.

18. Richard E. Morgan, *The Politics of Religious Conflict: Church and State in America* (New York: Pegasus Publishing Co., 1968).

19. Frank J. Sorauf, *The Wall of Separation* (Princeton, New Jersey: Princeton University Press, 1976) p. 82.

20. Sidney E. Mead, *The Nation with the Soul of a Church* (New York: Harper & Row, 1975), pp. 93-94. Even the titles of several cases illustrate this conflict among professional litigating groups: *Committee for Public Education and Religious Liberty v. Nyquist*, 93 S. Ct. 2955 (1973). *Cherry v. PEARL*, 93 S. Ct. 2955 (1973); and *Levitt v. PEARL*, 93 S. Ct. 2814 (1973).

21. The *Oxford Annotated Dictionary* defines "secular" as "1. Of or pertaining to the worldly or temporal as distinguished from the spiritual or eternal; . . . belonging to the state as distinguished from church; nonecclesiastical, civil . . .; not religious in character nor devoted to religious ends or uses." J. Coulson, ed., *Oxford Annotated Dictionary* (Oxford, Great Britain: Clarendon Press, 1975).

22. *Illinois ex rel McCollum v. Board of Education*, 333 U.S. 203 (1948); *Cantwell v. Connecticut*, 310 U.S. 296 (1940).

23. This interpretation departs from the original Kurland proposal in that it gives as much emphasis to "protection" as to "equal" in the Fourteenth Amendment clause.

24. Tussman and TenBroeck, "Equal Protection of Laws," p. 344.

25. Note "Forward: Equal Protection: Developments in the Law," *Harvard Law Review* 82 (1969): 1076.

26. See H. M. Hart and H. Sacks, *The Legal Process: Basic Problems in the Making and Application of Law* (Cambridge, Mass.: Harvard University Press, 1958), pp. 1413-16.

27. Tussman and TenBroeck, "Equal Protection of Laws," p. 354.

28. Note "Forward: Equal Protection," p. 1103.

29. *Brown v. Board of Education* II, 349 U.S. 294 (1955).

30. In other words, the Establishment Clause must be read as the Founding Fathers intended: what we would now call an equal protection doctrine.

31. Kenneth Culp Davis, *Administrative Law* (St. Paul: West Publishing Co., 1973), p. 305.

32. See *Gomillion v. Lightfoot*, 364 U.S. 339 at 347 (1960). "While in form this is merely an act redefining metes and bounds . . . the inescapable human effect of this essay in geometry and geography is to despoil colored citizens, and only colored citizens, of their theretofore enjoyed voting rights."

33. Giannella, "Religious Liberty II," p. 518. One example might be exempting Amish from drivers' license photographs, since they consider pictures to be "graven" images. See *Chicago Tribune*, 26 June 1976, section 1, p. 28.

34. Ibid.

35. See Kenneth L. Karst, "Equality as a Central Principle in the First Amendment," *University of Chicago Law Review* 43 (1975): 20.

36. We shall return to the definitional problem in chapter 8.

7

PUBLIC AID TO RELIGIOUS ORGANIZATIONS: SETTING LIMITS

Church-government fiscal relations take many forms. This book is not attempting to establish a definitive position for each of those multifarious relationships. Instead, our objective is to explore the extent to which neutrality will produce more consistent and equitable public policy. Chapter 5 explored many of the problems that arise from efforts to distinguish sectarian from nonsectarian organizations. Chapter 6 showed that fiscal neutrality provides a constitutional rationale for some economic assistance to religious and religiously affiliated organizations and provides constitutional limits. This chapter carries the exploration of fiscal neutrality further by providing practical examples of how it can be expected to affect church-government fiscal relations.

Three types of church-government issues will be examined. The question of paying taxes will be illustrated by a discussion of property taxes. The issue of reporting requirements and public sector impact on organizational revenue collection will be explored in relation to the federal income tax. Finally, the question of receiving public sector assistance directly will be discussed in the context of primary and secondary education.

PROPERTY TAX

Although much of existing policy on religious property tax exemptions meets the test of fiscal neutrality, the status quo does create an equity problem. Religious organizations are a comparatively small part of the problem, but because the neutralist approach is concerned with equity in general and with equal treatment for religious and nonreligious organizations similarly situated, the matter of unequal tax exemption burdens is worth at least brief mention.

Quigley and Stinson found exempt property to be more heavily concentrated in central cities than suburbs.[1] In some instances the accessibility to services offered by the central business district will greatly influence the location decision of exempt entities. For example, the new county court house is built downtown rather than out in the suburbs because all the necessary auxiliary services are more readily available at the center than at the periphery of the metropolitan area. Another factor affecting the location of exempt entities is property tax burden. High property taxes are capitalized into lower property values (*ceteris paribus*). That is to say, if two lots are identical in all important respects and the property taxes on lot A are twice the property taxes on lot B, buyers will offer less for lot A than lot B. However, if a buyer comes along who does not have to pay property taxes, he/she is willing to pay the same for either lot. Consequently, where property taxes are relatively high, tax exempt buyers have a distinct advantage in bidding against tax paying buyers. The higher the property taxes the greater the advantage the tax exempt buyer has. Property taxes are generally higher in central cities because central cities provide more services than most suburbs do. The result is that

. . . the percentage of real property value exempt and the concentration of exemptions beyond local government control are inversely related to median income and directly related to effective tax rates. The suburban income is generally one and one-half times the central city income and above the state median income, with both differences increasing over time. . . . Thus, when compared with suburbs, central cities tend to have less wealth, a greater property tax burden, and a greater proportion of exempt property, especially property beyond local government control whose benefits accrue to the region.[2]

Two fairly significant equity issues emerge from this analysis. First, economic forces cause jurisdictions taxing themselves hardest

and usually having the most fiscal difficulty to bear a dispropor-
tionate share of the tax-exempt load. It is a self-reinforcing cycle.
Those jurisdictions with the highest proportion of tax-exempt
property are often forced to use still higher property tax rates to
compensate for lost revenues. This in turn tends to drive away tax-
paying entities seeking to avoid these higher costs. At the same
time, exempt entities enjoy greater advantages in bidding for highly
taxed property. The problem promises to get worse before it gets
better.

Second, although local governments bear the cost of these tax
expenditures, it is often state governments that grant the exemption.[3] From the state's point of view the situation is ideal. Requests
from worthy groups for special treatment are met without cost to
the state. On the city's end it looks quite different. The city is
struggling to make ends meet when suddenly its tax base is reduced
because the state has granted some class of property owners some
sort of property tax exemption.

Clearly, one way to address both of these equity problems is to
have states reimburse local governments for revenues lost as a
result of state-imposed tax exemptions.[4] Exempt and nonexempt
entities alike would produce revenue for the local government and
that level of government making the policy would bear the cost.[5]
Putting this reform into operation, though, would require more
than just writing a few checks. Assessment information on exempt
properties is sparse. The incentive for local assessors would be to
set assessments on exempt properties as high as possible to get the
most money out of the state. Controlling this bias would not be
easy. Clear guidelines, sampling, effective sanctions, and the use of
objective comparative data wherever possible seem to be minimum
requirements.[6]

At least one desirable benefit of such an effort would be the collection and dissemination of better information about the level of
tax expenditures involved in property tax exemptions. Several
observers favor publishing more information about foregone
revenues,[7] perhaps doing it on an annual basis to parallel the
appropriations process for budgetary expenditures. Beneficiaries of
tax expenditures can be expected to oppose this proposal because
they prefer to have their benefits flow unnoticed and uninterrupted.

Too much publicity is perceived as a threat. While that concern is not entirely groundless,[8] the proposal can be supported with the argument that more information is helpful. Recognizing that public policy is made by mortals occasionally plagued by fallibility or eccentricity, it can nonetheless be hoped that decision makers with better information will make better decisions.

Potential technical difficulties notwithstanding, the state of Connecticut has demonstrated that it is possible to reimburse local governments for revenues lost through property tax exemptions. Church property was to be included in the program, but opposition from religious leaders resulted in churches being dropped from the formula. Local governments are now reimbursed by the state for twenty-five percent of the property tax revenues lost from exemptions granted to hospitals and colleges.[9] Excluding church property from a program of this sort is unnecessary and unwise. The revenues lost to a local government from tax exemptions to churches are every bit as real as the revenues lost from exemptions to hospitals and colleges. The nature of the tax expenditure is exactly the same. Fiscal neutrality would require that all such properties be treated equally.

Another way to cope with property tax exemptions is to charge for municipal services rendered. Virginia law, for example, "permits the governing body of any county, town or city to impose and collect a service charge on the owners of all real estate within its boundaries."[10] The charge may not exceed twenty percent of the local tax rate, but may be levied to pay for such services as police protection, fire protection, and solid waste collection and disposal. Certainly, church properties could be included among those paying service charges. In Virginia, however, church property alone is excluded from liability for the service charges. This is clearly not because church properties will be denied these services. Instead, it is another example of the free rider problem, with churches enjoying benefits accorded to no other similarly situated organizations. Fiscal neutrality does not require that churches make payments in lieu of property taxes for the services they receive, but it does require that churches enjoy no more tax benefits than other similar organizations within the taxing jurisdiction.

Turning to the more fundamental concerns of fiscal neutrality, such as defining similarly situated entities, we see the approach allowing considerable room for variation. What constitutes property similar to that owned by religious groups is a matter of legislative discretion. A long tradition already exists for some institutions and activities. What we propose is a logical extension of a common practice. State constitutional conventions, state legislatures, and local legislative bodies have long chosen to encourage sundry activities by exempting property used for those purposes from taxation. If one state decides to encourage religious, educational, and charitable activities, while another adds cultural activities to the list, it is very difficult to say that one state is wrong and another is right. Illinois' inclusion of agricultural and horticultural societies in the list of exempted properties is a policy no more right or wrong than classifying cities by population size or allowing right turns on red lights. The neutralist perspective does not prescribe the breadth of the public policy—in this case property tax exemption—only that there must be reasonable breadth. Religious organizations cannot be set apart for special advantage or disadvantage. Although it regulates another matter, Section 501(c) (3) of the Internal Revenue Code is an excellent model.

As property owners, religious groups are already subject to zoning codes, building codes, health codes, and other public regulations; simply because a structure is to be used as a place of worship does not mean the safety of people who gather there can be endangered by ignoring the building code. Free exercise arguments notwithstanding, public policies designed to protect the health and safety of the general public and communicants have largely prevailed.[11] From the fiscal neutrality perspective the important point is that "[A]s property owners, churches may not hope for much better treatment than that accorded other property owners under the due process clause. However, under the equal protection clause, they can certainly insist on being treated no worse."[12]

An examination of state constitutional and statutory provisions on property exemption summarized in table 7-1 indicates that by and large the general nature of the property tax exemption is the same for nonprofit groups—religious and nonreligious. For example, if the state constitution provides for property exemptions, there is usually mention of both religious and nonreligious groups.

Table 7-1
Property Tax Exemption Provisions in the Fifty States

	STATES GRANTING EXEMPTIONS[1]		STATES GRANTING EXEMPTIONS TO RELIGIOUS ORGANIZATIONS ONLY[4]
	Same for Religious & Nonreligious[2]	Different for Religious & Nonreligious[3]	
Property used for principle activity	48		
Property owned by organization	7	7	
necessary for organization's use	2	5	1
used for commercial purposes	4	1	4
used for social/recreational activities (camps)	2	2	
held for future construction	1	1	
site of construction in progress			1
used to raise produce			
other			
cemeteries	49		
parking lots	2	1	
hospitals	23		
orphanages	11	1	
publishing societies		1	
rest homes	7		
retreat houses	4		1
schools	43		
K-12			
colleges/universities			
seminaries	5		
dormitories	9		
residences (parsonage, convent, rectory)	2		30
attached			
not attached			
corporations and foundations	2		

Source: Compiled from state statutes.

[1]Number of states in which both religious and nonreligious organizations are granted property tax exemptions.

[2]The legal basis for granting the exemption (whether statutory or constitutional) is the same for both religious and nonreligious organizations.

[3]The legal basis for granting the exemption is not the same for both religious and nonreligious organizations (e.g., one may be constitutional and the other statutory).

[4]Number of states in which property tax exemption are granted only to religious organizations for the type of property specified.

In other words, there are few instances in which religious groups enjoy constitutional guarantees of property tax exemption while nonreligious groups must rely solely on statutory grants of exemptions, or vice versa.

Information at this level of analysis does not tell us whether religious organizations have a more or less difficult time winning a property tax exemption, or whether all religious groups have equal access to property tax exemptions.[13] Nonetheless, this examination does make it clear that the basis for seeking judicial relief and demanding equal treatment is the same for religious and nonreligious organizations. Taken at this level, the neutralist perspective requirements for property tax exemption policies seem already to be in place in most states. The fiscal neutrality perspective is not therefore a radical departure from the status quo. In the case of property tax exemption policies, states have long recognized the neutralist approach as the fairest and most workable. In *Walz* the Court mentioned the importance of tax exemptions being available to nonreligious as well as religious groups. Public policy now needs to recognize that a fiscal neutrality perspective can and should be applied to other church-government fiscal issues.

FEDERAL INCOME TAX

The justification for tax expenditures provided through the federal income tax is that the entities and activities benefited are worthy of public sector encouragement. The voluntary private sector, including religion, is expected to get more support when an income tax deduction reduces the cost of the contribution. However, one early study of these deductions concluded that the number of dollars lost in taxes is substantially greater than the number of dollars generated in additional voluntary contributions because of the deduction incentive.[14] Fund raisers were not convinced. Their own experience seemed to confirm beyond question that tax incentives play a role in decisions about philanthropic giving, especially for individuals with high incomes.[15]

Subsequent studies noted first more responsiveness to tax incentives,[16] and second a definite response to incentives.[17] The results differ, depending on the methods and data used, but it does seem that the price elasticity of charitable giving is greater than one. (Somewhere between − 1.2 and − 1.005.) This means that,

[I]f it is accepted that the price elasticity of charitable giving is about − 1.1 . . . the tax incentive for charitable giving induces more giving than it costs the government in forgone revenue. To illustrate, suppose that in the absence of any tax incentives, taxpayers would each give $1,000 to charity. If introducing the charitable deduction reduces the price of giving by 30 percent, this would induce taxpayers to increase their philanthropic giving to $1,480. The tax savings would be $444 (.3 × $1,480). This giving is increased by $480 at a cost to the government of $444. Put another way, repeal of the charitable deduction would reduce giving in this example by almost one-third.[18]

That is why officials of charitable organizations get worried when there is talk about possibly eliminating the deduction for contributions to their organizations. Reducing the tax incentive can be expected to produce a drop in contributions.

The size of the drop will depend on the extent to which contributions to that organization are spurred by tax incentives. Using Feldstein's estimates, the Commission on Private Philanthropy and Public Needs concluded that

[T]axpayers having incomes of $10,000 to $15,000 would reduce their gifts by 22 percent (from an average of $290 to $225). Taxpayers in the $100,000 to $500,000 class would cut back their giving by 75 percent, from average annual contributions of $9,184 to $2,246.[19]

In other words, the greatest impact would be felt by organizations most dependent on high income donors. As Table 7-2 shows, all kinds of philanthropic organizations would feel the pinch, but religious organizations would be less directly affected than most other types.[20]

Saying that an elimination of the deduction would hurt religious organizations less than other philanthropic organizations is not meant to imply that these deductions should be eliminated. On the contrary, we believe that public policy should continue to foster voluntary sector activities because they provide unique and vital contributions to the well-being of our society. And if other chari-

Table 7-2

Average Yearly Individual Giving to
Major Donee Areas by Income Levels, 1970

ADJUSTED GROSS INCOME	RELIGION	EDUCATION	HOSPITALS	HEALTH AND WELFARE	ALL OTHERS*
$5,000 and below	$63	$1	$0	$10	$15
$5,000 - $10,000	138	3	1	28	32
$10,000 - $15,000	191	5	2	43	43
$15,000 - $20,000	235	14	6	63	71
$20,000 - $50,000	349	48	25	114	152
$50,000 - $100,000	638	267	119	352	644
$100,000 - $500,000	1,322	1,791	615	1,203	4,251
$500,000 - $1,000,000	4,466	14,909	5,546	8,067	39,037
More than $1,000,000	7,073	45,865	14,688	14,430	175,219
Average Giving for all Incomes	$140	$9	$4	$34	$46

Source: Commission on Private Philanthropy and Public Needs, Research Papers. Vol. V: Regulation n.p. Department of the Treasury, 1977.

*Including giving to arts and cultural institutions and to private foundations.

table organizations are assisted, religious organizations ought not to be excluded.

Existing policy on charitable deductions is basically neutral with respect to religion. However, at least one recommendation made by the Commission on Private Philanthropy and Public Needs would increase the neutrality of current law, "that to increase inducements for charitable giving, all taxpayers who take the standard deduction should also be permitted to deduct charitable contributions as an additional, itemized deduction."[21]

Just as eliminating the deduction would have the least impact on religious organizations because so large a portion of religious giving comes from lower-income classes, so this recommendation would have the greatest effect on contributions to religious organizations. Even if the family takes the standard deduction, contributions dropped in the plate on Sunday morning could be a bonus deduction. The commission also recommends letting families with incomes less than $15,000 per year deduct charitable giving twice, and permitting families with incomes between $15,000 and $30,000 per year to deduct 150 percent of their charitable giving. These recommendations too would be a boon to religious organizations. That was not the aim of the commission; it was concerned with increasing philanthropic giving generally. Nonetheless, in light of what we know about the giving patterns of various income classes, it is clear that policy changes stated in broad language can have a selected impact on religious organizations—even if that was not the intent.

We believe that changes of the sort recommended by the Commission on Private Philanthropy and Public Needs, although they affect religious organizations more than many others, would be permissible because religion is not targeted as a special beneficiary, and the effect would be to move religious organizations closer to equity with nonreligious organizations with regard to the efficacy of contribution deductibility. As Henry Aaron observes,

The burden should . . . rest on those who would argue that the implicit federal matching grants should differ between those who itemize and those who do not. I confess that I cannot perceive any persuasive reason why rates should differ.[22]

Other general issues surrounding the tax treatment of philanthropic giving are not direct concerns of this inquiry. What to do about minimum tax requirements, appreciated property, bequests, corporate giving, maximum contribution ceilings, and others do not have an apparent differential impact on religious organizations beyond the sorts already discussed. A neutralist policy would simply require that any changes help or hurt religion no more than they help or hurt other charitable organizations.

The basic requirement for permissible deductions is currently that contributors receive no reciprocal economic benefit from their contributions. The money must go into the organization to provide for a general good in the community, and control of the contribution must shift to the organization. There must not be a *quid pro quo* for the contributor. This is not always easy to measure, but congressional intent has been clear on this matter since 1909. The only change came in 1916, when the word "income" was changed to "earnings." Other than that the language has been unaltered: ". . . no part of the net earnings of which inures to the benefit of any private shareholder or individual."[23]

When there is no reciprocal economic benefit and the recipient is a qualified charitable organization, deductions seem altogether justifiable. The special tax treatment, however, does impose some obligations on receiving organizations—which for our purposes mean religious organizations. Dean Kelley suggests some practical operating guidelines:

A church might set itself these limits in soliciting and receiving deductible contributions for designated purposes:

1. Contributions will not be received that are designated for non-exempt third parties;
2. Contributions will be received designated for particular purposes, programs, or projects of the church itself, which have been duly authorized in advance as part of its religious activity by the appropriate internal body;
3. Expenditure of such contributions for the purpose designated will be entirely within the discretion of the church or its appropriate internal body;
4. If the church cannot find a way to utilize such contributions within its own purposes and the donor's designation, it will return the donation to the donor with an explanation of the problem;

5. The church will determine the best means of carrying out its purposes with such contributions, and if an outside agency is utilized, will continue to exercise expenditure accountability to make sure that its funds are applied to its purposes by any contractor, agent, or grantee.[24]

To satisfy both members and outsiders that these guidelines are in fact being followed, it behooves religious organizations to keep reasonably accurate and detailed financial reports. The tendency, however, as we saw with informational tax returns, is to set religious organizations apart, exempting them from reporting requirements. For example, the Commission on Private Philanthropy and Public Needs recommends "[T]hat all larger tax-exempt organizations except churches and church affiliates be required to prepare and make readily available detailed annual reports on their finances, programs and priorities."[25] That was not the recommendation forwarded to the commission by an advisory committee of accountants. Their conclusion was that, "A single, uniform set of accounting principles, including those recommended by the committee in this report, should be adopted by *all* philanthropic organizations."[26] These recommendations appear to be both fair and sound. Their implementation should increase accountability, improve efficiency, and reduce intentional or unintentional mismanagement. There is no reason why religious organizations alone among charitable organizations should be deprived of these beneficial results or relieved of the reporting burden. Religious officials no doubt will not see it that way, but it is difficult to see how responsible financial accounting practices directly or substantially interfere with the development, teaching, and practice of religious beliefs.

AID TO EDUCATION

As mentioned in chapter 1, aid to nonpublic schools has been the single most intractable church-government fiscal problem the United States has faced. Chapter 2 explored in detail the failure of the Supreme Court to develop an equitable, consistent constitutional principle in this area. It is therefore with some trepidation that we offer two alternative forms of aid acceptable under the fiscal neutrality approach.

Before discussing the particular forms of aid, it may be well to explore the purposes of aid. The first objective is to provide equitable treatment to the children and parents who choose non-public school education. Two conflicting arguments are made in respect to equity. The first is that parents of students in nonpublic schools pay taxes to support public schools on the same basis as other citizens; in addition, they pay the full cost of private school education, even though the majority of that education is in fulfillment of *state-mandated* educational requirements. The opposing argument is that the state makes available free public schools to meet compulsory education requirements; if parents choose a private education for their children, they do it with the full knowledge that they must bear the expense of such an education. In this case, runs the argument, religious freedom has an additional price.

Both arguments have considerable merit and there is seemingly no mutually acceptable middle ground. Three constitutional principles are clear and may be considered settled law: the state does have the right to establish reasonable minimum educational requirements;[27] the state may not deny the freedom to attend nonpublic schools;[28] and the government may not finance religious education as such.[29] The question we raise is whether the secular education financed by the state must be in a secular environment or whether that same secular education may, if the parents so choose, be financed in a religious environment, provided the religious element is not financed by the state. We would argue that to insist upon a secular environment is to favor the nonreligious over the religious and to deny equitable treatment. In fact, we respectfully submit that Mr. Justice Stewart was in error in *Meek v. Pittenger* when he substituted a religious atmosphere test for the secular-sectarian distinction.[30] The atmosphere of a nonpublic school—Jewish, Presbyterian, Catholic, atheist, liberal, traditional, or any other—ought to be constitutionally irrelevant if other state requirements are met. Designing aid for secular education without directly financing religious study or the religious environment is the critical public policy issue we must address.

The second purpose of aid to nonpublic schools is fiscal efficiency. Certainly in the short term, it is less expensive to provide secular education within existing nonpublic schools than to absorb those students into the public school system. Such fiscal efficiency is a legitimate public policy objective.

A third and—in our minds—decisive purpose in providing aid to nonpublic schools is to assure a diversity of educational opportunities and allow a maximum of free choice for parents and children within constitutionally acceptable limits. Critics of aid to nonpublic schools claim there is already considerable diversity in public systems. This may be somewhat true in large metropolitan areas where there are many school districts—rich and poor, innovative and traditional. Consumers of public education could, in an ideal public choice model, "vote with their feet" by moving to the school district that provides the type of educational services they prefer. The theory sounds fine, but the economic reality is that few families can afford to move to the school district they prefer. The public choice model does not work for them.

For most families educational choice is highly restricted. Parents may not prefer to send their children to public schools, but other factors may leave no alternative—moving to another neighborhood or paying tuition is beyond their economic means or they prefer not to send their children to a sectarian school of a religious persuasion other than their own. In this context it is interesting to note that a poll conducted by Gallup found seventy-two percent of respondents in a nationwide sample agreeing that there should be private and parochial schools.[31] In communities where there were private and parochial schools, the favorable responses jumped to eighty-four percent. With so many people in favor of alternatives to public schools, why do nine out of ten students go to public schools? A majority of the Gallup poll respondents believed finances were the most important reason why parents send their children to public schools. When the financial factor was eliminated from consideration, as it was in the question posed in table 7-3, a majority of respondents in communities where there were already nonpublic schools said that they would prefer to send their children to nonpublic schools. From a policy point of view it is significant that respondents split very evenly in their preference for sectarian and nonsectarian nonpublic schools. Citizens apparently are not happy with their public schools, and if they could afford it they would make use of alternatives—with sectarian and nonsectarian being chosen in almost equal numbers.

It is against this background of the purposes of aid that we turn to tuition tax credits and educational vouchers. The idea for tax

Table 7-3

"If you had the money, or if your children could get free tuition, would you send them to a private school, to a church-related school (parochial), or to a public school?"

Nationally, the responses were as follows:

Would send children to private school	18%
Would send children to parochial school	22%
Would send children to public school	57%
No opinion	3%

The responses of those who live in areas where private and parochial schools exist are, of course, the most meaningful. In the private and parochial school areas these results were obtained:

Would send children to private school	30%
Would send children to parochial school	29%
Would send children to public school	41%

Source: How the Public Views Nonpublic Schools (Cambridge, Mass.: A Study of the American Independent School, 1969), p. 5.

credit is to provide a deduction from taxes due up to some stated maximum, usually $250 to $500, for parents who have children in school.[32] Debate over tuition tax credits has focused on two points, the wisdom of tax credits as public policy and their constitutionality. Let us look at each in turn.

The major public policy question is whether educational tax credits would harm public schools.[33] It is hypothesized that such harm could come in two ways. First, money which would have flowed to public schools would be diverted to private schools. Secondly, students otherwise forced by economic circumstances to attend public schools would elect to attend private schools. Concerning the first, proponents of tax credits argue that the program envisioned is not a grant of federal funds but credit against tax liability. While this would decrease federal revenues, it would not

displace current expenditures, and future aid would be most unlikely if all school children were not included. Concerning the
second, the counter argument is that competition, while initially
painful, would have the effect in the long run of strengthening
public schools by forcing administrators to develop more effective
programs. In any event, there is something profoundly disturbing
in the realization that public school students would flee to private
schools at considerable added expense if given even a modest
incentive.

A second policy issue is whether credits would be primarily a tax
break for the wealthy, since they would be generally available without a determination of financial need. Proponents of tax credits
argue that taxpayers who *together* make over $30,000 annually *and*
have children in school are a very small heavily taxed minority (less
than three percent), that middle-income people are the ones
primarily hit by inflation who need and will receive the vast prepon-
derance of the assistance of tax credits, and that simple equity
demands that those with students in private schools, since they also
support public schools, are entitled to some relief.[34] We agree.

A third policy concern is whether tax credits would aid segregated private academies. This issue was raised in an opinion issued
by the United States Commission on Civil Rights which states that
"passage of tuition tax credit legislation for students attending
private elementary and secondary schools would unconstitutionally
subsidize schools which discriminate on the basis of race."[35]
Proponents of tax credit rightly call the issue a red herring. A safeguard had been written into the original Packwood-Moynihan bill
but was eliminated when the House Ways and Means Committee
cut elementary and secondary schools out of the proposal. The
United States Catholic Conference, a proponent of tax credits, has
lobbied for *reinclusion* of the safeguard.[36] A spokesperson for the
Catholic League for Religion and Civil Liberties has argued that
tax credits would decrease discrimination by increasing the ability
of low-income people to attend nonpublic schools.[37] The Supreme
Court's ruling in *Norwood v. Harrison*,[38] holding a book loan
program violative of equal protection to the extent that it aided
racially segregated schools, would seem to be a controlling precedent in this regard.

A final policy issue is the cost of tax credits in lost revenue at a time when the government faces increasing deficits and is attempting to limit its own spending. This is certainly a significant consideration and involves both a choice between alternatives and a matter of priorities. Congress is in the difficult position of setting national priorities and making painful choices. Whether tax credit legislation is the best means to achieve educational equity we are not prepared to say. It is one way, and we would agree that equity ought not be a victim of inflation.

The traditional approach to discussing the constitutional issues in this area is to divide the questions into Free Exercise and Establishment Clause considerations. Since neutralists read the clauses together to express a single mandate we may show here how a neutralist approach can fit with previous constitutional tests. Although the clauses are in some measure overlapping, we may speak of five relevant tests: the narrowness of the benefited class, secular legislative purpose, principle and primary effect, entanglement, and the separability of secular and sectarian aid.

Committee for Public Education v. Nyquist, the most immediately relevant precedent, turned principally on the narrowness of the benefited class.[39] In that case over eighty percent of the students attended Catholic parochial schools.[40] Tax credits would make assistance equally available to all taxpayers with legitimate educational expenses without regard to the sectarian-nonsectarian, public-nonpublic, or higher-lower educational nature of the institutions within which the education is received, or the sectarian identification of the taxpayers. As such, tax credit legislation would seem to meet the breadth of benefited class principle established by the Court.[41]

Similarly, it seems clear that tax credit legislation could pass the secular purpose test. Since the stated purpose is to provide tax relief on a broad, nondiscriminatory basis, there is nothing in either the legislation or in legal precedents to indicate that the Court will deny the secularity of the purpose of Congress. Indeed, the Court has not stricken even a direct parochial aid measure on the basis that it involved a sectarian purpose. Secular purpose may be seen as a "low-threshold" test, and a substantial burden of proof rests on those who allege the absence of any secular purpose.[42]

In determining secular purpose it may be well to recall Mr. Justice Powell's concurring opinion in *Wolman*:

> Parochial schools, quite apart from their sectarian purpose have provided an educational alternative for millions of young Americans; they often afford wholesome competition with our public schools. . . . The State has, moreover, a legitimate interest in facilitating education of the highest quality for all children within its boundaries, whatever school their parents have chosen for them.[43]

The principle or primary effect test poses more substantial questions. The essence of the test is that

> if the essential *effect* of the government's action is to influence—either positively or negatively—the pursuit of a religious tradition or the expression of a religious belief, it should be struck down as violative of the free exercise clause if the effect is negative, and of the establishment clause if positive.[44]

In *Nyquist*, the Court observed that, "[o]ur cases simply do not support the notion that a law found to have a 'primary' effect to promote some legitimate end under the State's police power is immune from further examination to ascertain whether it also has the direct and immediate effect of advancing religion."[45] Tax credit legislation has the direct and immediate effect of relieving the burden of all taxpayers with tuition expenses to meet. As such it is general welfare legislation which does not directly aid any or all religious groups as such. Nor do benefits flow to religious institutions at all. On the other hand, there will most certainly be an indirect and incidental benefit to these schools. This type of aid was distinguished by Mr. Justice Powell in *Sloan v. Lemon*.[46] Tax credits have the further strength that the indirect, incidental aid does not flow uniquely or principally to religiously affiliated schools, but goes to all tuition-charging schools on all levels of education.[47] Unless the Court changes its mind on the validity of the principle and primary effect test, it could legitimately hold tax credit legislation constitutional in this regard.

The issue of entanglement is substantially less complicated. Tax credit legislation, utilizing revisions in the tax code instead of any direct grants or aids, avoids all direct government-religion involvement. According to William D. Valente,

> [The Packwood-Moynihan bill] involves no direct government-religion administrative involvement, no less *excessive* entanglement. The only condition for qualifying for the tax credit is educational expenditure at a state approved or certified school. Since state approval of schools is already a matter of state record and policy, no additional state involvement is required. No one can seriously contend that the present involvement of states in approving educational institutions to assure minimal standards in the public interest implicates an excessive supervision or entanglement. Indeed the Supreme Court . . . has repeatedly declared that the State has the right under its compulsory education laws to regulate and require schools to meet minimum standards of approval or certification. . . . Further, in the New York tax benefit case [Nyquist] the Court expressly declined to rule that the state law fostered any impermissible entanglement.[48]

The final test is the separability of the secular and sectarian impact. The Court may find this test inapplicable, since sectarian schools are not the direct recipients of aid. Indeed, one of the constitutional strengths of tax credits lies precisely in its avoidance of the distinctions for which the Court has often been criticized. If the Court were to take this route, it would find strong precedent in similar if less extensive federal programs such as the "G.I. Bill,"[49] the aid authorized for educationally disadvantaged veterans,[50] the educational aid granted to the families of dead or disabled veterans,[51] the payment of educational costs for pages of the Supreme Court and Congress and for all other minors who are congressional employees,[52] and the educational assistance payments to Senior Reserve Officers' Training Corps students.[53] In *each* of these programs the nature of the school attended—public, private, secular or religiously affiliated—is irrelevant. No court has ever condemned such federal programs.[54] Moreover, the economic benefits enjoyed by sectarian schools because of this exemption from property tax liability are much more direct aid than aid coming through students with either tax credits or vouchers.

On the other hand, the Supreme Court's decision in *Tilton v. Richardson*[55] and *Lemon v. Kurtzman*[56] depended heavily on separating secular and sectarian components in the educational process. This is not necessarily a stumbling block for tax credits. As the records in both *Tilton* and *Lemon* demonstrate, it is possible to develop separate budgets for the secular and sectarian components.[57] The courts could insist that credits be computed only on the basis of tuition paid for secular education at accredited institutions. Separate budgets could be neutrally evaluated by nongovernmental accrediting agencies as part of the normal accreditation process. Such a procedure need not involve excessive governmental entanglement and would certainly fit the fiscal neutrality model.

All the issues just discussed in connection with tax credits also apply to education vouchers. A system of education vouchers can provide increased educational options for parents in ways that do not favor one religion over another, or secular over nonsecular schools. The big difference between tax credits and education vouchers is that tax credits operate in a dual school system of separate public and nonpublic schools. A thoroughgoing voucher scheme, however, virtually eliminates distinctions between public and nonpublic schools. Probably the least complicated voucher plan is the one suggested by Nobel prize-winning economist Milton Friedman.

. . . He wishes to take the monies now devoted to financing public schools and use them to support free choice by parents. For each school-age child, parents would be issued a voucher. They would assign the voucher to the school of their choice—public, private, parochial, profit-making, or altruistic in organization. Schools would cash in the vouchers at the public treasury at rates publicly established. Parents could freely shop for the school they felt suited their child best, and alert entrepreneurs would widen the choices available by founding new schools better adjusted to the tastes of prospective customers.[58]

While they agree that something ought to be done about increasing parental choice in the delivery of educational services, liberals worry about the consequences of the free market approach Friedman proposes. In particular, there is a concern that unregulated voucher systems will have the following undesirable effects:

1. Racial segregation or class segregation may be exacerbated.
2. The traditional separation between church and state may be weakened.
3. Under a free-market arrangement, simple inflation of schooling costs

may occur, and the rich will use their own funds to supplement public funds in order to acquire superior schooling for their children, and thus the relative disadvantage of the poor will continue.

4. The public schools stand to become the dumping grounds or schools of last resort for those children who are rejected everywhere else.

5. Parents may not be able to make intelligent decisions because they cannot discern differences between schools or programs, or because they do not care to make schooling decisions.[59]

In response to these concerns, others have suggested a wide variety of voucher schemes.[60] Precisely what sort of voucher plan might actually be adopted is, of course, a question of political practicability. What political forces are most likely to shape a voucher plan? While one can only speculate, we do know that scattered experiments notwithstanding,[61] a fully regulated voucher plan has yet to be tried. Arons is probably correct when he observes that,

The basic difficulty with the voucher idea is that it requires a political commitment to values which are very weak and vulnerable in America today: a commitment to equality of wealth, power, and race; respect for and encouragement of real pluralism; nonintervention by government in substantial educational decisions; high regard for individuals and children; encouraging social integration; placing personalism and communitarianism above bureaucracy and technocratic values. It is likely that were a voucher scheme adopted by the states tomorrow, it would reflect the same values which are presently aggravating the abominable situation of American education.[62]

If minorities and the poor are not to be even more severely disadvantaged by a voucher plan, regulations will be needed to control the operation of the system. Unfortunately, it may be unrealistic to expect that the necessary controls will be politically acceptable. In light of fiscal neutrality's commitment to equity, it would be ironic indeed if a voucher plan instituted in the name of greater equality of educational opportunity were to work to the detriment of students already handicapped by the status quo. A voucher plan such as the family power equalizing proposal of Coons and Sugarman could increase educational choice in a way that conforms with the constitutional requirements of fiscal neutrality.[63] However, it must be recognized that the changes a controlled voucher plan would make in the delivery of educational services are so drastic that it is most reasonable to think about vouchers as long-range rather than short-range policy objectives.

It should be clear from the above discussion that the authors are somewhat undecided about educational vouchers. The *idea* is excellent and entirely consistent with fiscal neutrality. Given current social and political values and the inherent conservatism of large institutions such as public school systems, however, it is not entirely certain either that a voucher plan would significantly increase equality of treatment or that sufficient political support exists to get such a plan adopted. At the very least the plan deserves far more public debate than it has yet received.

CONCLUSION

The purpose of this chapter has been to illustrate how the principles of fiscal neutrality can be applied to church-government relations. The examples used highlight four basic points. First, something very much like fiscal neutrality is already in effect for property tax exemptions granted to religious organizations. The wide acceptance of this policy means that the seeds of approval for the basic tenets have already been sown across the nation.

Second, it is possible to extend fiscal neutrality's concern for equity to the resolution of related issues. For example, neutrality in church-government relations does not speak directly to the question of which level of government should bear the cost of religious property tax exemptions. However, it does follow that if religious and similarly situated organizations are to be treated equally, then all affected parties should be treated as equally as possible. In the case of property tax exemptions, equity demands that central cities not be forced to bear financial burdens greater than other local governments.

Third, the impact of any given policy is important. It is not enough to look at the putative objective of a given policy. What in fact does result or may result from that policy? Supplementing the standard deduction with an additional deduction for charitable contributions may seem on its face to be a neutral policy, but when we compare type of charitable contributions with income classes, we see that the effect of this policy change would be to benefit religious organizations more than charitable organizations. Assessment of that policy proposal must therefore be based on results that can reasonably be expected. Fiscal neutrality favors policies that produce more equality between religious and similarly situated organizations.

Fourth, equal treatment is often a function of administrative procedure. How religious organizations account for their money and how educational tax credits or educational vouchers are made available will go a long way in determining just how equal the treatment will be on a day-to-day basis. Concerns about equality will have many dimensions. Not the least of these must be the rather mundane, but very crucial, details of administrative control.

NOTES

1. John M. Quigley and Debra Stinson, *Levels of Property Tax Exemption*, Exchange Bibliography No. 840. (Monticello, Ill.: Council of Planning Librarians, July 1975).

2. Ibid., pp. 46-47.

3. As noted earlier, this is particularly true of religious property tax exemptions.

4. Alfred Balk, *The Free List: Property Without Taxes* (n.p.: Russell Sage Foundation, 1971); National Tax Association - Tax Institute of America, Report of the Property Taxation Committee, "The Erosion of the Ad Valorem Real Estate Tax Base," *Tax Policy* 40 (1973): 1-94; John M. Quigley and Roger W. Schmenner, "Property Tax Exemption and Public Policy," *Public Policy* 23 (Summer 1975): 259-97; Richard L. Gabler and John F. Shannon, "The Exemption of Religious, Educational, and Charitable Institutions from Property Taxation," The Commission on Private Philanthropy and Public Needs, *Research Papers*, vol. 4, *Taxes* (n.p.: Department of Treasury, 1977) pp. 2235-2564.

5. Shifting the power to grant or deny exemptions to local governments, as discussed by *Tax Policy* and Gabler and Shannon, neatly matches authority with fiscal responsibility, but exacerbates rather than ameliorates the interjurisdictional problems. As the Property Taxation Committee noted on pp. 44 and 45: "Although this alternative is logically neat, it would invite problems of overlapping local jurisdictions and the location of tax exempt organizations, consequences that may not be in the public interest. Local governments would find themselves in the position of competing with one another to attract tax exempt organizations that generate income such as colleges and to grant exemptions to business firms for the employment opportunities that they would afford the community. The result could be a significant decrease of the property tax burden on business property and a corresponding increase in the burden on residential property. For reasons of this kind

most of the alternatives to present exemption practices that would remedy the division of authority and responsibility lie in the direction of leaving the state with the authority to grant exemptions, but would increase state responsibility and accountability for its exempting actions.

6. See Appendix B for a discussion of one possible approach.

7. Alfred Balk, *Free List*; *Tax Policy*; Gabler and Shannon.

8. Gabler and Shannon note on p. 2561, "With a system of annual or periodic state government review, it can also be expected that there would be greater scrutiny of the activities of recipients of the tax-exempt status. Such scrutiny need not be subject to the charge of political interference. Rather, it can be restricted to providing the assurance that the exempt institution or organization is in fact providing the services and activities for which the original grant of exemption was provided. To the extent that review goes beyond this objective, the likelihood and validity of a charge of political interference becomes more germane."

9. James C. Rosapepe, "Tackling the Tax-Exempts," *E.P.O.* (March/April 1979), p. 51.

10. Kenneth T. Palmer and Roy W. Shin, "Compensatory Payment Plans in the States," *State Government* (Autumn 1975), p. 216.

11. A hierarchy of public concerns can be posited (see Paul J. Weber, "Religion and Equality: Understanding the First Amendment" [Ph.D. dissertation, University of Chicago, 1977], chapter 6). Public health and safety are very important and are not to be hastily dismissed in the name of religious freedom (see, for example, the Court's position on snake handling in *Pack v. Tennessee ex rel. Swann* 425 U.S. 954 (1975), cert. denied. Lower in the hierarchy would come public peace and order, followed by public welfare, public morality, civic duty, and finally, discomfort, inconvenience, and annoyance.

12. James E. Curry, *Public Regulation of the Religious Use of Land* (Charlottesville, Virginia: Michie, 1964), p. 335.

13. Hierarchal churches, such as Roman Catholic, apparently often encounter less difficulty obtaining an exemption for church properties used for administrative purposes than do nonhierarchial churches such as Baptist.

14. Michael K. Taussig, "Economic Aspects of the Personal Income Tax Treatment of Charitable Constitutions," *National Tax Journal* 20 (March 1967).

15. See, for example, Willard T. Hunter, *The Tax Climate for Philanthropy* (Washington, D.C.: American College Public Relations Association, 1968).

16. Robert A. Schwartz, "Personal Philanthropic Constitutions," *Journal of Political Economy* 78 (November-December 1970).

17. Michael J. Boskin and Martin S. Feldstein, "Effects of the Charitable Deduction Constitutions by Low-Income and Middle-Income Households: Evidence from the National Survey of Philanthropy," The Commission on Private Philanthropy and Public Needs, *Research Papers*, vol. 3: *Special Behavioral Studies, Foundations and Corporations*, (n.p.: Department of the Treasury, 1977), p. 1441-52.

18. Emil M. Sunley, Jr., "Federal State Tax Policies," in *Public Policy and Private Higher Education*, ed. David W. Brennan and Chester E. Finn, Jr. (Washington, D.C.: The Brookings Institution, 1978), pp. 281-320.

19. The Commission on Private Philanthropy and Public Needs, *Giving in America: Toward a Strong Voluntary Sector*, n.p., Commission on Private Philanthropy and Public Needs, 1975. p. 133.

20. Of course, an indirect result of reduced giving to educational and other organizations with a religious affiliation may well be to force increases in denominational subsidies.

21. *Giving in America*, p. 135.

22. Henry Aaron, "Federal Encouragement of Private Giving," in Tax Institute of America, *Tax Impacts on Philanthropy* (Princeton: Tax Institute of America, 1972), p. 212.

23. Act. of 23 September 1950. C. 994, 64 Stat. 906 § 332 (C).

24. Dean Kelley, "Operational Consequences of Church State Choices," *Social Problems* (January-February 1967), pp. 116-17.

25. *Giving U.S.A.*, p. 22.

26. Accounting Advisory Committee, "A Study of the Inadequacies of Present Financial Reporting by Philanthropic Organizations," in The Commission on Private Philanthropy and Public Needs, *Research Papers*, vol. 5, *Regulation*, (n.p.: Department of the Treasury, 1977), pp. 2869-2914.

27. *Wisconsin v. Yoder*, 406 U.S. 205 (1972).

28. *Pierce v. Society of Sisters*, 268 U.S. 510 (1925).

29. *Everson v. Board of Education*, 330 U.S. 1 (1947).

30. 421 U.S. 349 at 371-72 (1975).

31. *How the Public Views Nonpublic Schools* (Cambridge, Mass.: A Study of the American Independent School, 1969), p. 4.

32. One such bill before Congress was known as the Packwood-Moynihan Tuition Tax Credit Act (S. 2142) 95th Congress. Although other forms may vary, the principle remains basically the same.

33. This argument has been strongly advocated by the National Educational Association and the American Federation of Teachers. There may be less altrustic motives involved. The control of federal financing, at least as regards tax credits, would shift from HEW and the AFT would lose considerable political clout.

34. Interview with Senator William V. Roth, Jr., *U.S. News and World Report*, 3 April 1978, pp. 61-62.

35. See *Our Sunday Visitor*, 4 June 1978, p. 1.

36. Ibid.

37. Ibid.

38. 413 U.S. 455, 463-65 (1973).

39. 413 U.S. 756 (1973).

40. Lawrence H. Tribe has pointed out the significance of this test in several instances in *American Constitutional Law* (Mineola, N.Y., The Foundation Press, 1978), pp. 485-86, n. 33.

> In Committee for Public Education v. Nyquist . . . the Court, in striking down a voucher plan which extended aid only to low-income parents of *non-public school children* expressly distinguished Everson v. Board of Education . . . and

Board of Education v. Allen . . . on the ground that in "both cases the class of beneficiaries included *all* school children. . . ." Similarly, a program for the provision of certain auxiliary services to nonpublic school students *only* was struck down in Meek v. Pettinger. . . . And in Public Funds for Public Schools v. Marburger . . . the Supreme Court summarily affirmed the district court's invalidation of a New Jersey program which *lent* public school children their textbooks but *gave* reimbursement to parents of non-public school children for the *purchase* of secular, non-ideological textbooks. For such reimbursements to be valid, *exactly the same benefit* would have to be extended to parents of public school children.

41. That the Court continues to place importance on this principle may be seen in its affirmation of a Tennessee law which provided financial assistance to students in public and private (including church-related) colleges. *Americans United for the Separation of Church and State v. Blanton*, 433 F. Supp. 97 (M.D. Tenn. 1977) *sum. aff'd.*, 434 U.S. 803 (1977). Also *Public Funds for Public Schools of New Jersey v. Byrne*, 47 L.W. 3775, (1979) cert. denied.

42. See *Epperson v. Arkansas*, 393 U.S. 97 (1968).

43. 433 U.S. 229, 262 (1977) (Powell, J., concurring in part, concurring in the judgment in part, and dissenting in part).

44. L. Tribe, *American Constitutional Law*, p. 839.

45. 413 U.S. at 783-84, n. 39.

46. 413 U.S. 825, 832 (1973).

47. Both former HEW Secretary Califano and Attorney General Bell based their opinions that tax credits are unconstitutional in large measure on the principle or primary effect test. However, in requesting an opinion concerning constitutionality from the Justice Department, Secretary Califano asked the department to make "the assumption that the bill *applies only to elementary and secondary education*." Letter from Joseph Califano to Honorable Griffin B. Bell (8 February 1978) (emphasis added). This, of course, is a substantial distortion of the bills being considered.

48. *Hearings on S. 2142 Before the Subcomm. on Taxation and Debt Management Generally of the Senate Comm. on Finance*, 95th Cong., 2d Sess. 144 (1977-1978) (statement of William D. Valente).

49. 38 U.S.C. §§ 1651-98 (1976).

50. Ibid. §§ 1691-92.

51. Ibid. §§ 1733-34.

52. 2 U.S.C. §§ 88a-88b (1976).

53. 37 U.S.C. § 209 (1976; 10 U.S.C. § 2107 [1976]).

54. *Walz v. Tax Commission*, 397 U.S. 644 (1970).

55. 403 U.S. 672, 676-77 (1971).

56. 403 U.S. 602, 607, 612 (1971).

57. Ibid. at 666.

58. Robert M. Lekachman, "Education Report: Vouchers and Public Education," *New Leader* 54 (July 1971): 10.

59. Gary Bridge, "Citizen Choice in Public Services: Voucher Systems," in *Alternatives for Delivering Public Services*, ed. E.W. Savas (Boulder, Colo.: Westview Press, 1977), p. 82.

60. Various voucher proposals are discussed in the following: John E. Coons and Stephen D. Sugarman, *Education by Choice: The Case for Family Control* (Berkeley: University of California Press, 1978); George R. La Noue, ed., *Educational Vouchers: Concepts and Controversies* (New York: Teachers College Press of Columbia University, 1972); Steven Mintz, "Education Vouchers: Proposals and Prospects," A Staff Report to the President's Commission on School Finance, 1972; Laurence Byrnes, *Religion and Public Education* (New York: Harper and Row, 1975).

61. Bridge, "Citizen Choice," makes it clear that the experiment at Alum Rock, California was less than originally intended. The voucher plans in Vermont, New Hampshire, and Indianapolis mentioned by Coons and Sugarman are also less than complete models.

62. Stephen Arons, "The Peaceful Uses of Education Vouchers," in *Educational Vouchers: Concepts and Controversies*, ed. George R. La Noue (New York: Teachers College Press of Columbia University), pp. 95-96.

63. Coons and Sugarman's objection to religious organizations providing any funds to schools could well be met by requiring that no public money be used to support religious training and that all money received from religious organizations be used exclusively for religious purposes, as distinct from state-mandated secular training.

CONCLUSION

When we began this book, we knew that much about the subject matter was complicated, controversial, and to a large extent unknown. We began with the idea that the fiscal relationships between government and religious groups were precisely those which caused the most difficult legal and economic problems. Religious writers have tended to focus on the more dramatic issues of religious liberty: witch hunts, floggings, imprisonments, exiles, and other forms of persecution. Although these were certainly important if embarrassing episodes in American history, it was the fiscal issues, tax and spending policies, which provided the strongest impetus for change.

From the very beginnings of the nation, there has never been one commonly accepted understanding of the proper relationship between government and religion. The social contract-faith contract theory of Isaac Backus was profoundly important for the development of religious liberty in New England. The Virginia deism of Madison and Jefferson was equally influential. But neither form of separation won universal assent. Throughout the history of the nation, those who believed in accommodation have always made up in the strength of their numbers what they lacked in the eloquence of their leaders. Even when nonestablishment and religious liberty replaced the early New England compacts and the Act of Toleration that governed relations in Virginia, there was not one commonly accepted meaning of church-government separation. Jefferson's "wall of separation" provided a vivid metaphor, but even walls come in many heights and styles. One is tempted to point to Jefferson's famous serpentine wall around the University of Virginia: it had openings, and he envisioned extensive exchange and cooperation with adjacent schools of divinity. The wall was to be no barrier.

On the other hand, freedom and nonestablishment meant something. In our historical section we explored the attempts to find that elusive meaning. We can say two things with some certainty. Nonestablishment meant a structural and functional separation of governmental and religious organizations and religious freedom meant the end of privilege, coercion, and disability based on religious belief, affiliation, or activity. We draw the conclusion, relying heavily on Madison's *Memorial and Remonstrance* and the records of the First Congress, that equality of treatment is a critical element in both nonestablishment and religious liberty.

Our second conclusion in the historical section is that change and growth have been the rule in the area of church-government fiscal relations as in many other areas. Relationships have changed, perhaps pulsated is the word, between great and relative interdependence. Never have they remotely approached anything like "absolute separation," whatever that term may mean. Rather, there has been an evolution through types of interdependence: religious qualifications for public office; tax support for religious educators (as Patrick Henry delicately called them); religious or public responsibility for birth, death, and wedding records; the development of moral citizens and whatever education was available; tax exemptions, tax deductions, and the funding of many secular services in religious institutions.

Church-government fiscal relations have changed over time because governmental and religious institutions are both dynamic. Government has grown from an institution providing minimal protection to an expansive—even pervasive—taxing, welfare, and regulatory agency. To say that it has "invaded" areas once considered the religious domain is an understatement. The First Amendment has been applied to the states as part of the most far-reaching—if quiet—legal revolution the nation has ever experienced. For their part, religious groups have grown from isolated country chapels and itinerant preachers to multimillion-dollar organizations utilizing a multitude of government services, receiving government aids, and subject to myriad governmental regulations.

While our understanding of church-government fiscal interaction and interdependence has simultaneously grown and changed, it has not kept pace with day-to-day demands of policy. True, the courts began to replace the language of separation and accommodation with the language of neutrality, but the practical meaning of terms has remained elusive and their application sporadic.

Our third conclusion is that fiscal concerns and the resistance to fiscal pressures have triggered many of the changes both in the relationship of government and religion and in our understanding of that relationship. Backus saw the true light of religious liberty when the tax collector came knocking. The difference between the failure of Jefferson's *Bill for Establishing Religious Liberty* in 1779 and the success of Madison's *Memorial and Remonstrance* in 1785 was the prospect of an imminent increase in taxes. We do not argue, of course, that money has been the only significant variable, but it has been a major catalyst· in the development of both practice and principle.

The historical section included a discussion of the formation of the First Amendment religion clauses to make it unmistakably clear that the Founding Fathers wanted nonestablishment and religious liberty. As they struggled to find the right wording, neither separation nor aid was an issue. Their goal was a larger one: protection without privilege. We made the further point that the protection they sought was not merely to permit the individual to follow his conscience but to allow religious groups to participate in society with legally binding contracts and legally recognized identities. That was clearly the intent behind Huntington's objection to an early version of the First Amendment. When Madison heard the objection, he promptly offered a clarifying word, indicating his acceptance of Huntington's position. Therefore, even in the formulation of the First Amendment there was concern about protecting religion in its pragmatic fiscal relationships as well as in its expression of conscience and belief.

It is unfortunate that religion clause case law developed primarily around the least tractable area of church-government relations: aid to education. Historically this was an area so wrapped in conflict between ethnic and religious groups, in fears of persecution and potential domination, that it became a symbolic issue evaluated in terms of winners and losers. When the Supreme Court decreed that the religion clauses did indeed apply to the states, it tried to weave together two incompatible principles, the absolute separationist and the accommodationist, into a single constitutional doctrine. The result has been an ill-fitting pattern of inconsistencies, double standards, injustices, and distinctions without substance.

The Court's work has not been entirely in vain, however. It has begun to develop a doctrine of neutrality that is most promising and, in our opinion, most in keeping with the intent of the writers of the Constitution. We believe, however, that the development has not gone far enough. Elements of separation and accommodation remain, with the result that the Court engages in economic double-talk, and there is little incentive to generate the kind of data policy-makers need in order to make sound public policy.

Another price paid for the Court's inconsistency is the necessity for economic posturing, pretending that aid isn't aid, that indirect aid isn't as valuable as direct aid, that an exemption isn't a subsidy, and that religious institutions can justly be required to pay for services with divisible benefits but not for those with indivisible benefits. Such posturing undermines the Court's respectability and makes economic planning in this area a charade.

Why not admit that religious organizations receive enormous amounts of direct and indirect aid and have received them since before the establishment of the Republic? Then we can develop a constitutional doctrine that acknowledges the legitimacy of such aid and provides clear and strong safeguards against establishment (privilege, coercion, or disability). The consistency the authors seek is between constitutional doctrine and economic reality. We have tried to demonstrate that such a consistency is indeed attainable.

In chapter 4, "Aid to Religion: Who Gets What?" our attempts to assess the amounts of direct and indirect aid that flow from government to religious organizations may help to bury some myths. The first myth is that property exempted on the basis of religious ownership or use constitutes a very large proportion of tax-exempt property. Even in the largest cities the amount never exceeds 7.7 percent of the property tax base. If one includes rural and small town areas the percentage would be substantially less. By far the greatest amount of tax-exempt property is government-owned. As a consequence, the myth that taxing religious property would solve the fiscal problems of urban areas is exploded. Only in Hartford, Connecticut would taxation raise revenue by as much as 4.9 percent.

Another myth is that religious organizations are heavily dependent on income tax deductions. Since the percentage of charitable donations going directly to religious organizations decreases as income rises, and lower-income people are far more likely to use the standard deduction, the value of such a deduction to churches is far less than it is to other charitable institutions. In fact, we argue, if citizens were seriously concerned that religious groups be treated equally in this regard, tax law would allow deductions for charitable giving even to those who use the standard deduction. Senators Moynihan and Packwood introduced just such a bill (S.219) in the first session of the 96th Congress. Representatives Fisher, Conable, and Gradison introduced a similar bill in The House of Representatives (H.R.1785).

Finally, we hope our attempt to count the dollars flowing from government to religious or religiously affiliated organizations illustrates how very complex, indeed impossible, the task is. The availability of data varies from area to area. We know that overall, the annual flow of benefits from the public to the religious sector is enormous, just how enormous we simply do not know. The data base is exceedingly soft. Some change in government data collection requirements would lessen this problem, for example, disaggregating data to distinguish religious from nonreligious recipients. But is this necessary? We believe it is not, for our conclusion is that the exact amount of aid is irrelevant to the question of whether or not it is constitutional.

The reason lies in our discussion of fiscal neutrality. The fiscal neutrality doctrine simply means the religion clauses of the First Amendment must be read together to form a single principle: religion cannot be used as a legal classification to bestow a privilege or impose a burden. The free exercise of religion is a constitutionally protected right, but not a uniquely privileged one. Fiscal neutrality is based on an equal protection doctrine that protects free exercise without supporting establishment. Some may object that this allows a narrowing of the scope of freedom granted religious individuals and groups as long as similarly situated groups and individuals are likewise limited. To the contrary, the necessity of protecting a broad range of religious freedom demands that an equal freedom be available to all similarly situated individuals and groups. The protection of religious liberty then becomes a catalyst for broadening the scope of liberty rather than narrowing it. In those areas where religious groups would be obliged to give up unique privileges we argue that such perquisites are neither necessary nor appropriate. Religions have a constitutional right to be protected in their beliefs, associations, and activities. But they do not have a constitutional right to be free from the common burdens of life in an organized society. We do not argue that all organizations must share social burdens equally, only that those which are similarly situated must. So, for example, private, profit-making businesses may be taxed at one rate, individual wages may be taxed at another, and charitable, nonprofit organizations may be relieved of all taxation. This is fully consistent with the equal protection doctrine. Exactly how the burdens of society will be distributed is a separate matter of policy determination.

A concept of "similarly situated" is the key to the fiscal neutrality doctrine. Its acceptance depends on a recognition that religious individuals and institutions have many secular dimensions in common with other individuals and institutions. In those secular dimensions all such institutions may be both regulated and aided. In areas where religions are uniquely private (we would include creed, cult, styles of internal organization, and methods of selecting leadership), government has no proper role in regulating or aiding religion at all.

On the other hand, there may be areas where religion is both public and unique and where special provision must be made to protect equity. While the authors could conceive of several such issues in the area of religious liberty (exempting children from gym class on grounds of religious conviction, permitting the wearing of yarmulkas in court, not demanding pictures on driver's licenses, and so on), we were unable to find similar exceptions in church-government fiscal relations. We do leave open the possibility, however. If such areas are found, religion must be treated as a suspect class, and laws based on such classifications subjected to serious judicial scrutiny.

Our justification for acceptance of the fiscal neutrality doctrine is that it reflects the intent of the Founding Fathers, those who wrote and passed the First Amendment, and takes into account the realities of contemporary political, constitutional, religious, and economic development. In other words, it can form the basis for sound public policymaking.

Chapters 5 and 7 leave the high ground of theory and face the hard task of spelling out the specific implications of a fiscal neutrality doctrine. The general conclusion is that fiscal neutrality does not require radical departures from current practices. It would however, involve changes. Some would provide religious organizations with relatively more benefits than they now enjoy, and others would create new obligations to bring religious groups into line with similar organizations.

The first beneficial result would be to limit the need to define religion and religious affiliation. Specific definition is a problem only if religious organizations are set apart from other similar organizations and uniquely given or denied benefits or responsibilities by the public sector. We illustrated, through an analysis of colleges, the inherent difficulty in trying to draw lines between what is and is not religious affiliation. Any such distinction is far too arbitrary to be legally useful. It is far easier to provide an operational definition of nonprofit, charitable organizations and include religion along with other such groups. Both religious organizations functioning strictly as worshipping communities and religious affiliated groups can fit within that broader classification, ending the hopeless search for proper distinctions between the two.

One obligation that would accrue to religious organizations is the necessity to file informational tax returns. This is not unduly burdensome and is already an obligation incumbent upon all other similar groups. Neither compliance nor noncompliance poses any danger of excessive church-government entanglement. Likewise, the special treatment given to religious groups for the housing of ministers would end. Such a provision, available to no one else, is clearly a privilege granted on the basis of a religious classification and is inequitable. According to the fiscal neutrality doctrine it is also unconstitutional. The granting of exemptions from bond registration procedures would also be ended.

On the other hand, the restrictions on political activity imposed on religious activities through Section 501(c)(3) of the Internal Revenue Code, but not applicable to all nonprofit charitable groups, is an undue, and according to a fiscal neutrality approach, unconstitutional restriction. Religious groups should have the same right to participate in the political process as all other similar groups.

Most controversial of all church-government questions is the matter of public aid. Having set the stage by showing that aid has always been a fact of American life and that some forms of aid have been declared constitutional by the Supreme Court, we explored the limits of aid under the fiscal neutrality doctrine. Property tax law in general follows the doctrine to an admirable degree. It may well be for that reason that it is the source of so little church-government controversy. One issue we could not resist addressing is the inequity caused when states mandate exemptions from property taxes and municipalities are forced to pick up the burden. This includes all exempt properties and is not limited to churches. We support the recommendation that states reimburse localities for revenues lost on account of state-imposed exemptions. One beneficial effect of such a system—in addition to making legislators more responsible for their decisions—would be the collection and dissemination of information about the level of tax expenditures. It is one of our basic assumptions that public policy made with accurate information tends to be sounder than that based on guesswork and projection. Our general principle here, as elsewhere, is that property owned or used by religious organizations be treated as all similarly situated property is treated. Such limits ensure equity and are not unduly burdensome to religion.

We explored federal income tax deductions and concluded that religion is again generally treated in a manner consistent with fiscal neutrality. One notable point is that among those giving donations, citizens with lower incomes tend to favor giving to religious organizations, while higher-income donors direct their gifts to nonreligious recipients. Current policy allows those who itemize on their income tax returns to claim deductions but not citizens who file the standard form. As a result, many religious givers, being in lower-income brackets, cannot take a deduction because they do not itemize. A change in the law which would allow all citizens to deduct charitable giving, even those filing standard returns, would certainly benefit religious groups. Such a change would be permissible because religion is not classified so as to be the special beneficiary and the effect would be to increase their equity with nonreligious organizations *vis à vis* the efficacy of contribution deductibility. On the other hand, such a policy change is not constitutionally required since religion is also not the basis for a discriminatory classification. This is matter of legislative discretion.

The brief discussion about aid to education does not claim to end the controversy. If one begins by assuming that parents of private and public school students deserve equitable treatment, that fiscal efficiency is a public value, and that diversity of educational opportunities and a maximum of free choice among schools is sound public policy, it is clear that current public policy is deficient. Taking into account the judicial restrictions on aid to private schools, it appears that tuition tax credits and educational vouchers are alternative policies compatible with the fiscal neutrality doctrine. While tax credit legislation, properly constructed, seems to be a sound policy option, educational vouchers are more problematical. We are convinced that any voucher program, if it is not to create more problems than it solves, must be regulated. It seems clear that there is not enough political support presently available to institute the kinds of controls that would be necessary to make vouchers work equally well for all students. From the viewpoints of fiscal neutrality and educational equality, vouchers may be a good idea; however, it seems that their time has not yet come.

Some, no doubt, will say the same about fiscal neutrality. Treating religious and nonreligious organizations equally is sound constitutional doctrine, but undoubtedly opposition will be generated the first time some concession is required. Most religious organizations will be happy to accept more economic benefits from the public sector; filing informational tax returns, however, will be staunchly resisted. Certainly, we recognize that no advantage is ever happily relinquished, but that is not the overriding issue here.

We have, as a society, managed to construct an elaborate lexicon for calling pick-axes, case-knives and staircases lightning-rods. But we cannot deny that substantial church-government fiscal relations exist. They come in a wide variety of forms, many of them very complicated. Trying to pretend that these fiscal relations do not exist, or wishing that they were somehow less complicated than they are, is foolhardy. Policymakers have already waited too long to produce a fair and consistent policy that works.

This book argues that existing policies for church-government relations are not consistent with each other, with sound reasoning, or with the intentions of the writers of the First Amendment. A shift to fiscal neutrality may not always produce a drastic change in policy, but it will uniformly enhance equity. We find it encouraging that the application of fiscal neutrality to particular policy questions seems to impose new obligations on religious organizations as often as it provides new benefits. While it may draw fire on particular points from either accommodationists or separationists, fiscal neutrality does not work consistently to the advantage or disadvantage of either secular or sectarian interests. At the risk of sounding presumptuous, we will simply observe that the objectives and results of fiscal neutrality are well described by Webster's (Unabridged) definition of the golden mean: "the way of wisdom and safety between extremes."

APPENDIXES

FEDERAL AID TO RELIGIOUSLY
HIGHER EDUCATION FOR

[Dollar Amounts in Thousands]

RANK	INSTITUTION	TOTAL	USDA	COM	DOD
21	Yeshiva Univ	44,419	0	0	437
26	Duke Univ	35,244	10	0	826
44	Northestern U	25,853	19	39	934
45	Boston U	24,981	0	0	283
70	Emory U	17,218	0	0	68
100	Georgetown U	11,678	72	0	187
101	Meharry Med. C	11,543	0	0	0
112	Syracuse U	10,104	162	0	1,639
145	U of Denver	6,312	0	444	1,077
154	Boston C	5,695	0	0	1,387
163	Loma Linda U	5,209	0	0	0
167	Loyola U (Ill.)	4,903	0	0	40
172	U of Notre Dame	4,516	0	0	79
174	Creighton U	4,326	0	0	0
179	Catholic U of Am	3,884	0	19	1,008
181	U of the Pacific	3,831	0	0	0
184	Catholic U of PR	3,635	0	0	0
194	Xavier U of Louisiana	3,193	0	0	0
201	Central YMCA CC	3,040	0	0	0
209	Baylor U	2,869	0	0	0
211	Wilberforce U	2,846	0	0	0

*Key to abbreviations: USDA = US Department of Agriculture; COM = US Resource Development Administration; EPA = Environmental Protection Agency; NASA = National Aeronautics and Space Administration; NSF = National Science federal agencies.

APPENDIX A

AFFILIATED INSTITUTIONS OF FISCAL YEAR 1975*

ERDA	EPA	HEW	INT	NASA	NSF	DOT	OTHER*
50	0	43,287	0	11	634	0	0
964	351	30,209	161	133	2,590	0	0
790	153	18,393	66	102	5,103	243	11
135	0	22,492	0	132	1,196	552	191
67	0	16,800	0	140	143	0	0
39	2	11,065	0	13	259	0	41
0	42	11,398	0	0	103	0	0
205	503	5,182	76	52	2,107	178	0
489	22	1,772	199	522	1,699	88	0
50	196	3,613	0	0	443	0	6
0	0	5,209	0	0	0	0	0
43	0	4,753	0	0	67	0	0
1,169	170	1,724	0	173	1,201	0	0
0	0	4,322	0	0	4	0	0
0	0	2,291	0	98	439	29	0
0	0	3,827	0	0	4	0	0
0	0	3,635	0	0	0	0	0
0	0	3,157	0	30	6	0	0
0	0	3,040	0	0	0	0	0
18	0	2,797	0	0	54	0	0
0	0	2,809	0	20	17	0	0

Department of Commerce; DOD = US Department of Defense; ERDA = Energy HEW = Housing, Education and Welfare; INT = US Department of the Interior; Foundation; DOT = US Department of Transportation; OTHER = all other

RANK	INSTITUTION	TOTAL	USDA	COM	DOD
225	Marquette U	2,619	0	0	0
230	Clark C (Ga.)	2,547	0	0	0
236	U of Detroit	2,470	0	0	0
244	American U	2,387	0	0	1,168
247	Texas Chris. U	2,327	0	0	77
251	Fisk U	2,262	0	0	0
253	Knoxville C	2,243	0	0	0
256	Shaw U	2,218	0	0	0
257	Benedict C	2,218	0	0	0
260	Fordham U	2,131	0	0	0
270	Miles C	2,015	0	0	0
272	Canisils C	2,000	0	0	0
277	Virginia Union U	1,942	0	0	0
282	Rust C	1,822	0	0	0
290	Johnson C Smith U	1,744	0	0	0
291	Morris Brown C	1,744	0	0	0
292	Spelman C	1,738	0	0	0
293	Manhattan C	1,734	0	0	0
294	Morehouse C	1,733	0	0	0
296	St Augustines C	1,723	0	0	0
304	Bishop C	1,667	0	0	14
305	Bethune-Cookman C	1,663	0	0	0
317	So Methodist U	1,571	0	0	322
319	Ottawa U	1,552	0	0	0
321	W VA Wesleyn C	1,509	0	0	0
325	St Mary's U S An	1,485	0	0	0
326	Mary C	1,484	0	0	0
328	Baldwin-Wallace	1,469	0	0	0
330	Rockhurst C	1,458	0	0	0
331	Stillman C	1,452	0	0	0
337	Paine C	1,403	0	0	0
341	U of San Franc	1,384	0	0	0
346	Bethel C&Sem MN	1,352	0	0	0
347	Our Lady of the Lake C	1,348	0	0	0
356	DePaul U	1,328	0	0	0
360	Lane C	1,319	0	0	0
363	Seattle U	1,306	0	0	28
372	Dillard U	1,269	0	0	0
374	Pennett C (N.C.)	1,267	0	0	0
377	Morningside C	1,255	0	0	0

ERDA	EPA	HEW	INT	NASA	NSF	DOT	OTHER*
40	7	2,407	0	0	165	0	0
0	0	2,437	0	31	79	0	0
0	28	2,429	0	0	13	0	0
0	10	1,082	0	0	127	0	0
0	0	2,137	0	0	113	0	0
0	0	2,192	0	50	20	0	0
0	0	1,907	0	0	336	0	0
0	0	2,203	0	15	0	0	0
0	27	2,167	0	24	0	0	0
0	48	1,984	0	12	87	0	0
0	0	2,015	0	0	0	0	0
0	0	2,000	0	0	0	0	0
0	0	1,942	0	0	0	0	0
0	0	1,822	0	0	0	0	0
0	0	1,744	0	0	0	0	0
0	0	1,721	0	23	0	0	0
0	0	1,565	0	7	166	0	0
0	302	1,432	0	0	0	0	0
4	0	1,583	0	87	59	0	0
0	58	1,665	0	0	0	0	0
0	0	1,615	0	0	38	0	0
0	0	1,541	0	25	97	0	0
0	0	625	0	29	595	0	0
0	0	1,552	0	0	0	0	0
0	0	1,492	0	0	17	0	0
0	7	1,478	0	0	0	0	0
0	0	1,484	0	0	0	0	0
0	0	1,465	0	0	4	0	0
0	0	1,458	0	0	0	0	0
0	0	1,452	0	0	0	0	0
0	0	1,383	0	20	0	0	0
0	0	1,031	61	275	17	0	0
0	0	1,352	0	0	0	0	0
0	0	1,185	0	0	163	0	0
0	9	1,211	0	0	108	0	0
0	0	1,319	0	0	0	0	0
0	0	1,278	0	0	0	0	0
0	0	1,023	0	24	222	0	0
0	51	1,149	0	38	29	0	0
0	0	1,255	0	0	0	0	0

RANK	INSTITUTION	TOTAL	USDA	COM	DOD
380	IL Benedictine C	1,242	0	0	0
382	Aquinas C	1,240	0	0	0
385	St Paul's C (Va.)	1,208	0	0	0
390	LB Moyne-Owen C	1,182	0	0	0
398	Trinity U	1,141	0	0	0
401	Jarvis Christ C	1,133	0	0	0
407	C of Sacred Heart	1,104	0	0	0
411	Talladega C	1,087	0	0	0
413	Livingstone C	1,085	0	0	0
414	Duquesne U	1,083	0	0	0
422	Florida Mem C	1,060	0	0	0
423	St Peter's C	1,057	0	0	0
427	Claflin C	1,051	0	0	0
429	Brigham Young U	1,046	23	32	73
434	Catawba C	1,023	0	0	0
438	Voorhees C	1,017	0	0	0
445	Huston-Illotson C	999	0	0	0
451	C of St Benedict	966	0	0	0
453	Morris C	959	0	0	0
459	Pacone C	927	0	0	0
467	Allen U	912	0	0	0
468	Pasadena City C	910	0	0	0
470	Mercer U	903	0	0	0
474	St John's U (N.Y.)	894	0	0	0
481	Wiley C	882	0	0	0
482	Oakwood C	879	0	0	0
484	Drake U	873	0	0	0
492	Edward Waters C	848	0	0	0
495	U of Puget Sound	833	0	0	0
497	Texas C	833	0	0	0
498	Lees Jr C	832	2	0	0
506	Augustiana C (SC)	822	0	0	0
506	Fairfield U	817	0	0	0
513	Farber-Scotia C	798	0	0	0
527	Wittenberg U	757	0	0	0
530	Lewis & Clark C	751	0	0	0
532	Duachita Baptist U	751	0	0	0
533	Tusculum C	751	0	0	0
552	Seattle Pacific C	716	0	0	DOD
560	Seton Hall U	699	0	0	0

ERDA	EPA	HEW	INT	NASA	NSF	DOT	OTHER*
54	0	1,188	0	0	0	0	0
0	0	1,240	0	0	0	0	0
0	20	1,188	0	0	0	0	0
0	0	1,175	0	0	7	0	0
0	0	1,104	0	0	37	0	0
0	0	1,133	0	0	0	0	0
0	0	1,104	0	0	0	0	0
0	0	989	0	48	50	0	0
0	0	1,017	0	0	68	0	0
3	0	941	0	0	139	0	0
0	0	1,060	0	0	0	0	0
0	0	1,057	0	0	0	0	0
0	0	1,035	0	0	16	0	0
132	0	335	60	54	334	3	0
0	0	1,023	0	0	0	0	0
0	0	1,017	0	0	0	0	0
0	0	999	0	0	0	0	0
0	0	966	0	0	0	0	0
0	0	959	0	0	0	0	0
0	0	927	0	0	0	0	0
0	0	912	0	0	0	0	0
0	0	910	0	0	0	0	0
0	0	903	0	0	0	0	0
0	0	859	0	0	35	0	0
0	0	862	0	0	20	0	0
0	0	617	0	19	243	0	0
0	0	815	0	0	58	0	0
0	0	678	0	0	170	0	0
0	0	823	0	0	10	0	9
0	0	833	0	0	0	0	0
0	0	830	0	0	0	0	0
0	0	757	0	0	65	0	0
0	0	438	0	2	27	0	350
0	0	798	0	0	0	0	0
0	0	757	0	0	0	0	0
0	0	751	0	0	0	0	0
0	0	751	0	0	0	0	0
0	0	751	0	0	0	0	0
0	0	676	0	0	40	0	0
0	0	696	0	0	3	0	0

RANK	INSTITUTION	TOTAL	USDA	COM	DOD
563	Pepperdine U	697	0	0	0
566	So Cal C	687	0	0	0
570	Jamestown C	675	0	0	0
575	Viterbo C	670	0	0	0
579	Emmanuel C (Me.)	657	0	0	445
580	Philander Smith C	655	0	0	0
585	Mercy C of Detroit	649	0	0	0
586	Calvin C	641	0	0	0
589	Concordia C Moorhd	639	0	0	0
591	Loyola Marymount U	636	0	0	0
601	Daniel Payne C	621	0	0	0
605	Huron C	611	0	0	0
607	Rocky Mountain C	607	0	0	0
624	Briar Cliff C	588	0	0	0
627	Brevard Com C	585	0	0	0
630	Luther C	583	0	0	24
634	Salem C	579	0	0	0
646	Pacific U	553	0	0	0
649	Paul Quinn C	543	0	0	0
654	C of St Teresq	539	0	0	0
655	Providence C	539	0	0	0
658	Hiram C	536	0	0	0
662	Regis C	533	0	0	339
663	Chaminade C of Hono	532	0	0	0
664	Gannon C	531	0	0	0
665	Valparaiso U	529	0	0	0
678	Loyola U (La.)	516	0	0	2
681	St John's U (Minn.)	515	0	0	0
684	Kansas Newman C	511	0	0	0
695	Morristown C	503	0	0	0
698	St Edward's U	498	0	0	0
704	Mississippi Indus C	493	0	0	0
705	Arkansas C	493	0	0	0
706	Loretto Heights C	492	0	0	0
709	Marywood C	492	0	0	0
713	Davis & Elkins C	490	0	0	0
715	Sucmi C	488	0	0	0
726	Pikeville C	478	0	0	0
732	Cumberland C	473	0	0	0
735	St Anselm's C	472	0	0	0

ERDA	EPA	HEW	INT	NASA	NSF	DOT	OTHER*
0	0	697	0	0	0	0	0
0	0	687	0	0	0	0	0
0	0	675	0	0	0	0	0
0	0	662	0	0	8	0	0
0	0	212	0	0	0	0	0
0	0	655	0	0	0	0	0
0	0	619	0	0	30	0	0
0	0	637	0	0	4	0	0
0	0	639	0	0	0	0	0
0	0	632	0	0	4	0	0
0	0	471	0	0	150	0	0
0	0	611	0	0	0	0	0
0	0	607	0	0	0	0	0
0	0	588	0	0	0	0	0
0	0	585	0	0	0	0	0
0	0	531	0	0	28	0	0
0	0	579	0	0	0	0	0
0	0	542	0	0	11	0	0
0	0	543	0	0	0	0	0
0	0	539	0	0	0	0	0
0	0	529	0	0	10	0	0
0	0	517	0	0	19	0	0
0	0	194	0	0	0	0	0
0	0	509	0	0	23	0	0
0	0	531	0	0	0	0	0
0	0	522	0	0	7	0	0
0	0	428	0	0	86	0	0
0	0	507	0	0	8	0	0
0	0	511	0	0	0	0	0
0	0	333	0	0	170	0	0
0	0	498	0	0	0	0	0
0	0	290	0	0	203	0	0
0	0	474	0	0	19	0	0
0	0	492	0	0	0	0	0
0	0	492	0	0	0	0	0
0	0	490	0	0	0	0	0
0	0	488	0	0	0	0	0
0	0	478	0	0	0	0	0
0	0	473	0	0	0	0	0
0	0	472	0	0	0	0	0

RANK	INSTITUTION	TOTAL	USDA	COM	DOD
737	Oklahoma City U	471	0	0	0
748	Mary Holmes C	463	0	0	0
750	Baptist C at Charleston	462	0	0	0
751	MacMurray C	461	0	0	0
753	Ohio Wesleyan U	460	0	0	46
754	Upsala C	459	0	0	0
760	Hope C	455	0	0	0
761	Atlantic Christ C	455	0	0	0
765	Pacific Lutheran U	453	0	0	0
766	Illinois C	452	0	0	0
767	King C (Tenn.)	450	0	0	0
770	Incarnate Word C	448	0	0	0
771	N Park C Theol Sem	448	0	0	0
772	Marist C	447	0	0	0
780	Franklin & Marshall	439	0	0	0
782	U of Scranton	438	0	0	0
783	OK Baptist U	437	0	0	0
785	LaSalle C	437	0	0	0
786	Bethel C (Kans.)	437	0	0	0
795	Macalester C	433	0	0	0
802	Messiah C	427	0	0	0
806	So Missionary C	424	0	0	0
807	Alaska Methodist U	422	0	0	0
811	Sheldon Jackson JrC	418	0	0	0
812	Graceland C	418	0	0	0
813	C of St Scholastica	417	0	0	0
814	E Mennonite C	416	0	0	0
815	Mars Hill C	416	0	0	0
817	George Fox C	415	0	0	0
818	Huntingdon C (Ala.)	415	0	0	0
824	Springfield C (Ill.)	411	0	0	0
831	King's C (Pa.)	404	0	0	0
837	Seton Hill C	399	0	0	0
843	Spring Hill C	395	0	0	0
845	Gonzaga U	394	0	0	0
847	St Mary's C (Minn.)	393	0	0	0
849	St Mary's Jr C	392	0	0	0
850	Warren Wilson C	392	0	0	0
859	Chowan C	385	0	0	0
863	Barat C	384	0	0	0

ERDA	EPA	HEW	INT	NASA	NSF	DOT	OTHER*
0	0	465	0	0	6	0	0
0	0	463	0	0	0	0	0
0	0	462	0	0	0	0	0
0	0	461	0	0	0	0	0
0	0	410	0	0	4	0	0
0	0	459	0	0	0	0	0
0	0	273	0	0	182	0	0
0	0	455	0	0	0	0	0
0	0	384	0	0	69	0	0
0	0	452	0	0	0	0	0
0	0	450	0	0	0	0	0
0	0	448	0	0	0	0	0
0	0	411	0	0	37	0	0
0	0	447	0	0	0	0	0
0	0	361	0	0	78	0	0
27	0	397	0	0	14	0	0
0	0	432	0	0	5	0	0
0	0	437	0	0	0	0	0
0	0	437	0	0	0	0	0
0	0	412	0	0	21	0	0
0	0	427	0	0	0	0	0
0	0	424	0	0	0	0	0
0	0	422	0	0	0	0	0
0	0	418	0	0	0	0	0
0	0	418	0	0	0	0	0
0	0	417	0	0	0	0	0
0	0	416	0	0	0	0	0
0	0	416	0	0	0	0	0
0	0	415	0	0	0	0	0
0	0	404	0	0	11	0	0
0	0	411	0	0	0	0	0
0	0	404	0	0	0	0	0
0	0	399	0	0	0	0	0
0	0	395	0	0	0	0	0
0	0	373	0	0	21	0	0
0	0	386	0	0	7	0	0
0	0	392	0	0	0	0	0
0	0	392	0	0	0	0	0
0	0	385	0	0	0	0	0
0	0	375	0	0	9	0	0

RANK	INSTITUTION	TOTAL	USDA	COM	DOD
867	Bridgewater St C	381	0	0	0
872	Niagara U	379	0	0	0
875	Doane C	375	0	0	0
879	Wellesley C	372	0	0	0
893	Marymount C (Kans.)	361	0	0	0
898	Linfield C	358	0	0	0
901	Anderson C (Ind.)	357	0	0	0
909	Assumption C	351	0	0	0
910	Baker U	350	0	0	0
913	Alderson-Broadous	348	0	0	0
915	Shenandoah C	345	0	0	0
921	Maryville C (Tenn.)	343	0	0	0
925	William Jewell C	341	0	0	0
927	Hardin-Simmons U	339	0	0	0
928	C of Holy Cross	339	0	0	0
929	Alverno C	339	0	0	0
931	U of Tulsa	337	0	0	0
935	Beth Medrash Gevoha Amer	332	0	0	0
936	Pacific Union C	332	0	0	0
937	Marymount C (N.Y.)	331	0	0	0
940	Lemoyne C	330	0	0	0
944	Capital U	328	0	0	0
945	OK Christian C	328	0	0	0
947	Swarthmore C	327	0	0	0
950	St Joseph's C (Ind.)	323	0	0	0
951	Webster C	323	0	0	0
954	Marymount Manhattan	320	0	0	0
955	Northland C	318	1	0	0
959	Mt Marty C	318	0	0	0
961	SW Baptist C	316	0	0	0
962	Hesston C	316	0	0	0
966	Loyola C (Md.)	314	0	0	0
978	St Joseph's C (Pa.)	310	0	0	0
979	Marion C	310	0	0	0
980	Dallas Baptist C	309	0	0	0
981	Abilene Christ C	309	0	0	0
984	Goshen C	307	0	0	0
985	Alstin C	307	0	0	0
986	Avila C	306	0	0	0

ERDA	EPA	HEW	INT	NASA	NSF	DOT	OTHER*
0	0	381	0	0	0	0	0
0	0	369	0	0	10	0	0
0	0	375	0	0	0	0	0
0	0	370	0	0	2	0	0
0	0	361	0	0	0	0	0
0	0	349	0	0	9	0	0
0	0	329	0	0	28	0	0
0	0	351	0	0	0	0	0
0	0	350	0	0	0	0	0
0	0	348	0	0	0	0	0
0	0	345	0	0	0	0	0
0	0	343	0	0	0	0	0
0	0	341	0	0	0	0	0
0	0	262	0	65	12	0	0
0	0	281	0	0	58	0	0
0	0	339	0	0	0	0	0
0	60	225	23	0	29	0	0
0	0	332	0	0	0	0	0
0	0	332	0	0	0	0	0
0	0	331	0	0	0	0	0
0	0	330	0	0	0	0	0
0	0	328	0	0	0	0	0
0	0	328	0	0	0	0	0
0	0	166	0	0	161	0	0
0	0	323	0	0	0	0	0
0	0	297	0	0	26	0	0
0	0	317	0	0	3	0	0
0	0	317	0	0	0	0	0
0	0	275	0	0	43	0	0
0	0	316	0	0	0	0	0
0	0	316	0	0	0	0	0
0	0	314	0	0	0	0	0
0	0	297	0	0	13	0	0
0	0	304	0	0	6	0	0
0	0	309	0	0	0	0	0
0	0	302	0	0	7	0	0
0	0	307	0	0	0	0	0
0	0	307	0	0	0	0	0
0	0	306	0	0	0	0	0

RANK	INSTITUTION	TOTAL	USDA	COM	DOD
994	Xavier U	303	0	0	0
995	Walla Walla C	302	0	0	0
998	Findlay C	302	0	0	0
1001	Lee C (Tenn.)	299	0	0	0
1007	Stetson U	295	0	0	0
1008	St John C Cleveland	295	0	0	0
1010	Donnelly C	295	0	0	0
1013	Union C (Ky.)	294	0	0	0
1014	Willamette U	293	0	0	0
1015	Park C	293	0	0	0
1019	Harding C	291	0	0	0
1020	Lake Forest C	290	0	0	0
1025	St Michael's C	287	0	0	0
1029	Ohio Dominican C.	286	0	0	0
1033	St Mary's C (Ind.)	286	0	0	0
1036	Freed-Hardeman C	283	0	0	0
1037	Sch of Ozarks	280	0	0	0
1038	Dakota Wesleyan U	280	0	0	0
1043	William Carey C	277	0	0	0
1044	E Texas Baptist C	276	0	0	0
1046	U of Richmond	273	0	0	0
1048	Wilmington C (Ohio)	273	0	0	0
1049	U of Redlands	273	0	0	0
1050	C of St Thomas	272	0	0	0
1052	Madonna C	272	0	0	0
1055	Midway C	270	0	0	0
1060	Algsburg C	268	0	0	0
1061	St Olaf C	268	0	0	0
1062	Madison C	268	0	0	0
1064	Kansas Wesleyan	267	0	0	0
1069	Keuka C	265	0	0	0
1078	C of Ozarks	263	0	0	0
1079	Notre Dame C (N.H.)	263	0	0	0
1083	Whitworth C	262	0	0	0
1090	La Grange C	258	0	0	0
1093	Carson-Newman C	258	0	0	0
1098	Hamline U	256	0	0	0
1099	St Vincent C	255	0	0	0
1102	St Francis C (Pa.)	255	0	0	DOD
1103	VA Wesleyan C	255	0	0	0

ERDA	EPA	HEW	INT	NASA	NSF	DOT	OTHER*
0	0	241	0	0	62	0	0
0	0	297	0	0	5	0	0
0	0	302	0	0	0	0	0
0	0	299	0	0	0	0	0
0	0	262	0	0	33	0	0
0	0	295	0	0	0	0	0
0	0	295	0	0	0	0	0
0	0	294	0	0	0	0	0
0	0	287	0	0	6	0	0
0	0	291	0	0	2	0	0
0	0	235	0	43	13	0	0
0	0	290	0	0	0	0	0
0	0	282	0	0	5	0	0
0	0	265	0	0	21	0	0
0	0	277	0	0	9	0	0
0	0	283	0	0	0	0	0
0	0	280	0	0	0	0	0
0	0	257	0	0	23	0	0
0	0	277	0	0	0	0	0
0	0	276	0	0	0	0	0
0	0	264	0	0	9	0	0
0	0	247	0	0	26	0	0
0	0	265	0	0	8	0	0
0	0	272	0	0	0	0	0
0	0	272	0	0	0	0	0
0	0	270	0	0	0	0	0
0	0	264	0	0	4	0	0
0	0	250	0	0	18	0	0
0	0	245	0	0	23	0	0
0	0	267	0	0	0	0	0
0	0	265	0	0	0	0	0
0	0	263	0	0	0	0	0
0	0	263	0	0	0	0	0
0	0	262	0	0	0	0	0
0	0	247	0	0	11	0	0
0	0	239	0	0	19	0	0
0	0	253	0	0	3	0	0
0	65	182	0	0	8	0	0
0	0	248	0	0	7	0	0
0	0	255	0	0	0	0	0

RANK	INSTITUTION	TOTAL	USDA	COM	DOD
1106	Otterbein C	253	0	0	0
1110	St Xavier C	252	0	0	0
1113	Trinity C (Ct.)	251	0	0	0
1118	Pacific C	250	0	0	0
1120	Concordia C (DRF)	249	0	0	0
1121	Mississippi C	248	0	0	0
1135	Lambuth C	245	0	0	0
1136	Drury C	244	0	0	0
1137	Greenville C	244	0	0	0
1140	Howard Payne C	243	0	0	0
1144	Ferrum C	241	0	0	0
1145	Haverford C	240	0	0	0
1154	So Baptist C	237	0	0	0
1157	Farlham C	237	0	0	0
1158	Benedictine C	237	0	0	0
1163	Wagner C	236	0	0	0
1171	St Andrews Presb C	233	0	0	0
1175	John Carroll U	232	0	0	40
1177	Loras C	231	0	0	0
1178	Bethany C (Kans.)	231	0	0	0
1179	Tarkio C	231	0	0	0
1180	W Maryland C	231	0	0	0
1188	Barry C	229	0	0	0
1189	Bluffton C	229	0	0	0
1191	Simpson C (La.)	227	0	0	0
1193	Lawrence U	227	0	0	0
1194	C of St Catherine	227	0	0	0
1197	Christ Brothers C	226	0	0	0
1198	Immaculate Heart C	225	0	0	0
1201	U of Portland	224	0	0	0
1203	Columbia Union C	224	0	0	0
1207	Mt St Mary's C (Calif.)	223	0	0	0
1209	McPherson C	222	0	0	0
1211	Westmar C	222	0	0	0
1212	Northwestern C (Iowa)	222	0	0	0
1214	Butler U	221	0	0	0
1216	Wayland Baptist C	221	0	0	0
1225	U of St Thomas	218	0	0	0
1227	Blackburn C	218	0	0	DOD
1231	Elmhurst C	217	0	0	0

ERDA	EPA	HEW	INT	NASA	NSF	DOT	OTHER*
0	0	253	0	0	0	0	0
0	0	252	0	0	0	0	0
0	0	251	0	0	0	0	0
0	0	250	0	0	0	0	0
0	0	249	0	0	0	0	0
0	0	228	0	0	20	0	0
0	0	245	0	0	0	0	0
0	0	236	0	0	8	0	0
0	0	221	0	23	0	0	0
0	0	243	0	0	0	0	0
0	0	241	0	0	0	0	0
0	0	225	0	0	15	0	0
0	0	237	0	0	0	0	0
0	0	227	0	0	10	0	0
0	0	237	0	0	0	0	0
0	0	236	0	0	0	0	0
0	0	233	0	0	0	0	0
0	0	184	0	8	0	0	0
0	0	231	0	0	0	0	0
0	0	231	0	0	0	0	0
0	0	231	0	0	0	0	0
0	0	231	0	0	0	0	0
0	0	229	0	0	0	0	0
0	0	199	0	0	30	0	0
0	0	226	0	0	1	0	0
0	0	173	0	0	54	0	0
0	0	227	0	0	0	0	0
0	0	154	0	0	72	0	0
0	0	225	0	0	0	0	0
0	0	224	0	0	0	0	0
0	0	169	0	0	55	0	0
0	0	223	0	0	0	0	0
0	0	222	0	0	0	0	0
0	0	222	0	0	0	0	0
0	0	222	0	0	0	0	0
0	0	221	0	0	0	0	0
0	0	221	0	0	0	0	0
0	0	218	0	0	0	0	0
0	0	218	0	0	0	0	0
0	0	217	0	0	0	0	0

RANK	INSTITUTION	TOTAL	USDA	COM	DOD
1234	Spartanburg Jr C	216	0	0	0
1236	Occidental C	215	0	0	0
1238	Allegheny C	214	0	0	0
1239	Marian C of Fond Du Lac	214	0	0	0
1240	SW Christian C	214	0	0	0
1243	Campbell C	212	0	0	0
1246	Westminster C (Utah)	212	0	0	0
1247	Roanoke C	211	0	0	0
1248	Hartwick C	211	0	0	0
1255	St Mary's Domin C	210	0	0	0
1258	SW C (Ks.)	209	0	0	0
1262	Mt St Mary C (N.Y.)	207	0	0	0
1264	C of New Rochelle	207	0	0	0
1265	Kalamazoo C	207	0	0	0
1268	Coe C	206	0	0	0
1269	Andrews U	206	0	0	0
1273	Greensboro C	205	0	0	0
1275	Wartburg C	204	0	0	0
1277	Presbyterian C	203	0	0	0
1278	Gustavus Adolphus C	203	0	0	0
1282	Neb Wesleyan U	202	0	0	0
1285	St Gregory's C	201	0	0	0
1288	Ashland C	200	0	0	0
1290	C of Great Falls	200	0	0	0
1292	Olivet Nazarene C	200	0	0	0
1293	Holy Name C	199	0	0	0
1294	Thomas More C	199	0	0	0
1295	Mt Mercy C	198	0	0	0
1297	IL Wesleyan U	198	0	0	0
1301	C of Idaho	197	0	0	0
1310	Dordt C	195	0	0	0
1311	Monmouth C (N.J.)	195	0	0	0
1312	Covenant C	193	0	0	0
1315	Siena Heights C	193	0	0	0
1318	Spalding C	193	0	0	0
1321	Columbia C (S.C.)	191	0	0	0
1324	Geneva C	189	0	0	0
1332	Texas Lutheran C	186	0	0	0
1333	Manchester C	186	0	0	0
1338	McMurry C	184	0	0	0

ERDA	EPA	HEW	INT	NASA	NSF	DOT	OTHER*
0	0	216	0	0	0	0	0
0	0	201	0	0	14	0	0
0	0	188	0	0	26	0	0
0	0	214	0	0	0	0	0
0	0	214	0	0	0	0	0
0	0	212	0	0	0	0	0
0	0	212	0	0	0	0	0
0	0	207	4	0	0	0	0
0	0	202	0	0	9	0	0
0	0	210	0	0	0	0	0
0	0	202	0	0	7	0	0
0	0	207	0	0	0	0	0
0	0	200	0	0	7	0	0
0	0	199	0	0	8	0	0
0	0	186	0	0	20	0	0
0	0	195	0	0	11	0	0
0	0	205	0	0	0	0	0
0	0	193	0	0	11	0	0
0	0	203	0	0	0	0	0
0	0	193	0	0	10	0	0
0	0	118	0	0	84	0	0
0	0	201	0	0	0	0	0
0	0	200	0	0	0	0	0
0	0	200	0	0	0	0	0
0	0	175	0	0	25	0	0
0	0	199	0	0	0	0	0
0	0	184	0	0	15	0	0
0	0	198	0	0	0	0	0
0	0	196	0	0	2	0	0
0	0	197	0	0	0	0	0
0	0	195	0	0	0	0	0
0	0	194	0	0	1	0	0
0	0	193	0	0	0	0	0
0	0	193	0	0	0	0	0
0	0	193	0	0	0	0	0
0	0	186	0	0	5	0	0
0	0	189	0	0	0	0	0
0	0	186	0	0	0	0	0
0	0	186	0	0	0	0	0
0	0	184	0	0	0	0	0

RANK	INSTITUTION	TOTAL	USDA	COM	DOD
1339	Ripon C	184	0	0	0
1343	Maryville C (Mo.)	183	0	0	0
1345	Mt. Union C	183	0	0	0
1346	Bethany C (W.V.)	182	0	0	0
1347	Taylor U	182	0	0	0
1348	Campbellsville C	182	0	0	0
1349	S-E Bible C	182	0	0	0
1350	Warner Pacific C	181	0	0	0
1353	Bellarmine-Ursuline	180	0	0	0
1361	Susquehanna U	177	0	0	0
1362	William Penn C	177	0	0	0
1365	Lubbock Christian C	176	0	0	0
1370	Drew U	174	0	0	0
1371	C of Wooster	174	0	0	0
1378	Lynchburg C	172	0	0	0
1382	Alma C	172	0	0	0
1384	Manhattanvl C	171	0	0	0
1392	Spertls C of Judai	168	0	0	0
1395	Sterling C	167	0	0	0
1397	Heidelberg C	167	0	0	0
1398	Furman U	167	0	0	0
1399	Newberry C	166	0	0	0
1401	Defiance C	166	0	0	0
1403	Central Methodist C	166	0	0	0
1404	LA Verne C	166	0	0	0
1406	Whittier C	165	0	0	0
1407	Oral Roberts U	165	0	0	0
1408	C of St Elizabeth	165	0	0	0
1409	Ruena Vista C	165	0	0	0
1411	Union C (Neb.)	164	0	0	0
1413	E Nazarene C	164	0	0	0
1419	Fureka C	163	0	0	0
1426	Carroll C (Wisc.)	161	0	0	0
1432	Hobart & WM Smith C	160	0	0	0
1434	Wheeling C	159	0	0	0
1438	Salve Regina C	159	0	0	0
1439	Muckingum C	158	0	0	0
1444	DePauw U	156	0	0	0
1450	Walsh C	155	0	0	0
1451	Hiwassee C	155	0	0	0

ERDA	EPA	HEW	INT	NASA	NSF	DOT	OTHER*
0	0	184	0	0	0	0	0
0	0	183	0	0	0	0	0
0	0	183	0	0	0	0	0
0	0	182	0	0	0	0	0
0	0	182	0	0	0	0	0
0	0	182	0	0	0	0	0
0	0	182	0	0	0	0	0
0	0	181	0	0	0	0	0
0	0	180	0	0	0	0	0
0	0	173	0	0	4	0	0
0	0	177	0	0	0	0	0
0	0	176	0	0	0	0	0
0	0	167	0	0	7	0	0
0	0	161	0	0	13	0	0
1	0	171	0	0	0	0	0
0	0	149	0	0	23	0	0
0	0	171	0	0	0	0	0
0	0	168	0	0	0	0	0
0	0	167	0	0	0	0	0
0	0	146	0	0	21	0	0
0	0	140	0	0	27	0	0
0	0	159	0	0	7	0	0
0	0	166	0	0	0	0	0
0	0	166	0	0	0	0	0
0	0	166	0	0	0	0	0
0	0	165	0	0	0	0	0
0	0	158	0	0	7	0	0
0	0	165	0	0	0	0	0
0	0	165	0	0	0	0	0
0	0	164	0	0	0	0	0
0	0	156	0	0	8	0	0
0	0	163	0	0	0	0	0
0	0	161	0	0	0	0	0
0	0	158	0	0	2	0	0
0	0	148	0	0	11	0	0
0	0	159	0	0	0	0	0
0	0	126	0	0	32	0	0
0	0	156	0	0	0	0	0
0	0	155	0	0	0	0	0
0	0	155	0	0	0	0	0

RANK	INSTITUTION	TOTAL	USDA	COM	DOD
1459	Atlantic Union C	153	0	0	0
1460	Partlesville Wes C	153	0	0	0
1461	Letourneau C	153	0	0	0
1463	Waldorf C	153	0	0	0
1467	Wheaton C (Ill.)	152	0	0	0
1468	Cornell C	151	0	0	0
1476	Aurora C	149	0	0	0
1477	AL Lutheran Acad & C	148	0	0	0
1487	Sioux Falls C	146	0	0	0
1490	Mercyhurst C	145	0	0	0
1493	U of South	145	0	0	0
1495	SW at Memphis	144	0	0	0
1501	Gardner Webb C	143	0	0	0
1503	Mary Baldwin C	143	0	0	0
1504	St Francis C (N.Y.)	142	0	0	0
1506	Grand View C	142	0	0	0
1510	Beaver C	142	0	0	0
1512	Dickinson C	141	0	0	0
1513	Beloit C	141	0	0	0
1515	Rosary Hill C	141	0	0	0
1517	St. Norbert C	141	0	0	0
1518	Trevecca Nazarene C	141	0	0	0
1520	IN Central C	140	0	0	0
1529	Millsaps C	138	0	0	0
1531	Iona C	137	0	0	0
1536	Midland Lutheran C	135	0	0	0
1538	Wesley C	135	0	0	0
1540	Chapman C	135	0	0	0
1542	Wofford C	134	0	0	0
1545	C Misericorcia	133	0	0	0
1547	Stonehill C	132	0	0	0
1548	Marycrest C	132	0	0	0
1551	Houghton C	131	0	0	0
1554	Lenoir-Rhyne C	131	0	0	0
1556	Friends U	131	0	0	0
1557	Phillips U	130	0	0	0
1562	Mercy C	129	0	0	0
1564	Fontbonne C	128	0	0	0
1566	Barrington C	128	0	0	0
1569	Bryan C	127	0	0	0

ERDA	EPA	HEW	INT	NASA	NSF	DOT	OTHER*
0	0	153	0	0	0	0	0
0	0	153	0	0	0	0	0
0	0	153	0	0	0	0	0
0	0	153	0	0	0	0	0
0	0	152	0	0	0	0	0
0	0	144	0	0	7	0	0
0	0	149	0	0	0	0	0
0	0	0	0	0	148	0	0
0	0	146	0	0	0	0	0
0	0	145	0	0	0	0	0
0	0	141	0	0	4	0	0
0	0	127	0	0	17	0	0
0	0	143	0	0	0	0	0
0	0	53	0	8	82	0	0
0	0	142	0	0	0	0	0
0	0	142	0	0	0	0	0
0	0	75	0	0	67	0	0
0	0	141	0	0	0	0	0
0	0	131	0	0	10	0	0
0	0	141	0	0	0	0	0
0	0	141	0	0	0	0	0
0	0	141	0	0	0	0	0
0	0	140	0	0	0	0	0
0	0	138	0	0	0	0	0
0	0	137	0	0	0	0	0
0	0	135	0	0	0	0	0
0	0	135	0	0	0	0	0
0	0	135	0	0	0	0	0
0	0	134	0	0	0	0	0
0	0	133	0	0	0	0	0
0	0	132	0	0	0	0	0
0	0	132	0	0	0	0	0
0	0	131	0	0	0	0	0
0	0	121	0	0	10	0	0
0	0	131	0	0	0	0	0
0	0	130	0	0	0	0	0
0	0	129	0	0	0	0	0
0	0	128	0	0	0	0	0
0	0	128	0	0	0	0	0
0	0	121	0	0	6	0	0

RANK	INSTITUTION	TOTAL	USDA	COM	DOD
1570	Rabbinical C Telshe	127	0	0	0
1572	Yankton C	126	0	0	0
1574	Texas Wesleyan C	126	0	0	0
1577	Regis C	125	0	0	0
1581	Evangel C	125	0	0	0
1588	Meredith C	122	0	0	0
1590	Houston Baptist C	122	0	0	0
1591	C of St Mary	122	0	0	0
1592	St Martin's C	121	0	0	0
1594	C of St Rose	121	0	0	0
1595	Millikin U	121	0	0	0
1599	Merrimack C	120	0	0	0
1600	NW Nazarene C	120	0	0	0
1602	CO Women's C	120	0	0	0
1606	Averett C	120	0	0	0
1609	Molloy C	119	0	0	0
1611	Emory & Henry C	119	0	0	0
1620	St John Fisher C	117	0	0	0
1622	Hood C	116	0	0	0
1623	Flon C	116	0	0	0
1626	Trinity C (Vt.)	116	0	0	0
1629	Grace Theol Sem	115	0	0	0
1632	Mt Vernon Naz C	115	0	0	0
1637	Juniata C	115	0	0	0
1640	Mary Hardin-Baylor C	114	0	0	0
1643	Concordia Tchrs C (Neb.)	113	0	0	0
1648	Villa Maria C	111	0	0	0
1651	Trinity C (D.C.)	111	0	0	0
1654	U of Duruque	110	0	0	0
1655	Augustana C (Ill.)	110	0	0	0
1656	Missouri Valley C	110	0	0	0
1657	C of Mt St Vincent	110	0	0	0
1661	Piedmont C	109	0	0	0
1663	Asbury C	109	0	0	0
1667	Grinneli C	109	0	0	0
1668	VA Intermont C	109	0	0	0
1673	Lees-McRae C	107	0	0	0
1675	C of Steubenville	107	0	0	0
1678	Bethany Bible C	106	0	0	0
1679	Beth Jacob Hebr Tchrs C	106	0	0	0

ERDA	EPA	HEW	INT	NASA	NSF	DOT	OTHER*
0	0	127	0	0	0	0	0
0	0	126	0	0	0	0	0
0	0	126	0	0	0	0	0
0	0	125	0	0	0	0	0
0	0	125	0	0	0	0	0
0	0	122	0	0	0	0	0
0	0	82	0	40	0	0	0
0	0	122	0	0	0	0	0
0	0	121	0	0	0	0	0
0	0	121	0	0	0	0	0
0	0	109	0	0	12	0	0
0	0	120	0	0	0	0	0
0	0	116	0	0	4	0	0
0	0	120	0	0	0	0	0
0	0	120	0	0	0	0	0
0	0	119	0	0	0	0	0
0	0	108	0	0	11	0	0
0	0	108	0	0	9	0	0
0	0	94	0	0	22	0	0
0	0	116	0	0	0	0	0
0	0	116	0	0	0	0	0
0	0	115	0	0	0	0	0
0	0	115	0	0	0	0	0
0	0	87	0	0	28	0	0
0	0	114	0	0	0	0	0
0	0	113	0	0	0	0	0
0	0	111	0	0	0	0	0
0	0	111	0	0	0	0	0
0	0	110	0	0	0	0	0
0	0	110	0	0	0	0	0
0	0	110	0	0	0	0	0
0	0	110	0	0	0	0	0
0	0	109	0	0	0	0	0
0	0	109	0	0	0	0	0
0	0	66	0	0	43	0	0
0	0	109	0	0	0	0	0
0		107	0	0	0	0	0
0	0	107	0	0	0	0	0
0	0	106	0	0	0	0	0
0	0	106	0	0	0	0	0

RANK	INSTITUTION	TOTAL	USDA	COM	DOD
1683	KY Christian C	105	0	0	0
1690	Georgetown C	104	0	0	0
1693	Florida So C	104	0	0	0
1695	Immaculata C	103	0	0	0
1696	Cen Yesh Tom Imimim Lubuz	103	0	0	0
1697	Notre Dame C (Ohio)	103	0	0	0
1699	Centre C of Ky.	102	0	0	0
1701	C of Our Lady Elms	102	0	0	0
1703	Rosary C	102	0	0	0
1704	St Mary of Plains C	101	0	0	0
1708	St Mary's C Cal.	101	0	0	0
1709	Mt Olive C	101	0	0	0
1710	Brescia C	101	0	0	0
1711	Mirrer Yeshiva Cent Inst	101	0	0	0
1712	TN Temple C	101	0	0	0
1713	Bethany-Naz C	100	0	0	0
1714	Spring Arbor C	100	0	0	0
1716	Chorter C (Ark.)	100	0	0	0
1719	Pffiffer C	100	0	0	0
1721	C of St Francis	100	0	0	0
1722	Fort Wayne Bible C	100	0	0	0
1723	Louisiana C	99	0	0	0
1725	Wingate C	99	0	0	0
1726	NC Wesleyan C	99	0	0	0
1728	Marian C	99	0	0	0
1737	U of San Diego	98	0	0	0
1739	Roberts Wesleyan C	97	0	0	0
1740	Westminster C (Pa.)	97	0	0	0
1741	Hendrix C	97	0	0	0
1743	Albion C	96	0	0	0
1747	Presentation C	96	0	0	0
1748	Davidson C	96	0	0	0
1762	David Liescomb C	94	0	0	0
1764	Dana C	94	0	0	0
1768	Iowa Wesleyan C	93	0	0	0
1769	Belmont Abbey C	93	0	0	0
1771	United Theo Sem (Ohio)	92	0	0	0
1776	Mes Tor Vodaath Rabin Sem	91	0	0	0

ERDA	EPA	HEW	INT	NASA	NSF	DOT	OTHER*
0	0	105	0	0	0	0	0
0	0	104	0	0	0	0	0
0	0	104	0	0	0	0	0
0	0	103	0	0	0	0	0
0	0	103	0	0	0	0	0
0	0	31	0	0	72	0	0
0	0	102	0	0	0	0	0
0	0	102	0	0	0	0	0
0	0	102	0	0	0	0	0
0	0	101	0	0	0	0	0
0	0	56	0	0	45	0	0
0	0	101	0	0	0	0	0
0	0	101	0	0	0	0	0
0	0	101	0	0	0	0	0
0	0	101	0	0	0	0	0
0	0	100	0	0	0	0	0
0	0	100	0	0	0	0	0
0	0	100	0	0	0	0	0
0	0	90	0	0	10	0	0
0	0	100	0	0	0	0	0
0	0	100	0	0	0	0	0
0	0	99	0	0	0	0	0
0	0	99	0	0	0	0	0
0	0	99	0	0	0	0	0
0	0	99	0	0	0	0	0
0	0	98	0	0	0	0	0
0	0	97	0	0	0	0	0
0	0	97	0	0	0	0	0
0	0	92	0	0	5	0	0
0	0	96	0	0	0	0	0
0	0	96	0	0	0	0	0
0	0	96	0	0	0	0	0
0	0	94	0	0	0	0	0
0	0	94	0	0	0	0	0
0	0	93	0	0	0	0	0
0	0	93	0	0	0	0	0
0	0	92	0	0	0	0	0
0	0	91	0	0	0	0	0

RANK	INSTITUTION	TOTAL	USDA	COM	DOD
1777	Gwynedo-Mercy C	91	0	0	0
1778	Allntwn C St Fr Desales	91	0	0	0
1779	Centenary C of Louis	91	0	0	0
1780	Cal Lutheran C	91	0	0	0
1782	Mt Angel C	90	0	0	0
1786	Ottumwa Heights C	89	0	0	0
1787	C Mt St Joseph-Ohio	89	0	0	0
1790	Athens C	89	0	0	35
1794	Trinity C (Ill.)	88	0	0	0
1795	Maria C of Albany	88	0	0	0
1797	Rabbinicl Acad M R Berlin	88	0	0	0
1798	Mt St Mary C (N.H.)	88	0	0	0
1799	Central Bible C	88	0	0	0
1800	Culver-Stockton C	88	0	0	0
1803	Mundelein C	87	0	0	0
1805	Huntington C (Ind.)	87	0	0	0
1807	Mt Aloysius Jr C	87	0	0	0
1812	C St Joseph Prov	86	0	0	0
1815	Mid-Amer Naz C	86	0	0	0
1819	St Bonaventure U	85	0	0	0
1820	Anderson C (S.C.)	85	0	0	0
1823	U of Dallas	85	0	0	0
1827	Villa Julie C	84	0	0	0
1830	Episcopal Theo Sch	83	0	0	0
1832	Malone C	83	0	0	0
1835	Olivet C	83	0	0	0
1837	Bridgewater C	82	0	0	0
1838	Sacred Heart U	82	0	0	0
1839	Ursinus C	82	0	0	0
1840	Reinhardt C	82	0	0	0
1841	Monmouth C (Ill.)	82	0	0	0
1844	Marymount C (Va.)	82	0	0	0
1847	Grand Canyon C	81	0	0	0
1849	Methodist C	81	0	0	0
1852	Louisburg C	80	0	0	0
1853	Moravian C	80	0	0	0
1859	St. Catherine C	79	0	0	0
1861	Tabor C	79	0	0	0
1862	Bates C	79	0	0	0

ERDA	EPA	HEW	INT	NASA	NSF	DOT	OTHER*
0	0	91	0	0	0	0	0
0	0	91	0	0	0	0	0
0	0	91	0	0	0	0	0
0	0	91	0	0	0	0	0
0	0	90	0	0	0	0	0
0	0	89	0	0	0	0	0
0	0	89	0	0	0	0	0
0	0	22	0	32	0	0	0
0	0	88	0	0	0	0	0
0	0	88	0	0	0	0	0
0	0	88	0	0	0	0	0
0	0	70	0	0	18	0	0
0	0	88	0	0	0	0	0
0	0	88	0	0	0	0	0
0	0	87	0	0	0	0	0
0	0	86	0	0	1	0	0
0	0	87	0	0	0	0	0
0	0	86	0	0	0	0	0
0	0	86	0	0	0	0	0
0	0	85	0	0	0	0	0
0	0	85	0	0	0	0	0
0	0	85	0	0	0	0	0
0	0	84	0	0	0	0	0
0	0	83	0	0	0	0	0
0	0	83	0	0	0	0	0
0	0	83	0	0	0	0	0
0	0	82	0	0	0	0	0
0	0	78	0	0	4	0	0
0	0	82	0	0	0	0	0
0	0	82	0	0	0	0	0
2	0	80	0	0	0	0	0
0	0	82	0	0	0	0	0
0	0	81	0	0	0	0	0
0	0	81	0	0	0	0	0
0	0	80	0	0	0	0	0
0	0	80	0	0	0	0	0
0	0	79	0	0	0	0	0
0	0	75	0	0	4	0	0
0	0	64	0	0	15	0	0

RANK	INSTITUTION	TOTAL	USDA	COM	DOD
1866	Waynesburg C	79	0	0	0
1868	Randolph-Macon Womens C	78	0	0	0
1873	North Central C	77	0	0	0
1874	Siena C	77	0	0	0
1875	Rosemont C	77	0	0	0
1879	KY Wesleyan C	76	0	0	0
1883	Elizabethtown C	76	0	0	0
1884	Central Wesleyan C	76	0	0	0
1888	Villa Maria C Buffa	75	0	0	0
1891	Thiel C	75	0	0	0
1892	NE Bible Inst	75	0	0	0
1893	St Ambrose C	75	0	0	0
1895	LA Baptist C&Sem	75	0	0	0
1896	St Marys C O'Fallon	75	0	0	0
1898	Emmanuel C (Ga.)	74	0	0	0
1899	Martin C	74	0	0	0
1900	St Joseph C (Ct.)	74	0	0	0
1903	St Bernard C	74	0	0	0
1906	Franklin C	73	0	0	0
1908	Denison U	73	0	0	0
1916	William Woods C	72	0	0	0
1917	SW U (Tex.)	72	0	0	0
1918	Marygrove C	72	0	0	0
1919	Wilmington C	72	0	0	0
1922	Mesiviha Tifereth Jeru AM	71	0	0	0
1923	St Joseph's C (Me.)	71	0	0	0
1924	Concordia C-St Paul	71	0	0	0
1929	Lakeland C	71	0	0	0
1933	United Wesleyan C	70	0	0	0
1934	Evangel Luth Theo S	69	0	0	0
1939	York C	69	0	0	0
1946	Caldwell C	67	0	0	0
1948	N Greenville C	67	0	0	0
1949	Grand Rapids Bapt C	66	0	0	0
1955	St Francis C (Ind.)	65	0	0	0
1957	Cabrini C	65	0	0	0
1958	Gettysburg C	65	0	0	0
1960	Holy Family C	65	0	0	0

Appendix A

ERDA	EPA	HEW	INT	NASA	NSF	DOT	OTHER*
0	0	71	0	0	8	0	0
0	0	64	0	0	14	0	0
0	0	77	0	0	0	0	0
0	0	75	0	0	2	0	0
0	0	77	0	0	0	0	0
0	0	72	0	0	4	0	0
0	0	41	0	0	35	0	0
0	0	76	0	0	0	0	0
0	0	75	0	0	0	0	0
0	0	75	0	0	0	0	0
0	0	75	0	0	0	0	0
0	0	75	0	0	0	0	0
0	0	75	0	0	0	0	0
0	0	75	0	0	0	0	0
0	0	74	0	0	0	0	0
0	0	74	0	0	0	0	0
0	0	68	0	0	6	0	0
0	0	74	0	0	0	0	0
0	0	73	0	0	0	0	0
5	0	63	0	0	5	0	0
0	0	72	0	0	0	0	0
0	0	72	0	0	0	0	0
0	0	61	0	0	11	0	0
0	0	72	0	0	0	0	0
0	0	71	0	0	0	0	0
0	0	71	0	0	0	0	0
0	0	71	0	0	0	0	0
0	0	71	0	0	0	0	0
0	0	70	0	0	0	0	0
0	0	69	0	0	0	0	0
0	0	69	0	0	0	0	0
0	0	67	0	0	0	0	0
0	0	67	0	0	0	0	0
0	0	66	0	0	0	0	0
0	0	65	0	0	0	0	0
0	0	65	0	0	0	0	0
0	0	39	0	0	26	0	0
0	0	65	0	0	0	0	0

RANK	INSTITUTION	TOTAL	USDA	COM	DOD
1962	Rabncl C Chsan Sofer	65	0	0	0
1964	Union U	65	0	0	0
1966	SW Assemb God C	63	0	0	0
1971	Wood Jr C	62	0	0	0
1972	Tift C	62	0	0	0
1973	Cin Bible Sem	62	0	0	0
1974	Westmont C	62	0	0	0
1980	Lewis & Clark St C	62	0	0	0
1981	McKendree C	61	0	0	0
1982	Belhaven C	61	0	0	0
1983	Clarke C (Iowa)	61	0	0	0
1984	Ark Baptist C	61	0	0	0
1985	Wesleyan C	61	0	0	0
1986	St Francis C (Me.)	61	0	0	0
1991	Schreiner C	61	0	0	0
1995	Wilson C	61	0	0	0
1996	Transylvania U	60	0	0	0
2002	Anna Maria C	60	0	0	0
2005	Kendall C	59	0	0	0
2007	Sue Bennett C	59	0	0	0
2011	Trinity Christn C	58	0	0	0
2013	St Mary C (Kans.)	58	0	0	0
2015	Bethel C (Ind.)	58	0	0	0
2016	Peace C	58	0	0	0
2020	Chestnut Hill C	57	0	0	0
2023	Lebanon Valley C	57	0	0	0
2024	Erskine C	57	0	0	0
2026	Central Baptist C	56	0	0	0
2029	Lindsey Wilson C	56	0	0	0
2030	Lycoming C	56	0	0	0
2031	Ner Israel Rabncl C	55	0	0	0
2033	Mt St Marys C (Md.)	55	0	0	0
2038	Rivier C	54	0	0	0
2039	Be'er Shmuel Talmudical A	54	0	0	0
2040	Naz C of Rochester	54	0	0	0
2041	Birmingham-So C	54	0	0	0
2043	Cedar Crest C	54	0	0	0
2045	NE Christn Jr C	53	0	0	0
2047	Belmont C	53	0	0	0

ERDA	EPA	HEW	INT	NASA	NSF	DOT	OTHER*
0	0	65	0	0	0	0	0
0	0	59	0	0	6	0	0
0	0	63	0	0	0	0	0
0	0	62	0	0	0	0	0
0	0	62	0	0	0	0	0
0	0	62	0	0	0	0	0
0	0	62	0	0	0	0	0
0	0	62	0	0	0	0	0
0	0	61	0	0	0	0	0
0	0	61	0	0	0	0	0
0	0	60	0	0	1	0	0
0	0	61	0	0	0	0	0
34	0	27	0	0	0	0	0
0	0	61	0	0	0	0	0
0	0	61	0	0	0	0	0
0	0	61	0	0	0	0	0
0	0	60	0	0	0	0	0
0	0	60	0	0	0	0	0
0	0	59	0	0	0	0	0
0	0	59	0	0	0	0	0
0	0	58	0	0	0	0	0
0	0	58	0	0	0	0	0
0	0	58	0	0	0	0	0
0	0	58	0	0	0	0	0
0	0	57	0	0	0	0	0
0	0	57	0	0	0	0	0
0	0	57	0	0	0	0	0
0	0	56	0	0	0	0	0
0	0	56	0	0	0	0	0
0	0	56	0	0	0	0	0
0	0	55	0	0	0	0	0
0	0	52	0	0	3	0	0
0	0	54	0	0	0	0	0
0	0	54	0	0	0	0	0
0	0	54	0	0	0	0	0
0	0	54	0	0	0	0	0
0	0	54	0	0	0	0	0
0	0	53	0	0	0	0	0
0	0	45	0	0	8	0	0

RANK	INSTITUTION	TOTAL	USDA	COM	DOD
2052	Ladycliff C	53	0	0	0
2053	St Paul Bible C	52	0	0	0
2054	Lon Morris C	52	0	0	0
2057	Shorter C (Ga.)	52	0	0	0
2058	Elizabeth Seton C	52	0	0	0
2061	Concordia C (N.Y.)	51	0	0	0
2062	Lincoln Christian C	51	0	0	0
2066	Sacred Heart C	51	0	0	0
2071	Young Harris C	50	0	0	0
2072	Columbia Christn C	50	0	0	0
2076	Albertus Magnus C	50	0	0	0
2077	St Meinrad C	50	0	0	0
2079	Bluefield C	50	0	0	0
2082	Marymount C (Fla.)	50	0	0	0
2083	Bicker C	50	0	0	0
2084	Rab C Bobover Yeshiva	49	0	0	0
2092	Mater Dei C	48	0	0	0
2095	Westminster C (Md.)	48	0	0	0
2096	Princeton Theol Sem	48	0	0	0
2098	St Thomas Aquinas C	48	0	0	0
2102	Simpson C (Calif.)	47	0	0	0
2103	CA Baptist C	47	0	0	0
2105	Hastings C	47	0	0	0
2107	ALA Christian C	46	0	0	0
2109	Randolph-Macon C	46	0	0	0
2110	Edgewood C	46	0	0	0
2112	Pontifical C Josephinup	46	0	0	0
2113	N Central Bible C	45	0	0	0
2115	Georgian Court C	45	0	0	0
2125	Immac Concep Sem-N.J.	44	0	0	0
2130	Milligan C	43	0	0	0
2132	Rabbi Joseph Rabncl	43	0	0	0
2134	Belzer Yesh-Machzikel Sem	43	0	0	0
2135	Lindenwood C	43	0	0	0
2136	Queens C	43	0	0	0
2140	Adrian C	42	0	0	0
2143	St Marys C of Md.	42	0	0	0
2153	Mt Mary C	41	0	0	0
2155	Bethel C (Tenn.)	41	0	0	0

ERDA	EPA	HEW	INT	NASA	NSF	DOT	OTHER*
0	0	53	0	0	0	0	0
0	0	52	0	0	0	0	0
0	0	52	0	0	0	0	0
0	0	52	0	0	0	0	0
0	0	52	0	0	0	0	0
0	0	51	0	0	0	0	0
0	0	51	0	0	0	0	0
0	0	51	0	0	0	0	0
0	0	50	0	0	0	0	0
0	0	50	0	0	0	0	0
0	0	50	0	0	0	0	0
0	0	50	0	0	0	0	0
0	0	50	0	0	0	0	0
0	0	50	0	0	0	0	0
0	0	50	0	0	0	0	0
0	0	49	0	0	0	0	0
0	0	48	0	0	0	0	0
0	0	48	0	0	0	0	0
0	0	48	0	0	0	0	0
0	0	48	0	0	0	0	0
0	0	47	0	0	0	0	0
0	0	47	0	0	0	0	0
0	0	47	0	0	0	0	0
0	0	46	0	0	0	0	0
0	0	39	0	0	7	0	0
0	0	46	0	0	0	0	0
0	0	46	0	0	0	0	0
0	0	45	0	0	0	0	0
0	0	45	0	0	0	0	0
0	0	44	0	0	0	0	0
0	0	43	0	0	0	0	0
0	0	43	0	0	0	0	0
0	0	43	0	0	0	0	0
0	0	43	0	0	0	0	0
0	0	43	0	0	0	0	0
0	0	30	0	0	12	0	0
0	0	42	0	0	0	0	0
0	0	41	0	0	0	0	0
0	0	41	0	0	0	0	0

RANK	INSTITUTION	TOTAL	USDA	COM	DOD
2156	St Leo C	40	0	0	0
2160	Central C	40	0	0	0
2162	Gulf Coast Bible C	39	0	0	0
2163	Bard C	39	0	0	0
2164	Concordia Luth Jr C	39	0	0	0
2165	Rabb C of Kamenitz Yesh	39	0	0	0
2166	Pacific Oaks C	39	0	0	0
2168	Divine Word C	39	0	0	0
2169	Cardinal Stritch C	38	0	0	0
2171	Rabbncl Sem of Amer	38	0	0	0
2174	Maria Regina C	38	0	0	0
2178	Pacific Christn C	37	0	0	0
2180	Albright C	37	0	0	0
2182	Bethany Luth C	37	0	0	0
2186	Concordia C (Wisc.)	36	0	0	0
2187	Green Mountain C	36	0	0	0
2194	Concordia Luth C Tex.	36	0	0	0
2200	Andrew C	35	0	0	0
2204	Dominican C Blauvelt	35	0	0	0
2206	Concordia Sem	34	0	0	0
2207	St Josephs C (N.Y.)	34	0	0	0
2208	Rab Sem Netzach Isr Ram	34	0	0	0
2215	Hillsdale C	34	0	0	0
2216	Bapt Bible C of Pa.	34	0	0	0
2218	C of Notre Dame (Calif.)	33	0	0	0
2219	Luther Theol Sem	33	0	0	0
2222	SW Union C	32	0	0	0
2225	Carthage C	32	0	0	0
2226	Ursuline C	32	0	0	0
2235	Blue Mountain C	31	0	0	0
2236	NW Christian C	31	0	0	0
2237	C of Notre Dame Md.	30	0	0	0
2240	Kenyon C	30	0	0	0
2241	St Charles Borromed Sem	30	0	0	0
2244	Notre Dame Sem	29	0	0	0
2245	Our Lady of Angels C	29	0	0	0
2246	Garrett Biblical Ins	29	0	0	0
2248	Hampden-Sydney C	28	0	0	0

ERDA	EPA	HEW	INT	NASA	NSF	DOT	OTHER*
0	0	40	0	0	0	0	0
0	0	40	0	0	0	0	0
0	0	39	0	0	0	0	0
0	0	39	0	0	0	0	0
0	0	39	0	0	0	0	0
0	0	39	0	0	0	0	0
0	0	39	0	0	0	0	0
0	0	39	0	0	0	0	0
0	0	38	0	0	0	0	0
0	0	38	0	0	0	0	0
0	0	38	0	0	0	0	0
0	0	37	0	0	0	0	0
0	0	37	0	0	0	0	0
0	0	37	0	0	0	0	0
0	0	36	0	0	0	0	0
0	0	36	0	0	0	0	0
0	0	36	0	0	0	0	0
0	0	35	0	0	0	0	0
0	0	35	0	0	0	0	0
0	0	34	0	0	0	0	0
0	0	34	0	0	0	0	0
0	0	34	0	0	0	0	0
0	0	34	0	0	0	0	0
0	0	34	0	0	0	0	0
0	0	33	0	0	0	0	0
0	0	33	0	0	0	0	0
0	0	32	0	0	0	0	0
0	0	32	0	0	0	0	0
0	0	31	0	0	1	0	0
0	0	31	0	0	0	0	0
0	0	31	0	0	0	0	0
0	0	30	0	0	0	0	0
0	0	30	0	0	0	0	0
0	0	30	0	0	0	0	0
0	0	29	0	0	0	0	0
0	0	29	0	0	0	0	0
0	0	29	0	0	0	0	0
0	0	22	0	0	6	0	0

RANK	INSTITUTION	TOTAL	USDA	COM	DOD
2250	Martin Luther C	28	0	0	0
2251	Lutheran Theol Sem Gettys	28	0	0	0
2252	Muhlenberg C	27	0	0	0
2253	St Thomas Sem C (Colo.)	27	0	0	0
2254	NE Bible C	27	0	0	0
2260	Silver Lake C Holy Fmly	26	0	0	0
2269	Hannibal La Grange C	25	0	0	0
2272	St Mary-of-the-Woods C	24	0	0	0
2276	Interdenomina Theo C	24	0	0	0
2278	Concordia Senior C	24	0	0	0
2281	Aquinas Jr C	23	0	0	0
2285	Alvernia C	23	0	0	0
2287	Saints C	22	0	0	0
2291	Mary Manse C	22	0	0	0
2292	Derech Ayson Rabbin Sem	22	0	0	0
2294	St Marys Sem & U	22	0	0	0
2296	Methodist Theo Sch Ohio	21	0	0	0
2298	Brevard C	21	0	0	0
2300	Mt St Joseph C	21	0	0	0
2306	Annhurst C	20	0	0	0
2307	St Pauls C (Mo.)	20	0	0	0
2312	Tenn Wesleyan C	20	0	0	0
2314	St Joseph Sem (La.)	20	0	0	0
2316	SEastn Christian C	20	0	0	0
2320	Sem of St Pius X	19	0	0	0
2321	Berkshire Christn C	19	0	0	0
2324	Athenaeum of Ohio	18	0	0	0
2325	Crosier Sem	18	0	0	0
2327	Lafayette C	18	0	0	0
2328	Natchez Jr C	18	0	0	0
2329	Hebrew Theol C	18	0	0	0
2331	So CA Sch Theol	18	0	0	0
2332	Holy Cross Jr C	18	0	0	0
2335	St Johns C (Kans.)	17	0	0	0
2336	Our Lady Holy Cross C	17	0	0	0
2341	Judson C (Ala.)	17	0	0	0
2349	Whitworth C	16	0	0	0

ERDA	EPA	HEW	INT	NASA	NSF	DOT	OTHER*
0	0	28	0	0	0	0	0
0	0	28	0	0	0	0	0
0	0	25	0	0	2	0	0
0	0	27	0	0	0	0	0
0	0	27	0	0	0	0	0
0	0	26	0	0	0	0	0
0	0	25	0	0	0	0	0
0	0	24	0	0	0	0	0
0	0	24	0	0	0	0	0
0	0	24	0	0	0	0	0
0	0	23	0	0	0	0	0
0	0	23	0	0	0	0	0
0	0	22	0	0	0	0	0
0	0	22	0	0	0	0	0
0	0	22	0	0	0	0	0
0	0	22	0	0	0	0	0
0	0	21	0	0	0	0	0
0	0	21	0	0	0	0	0
0	0	21	0	0	0	0	0
0	0	20	0	0	0	0	0
0	0	20	0	0	0	0	0
0	0	20	0	0	0	0	0
0	0	20	0	0	0	0	0
0	0	20	0	0	0	0	0
0	0	19	0	0	0	0	0
0	0	19	0	0	0	0	0
0	0	18	0	0	0	0	0
0	0	18	0	0	0	0	0
0	0	8	0	0	10	0	0
0	0	18	0	0	0	0	0
0	0	18	0	0	0	0	0
0	0	18	0	0	0	0	0
0	0	18	0	0	0	0	0
0	0	17	0	0	0	0	0
0	0	17	0	0	0	0	0
0	0	17	0	0	0	0	0
0	0	16	0	0	0	0	0

RANK	INSTITUTION	TOTAL	USDA	COM	DOD
2350	OHR Hameir Theo Sem	15	0	0	0
2351	St Marys C (Mich.)	15	0	0	0
2352	Cath C Immac Concep	15	0	0	0
2360	High Point C	14	0	0	0
2366	Dominican C	13	0	0	0
2367	Friends Bible C	13	0	0	0
2368	Immac Concep Sem (Mo.)	13	0	0	0
2370	Notre Dame C (Mo.)	13	0	0	0
2372	St Meinrad Sch-Theol	13	0	0	0
2375	Mt St Clare C	12	0	0	0
2377	Louisvl Pres Theo Sm	12	0	0	0
2378	Wartburg Theol Sem	12	0	0	0
2381	St Johns Sem	12	0	0	0
2387	Dominican C San Rafael	12	0	0	0
2389	Hanover C	11	0	0	0
2390	Iliff Sch of Theol	11	0	0	0
2392	Chicago Theol Sem	11	0	0	0
2393	Shimer C	11	0	0	0
2395	Agnes Scott C	11	0	0	0
2397	Sacred Heart Sem	11	0	0	0
2399	Concordia Tchrs C Ill.	11	0	0	0
2402	Aquinas Inst of Theo	10	0	0	0
2406	Don Bosco C	10	0	0	0
2410	Freeman Jr C	9	0	0	0
2412	Salem C	9	0	0	0
2414	Luth Sch of Theol	9	0	0	0
2418	Immac C of Wash	8	0	0	0
2420	McCormick Theol Sem	8	0	0	0
2421	Eden Theol Sem	8	0	0	0
2423	Pres Sch Christn Ed	8	0	0	0
2425	Nazarene Theol Sem	8	0	0	0
2427	Manor Jr C	7	0	0	0
2429	St Marys C (N.C.)	7	0	0	0
2432	Borromeo C of Ohio	7	0	0	0
2434	Church Div Sch Pacific	6	0	0	0
2439	United Theol Sem	5	0	0	0
2440	Sem of St Vincent De Paul	5	0	0	0

ERDA	EPA	HEW	INT	NASA	NSF	DOT	OTHER*
0	0	15	0	0	0	0	0
0	0	15	0	0	0	0	0
0	0	15	0	0	0	0	0
0	0	14	0	0	0	0	0
0	0	13	0	0	0	0	0
0	0	13	0	0	0	0	0
0	0	13	0	0	0	0	0
0	0	13	0	0	0	0	0
0	0	13	0	0	0	0	0
0	0	12	0	0	0	0	0
0	0	12	0	0	0	0	0
0	0	12	0	0	0	0	0
0	0	12	0	0	0	0	0
0	0	10	0	0	2	0	0
0	0	11	0	0	0	0	0
0	0	11	0	0	0	0	0
0	0	11	0	0	0	0	0
0	0	11	0	0	0	0	0
0	0	0	0	0	11	0	0
0	0	11	0	0	0	0	0
0	0	11	0	0	0	0	0
0	0	10	0	0	0	0	0
0	0	10	0	0	0	0	0
0	0	8	0	0	1	0	0
0	0	9	0	0	0	0	0
0	0	9	0	0	0	0	0
0	0	8	0	0	0	0	0
0	0	8	0	0	0	0	0
0	0	8	0	0	0	0	0
0	0	8	0	0	0	0	0
0	0	8	0	0	0	0	0
0	0	7	0	0	0	0	0
0	0	7	0	0	0	0	0
0	0	7	0	0	0	0	0
0	0	6	0	0	0	0	0
0	0	5	0	0	0	0	0
0	0	5	0	0	0	0	0

RANK	INSTITUTION	TOTAL	USDA	COM	DOD
2442	St Bernards Sem	4	0	0	0
2444	Holy Redeemer C	4	0	0	0
2446	Felician C (Ill.)	4	0	0	0
2450	Sulpician Sem NW	4	0	0	0
2453	Marylhurst C	4	0	0	0
2454	St Marys C (Ky.)	4	0	0	0
2457	Centenary C Women	4	0	0	0
2458	St Alphonsus C	4	0	0	0
2460	St Fidelis C	4	0	0	0
2463	Duns Socils C	4	0	0	0
2466	Hebrew Tchrs C	3	0	0	0
2471	N Bapt Theol Sem	3	0	0	0
2476	Minn Bible C	2	0	0	0
2477	Scarritt C Christn Wkrs	2	0	0	0
2479	NY Theol Sem	1	0	0	0
2481	Platte Valley Bible C	1	0	0	0
2482	Angilla Domini C	1	0	0	0
2483	Jewish Theol Sem of Amer	1	0	0	0
2485	Seabury-Western Theol Sem	1	0	0	0
2486	Spencerian C	1	0	0	0

Source: National Science Foundation, Division of Science Resources Studies, Uni-*versities, Colleges, and Selected Nonprofit Institutions, Fiscal Year 1975,* (Washington, D.C.: Government Printing Office, 1977).

ERDA	EPA	HEW	INT	NASA	NSF	DOT	OTHER*
0	0	4	0	0	0	0	0
0	0	4	0	0	0	0	0
0	0	4	0	0	0	0	0
0	0	4	0	0	0	0	0
0	0	4	0	0	0	0	0
0	0	4	0	0	0	0	0
0	0	4	0	0	0	0	0
0	0	4	0	0	0	0	0
0	0	4	0	0	0	0	0
0	0	4	0	0	0	0	0
0	0	3	0	0	0	0	0
0	0	3	0	0	0	0	0
0	0	2	0	0	0	0	0
0	0	2	0	0	0	0	0
0	0	1	0	0	0	0	0
0	0	1	0	0	0	0	0
0	0	1	0	0	0	0	0
0	0	1	0	0	0	0	0
0	0	1	0	0	0	0	0
0	0	1	0	0	0	0	0

versities and Nonprofit Institutions Study Group, *Federal Support to Uni-*
by J.G. Huckenpahler, Surveys of Science Resources Series, NSF 77-311

APPENDIX B
CURRENT ACCOUNTING AND PUBLIC REPORTING PRACTICE AND COMMITTEE'S CONCLUSIONS

"Recently, Rountree and Associates developed a methodology that illustrates the type of calculations necessary for a state reimbursement program of this type.[1] To determine the state payment, Rountree and Associates developed two concepts—a revenue capacity factor (RCF) and a payment in lieu of tax factor (PILT). To develop the RCF, the following data are needed for each taxing jurisdiction: (1) the acreage of each taxable parcel of real property, (2) the gross square footage of all improvements to taxable parcels, (3) the acreage of each tax-exempt parcel of real estate, (4) the gross square footage of all improvements to tax-exempt parcels, and (5) the portion of total property tax revenues accruing separately to land and improvement.

To derive the RCF for each jurisdiction, the total revenue generated by taxable land is divided by the total square footage of taxable land, giving the revenue capacity factor for land. As a second step, a revenue capacity factor for improvements is calculated by dividing the total revenue generated by improvements by the total gross square footage of taxable improvements.

This gives an average value on a communitywide basis for land and improvements for all taxable property. Since it is calculated on a square-footage basis, each of these average values—for land and improvements—can be applied to the square footage of tax-exempt property to yield a revenue raising potential for such properties. As Rountree and Associates state:

> The Revenue Capacity Factor represents a standard measurement, on a community-wide basis, of the revenue generating ability associated

with any single square foot of land or improvement, taxable or tax-exempt, in each individual jurisdiction. On this basis, the revenue capacity factors may be applied to tax-exempt land improvements to determine their potential revenue generating ability of not exempt. It should be noted that the revenue figure generated by the formula is essentially equivalent to the average full value of the property tax which would normally be levied on the parcel were it taxable.[2]

The second step in this overall procedure is to develop the payment due by the state. For this component, Rountree and Associates use six types of local expenditures as reflecting "the effective cost to each jurisdiction for providing certain vital functions whose benefits accrue to all real property in the locality, whether taxable or tax exempt. . . ." These expenditures are general administration, assessment of taxes, administration of justice, crime prevention and detection, fire prevention and extinction, and maintenance of buildings and grounds. The sum of these six items is then divided by the total property tax revenue to total local source revenue. This is termed the payment-in-lieu-of-taxes coefficient. If the exempt property is also valued, then the PILT coefficient can be applied to this value and establishes the limit of in-lieu payments to the particular locality.

This approach to the state reimbursement issue can rest here and thus constitute a state payment solely for the presence of tax-exempt property."[3]

It may well be that the larger answer to these equity problems is a shift from dependence on property tax to some other base, such as income. After looking at a number of alternatives, Quigley and Schmenner conclude that, "The analysis indicates that the replacement of property taxation with income taxation would reduce many of these distortions . . ."[4] Gilbert (1979),[5] and Bahl and Vogt (1975)[6] reach similar conclusions about the capacity of property tax alterations to solve central city/outside central city equity problems even on a regional level. However, while shifting to an income base at a regional or state level may ultimately reduce equity problems, it does not alter short-run effects of existing property tax exemption policies.

NOTES

1. Rountree and Associates, *Real Property Taxation and Relief*, 2 vols. (Richmond, Va.: 1972, n.p.)

2. Ibid., p. 111.

3. L. Richard Gabler and John Shannon, "The Exemption of Religious, Educa-

tional, and Charitable Institutions from Property Taxation," in *Research Papers*, vol. 4: *Taxes*, The Commission on Private Philanthropy and Public Needs (n.p.: Department of the Treasury, 1977), pp. 2556-57.

4. John Quigley and Roger W. Schmenner, "Property Tax Exemption and Public Policy," *Public Policy* 23 (Summer 1975): 293.

5. D. A. Gilbert, "Property Tax Base Sharing: An Answer to Central City Fiscal Problems?" *Social Science Quarterly* 59 (March 1979): 681-89.

6. Roy W. Bahl and Walter Vogt, *Fiscal Centralization and Tax Burdens* (Cambridge, Mass.: Ballinger, 1975).

BIBLIOGRAPHY

BOOKS

Ahlstrom, Sidney E. *A Religious History of the American People.* New Haven: Yale University Press, 1972.

Antieau, Chester J.; Arthur Downey; and Edward C. Roberts. *Freedom from Federal Establishment: Formation and Early History of the First Amendment Religion Clauses.* Milwaukee: Bruce Publishing, 1964.

Antieau, Chester J.; Philip M. Carroll; and Thomas C. Burke. *Religion Under the State Constitutions.* Brooklyn: Central Book, 1965.

Backus, Isaac. *A Church History of New England, With Particular Reference to the Denomination of Christians Called Baptists.* Vols. 1-3. Boston: n.p., 1796.

Bahl, Roy W., and Walter Vogt. *Fiscal Centralization and Tax Burdens.* Cambridge, Mass.: Ballinger, 1975.

Balk, Alfred. *The Free List: Property Without Taxes.* New York: Russell Sage Foundation, 1971.

———. *The Religious Business.* Richmond, Va.: John Knox Press, 1968.

Bartell, Ernest J.; Kenneth M. Brown; Arthur J. Corazzini; Dennis J. Dugan; and Thomas R. Swartz. *Catholic Education in the Archdiocese of St. Louis: Allocation and Distribution of Human and Financial Resources.* Notre Dame, Ind.: Office for Educational Research, University of Notre Dame, 1970.

Beaver, R. Pierce. *Church, State and the American Indians.* St. Louis: Concordia Publishing House, 1966.

Becker, Theodore L., and Malcolm M. Feeley, eds. *The Impact of Supreme Court Decisions.* 2d ed. New York: Oxford University Press, 1973.

Berger, Peter. *The Sacred Canopy: Elements of a Sociological Theory of Religion*. Garden City, N.J.: Doubleday & Co., 1969.

Berman, Harold. *The Interaction of Law and Religion*. Nashville: Abingdon Press, 1974.

Billington, Ray A. *The Protestant Crusade: A Study of the Origins of American Nativism*. New York: The MacMillan Co., 1938.

Blanshard, Paul. *American Freedom and Catholic Power*. 2d ed. Boston: Beacon Press, 1958.

Blau, Joseph L., ed. *Cornerstones of Religious Freedom in America*. Boston: Beacon Press, 1949.

Blum, Virgil, S. J. *Freedom of Choice in Education*. Milwaukee: Bruce Publishing Co., 1959.

Bowen, Howard R., and John W. Minter. *Private Higher Education*. Washington, D.C.: Association of American Colleges, 1975.

Boyd, Julian P., ed. *The Papers of Thomas Jefferson*. Vol. 1. Princeton: Princeton University Press, 1950.

Brown, Kenneth M. *Catholic Education in the Archdiocese of Atlanta: An Economic and Financial Analysis*. Notre Dame, Ind.: Office for Educational Research, University of Notre Dame, 1971.

Byrnes, Lawrence. *Religion and Public Education*. New York: Harper & Row, 1975.

Cole, Marley. *Jehovah's Witnesses: The New World Society*. New York: The Vantage Press, 1955.

Coons, John E., and Stephen D. Sugarman. *Education by Choice: The Case for Family Control*. Berkeley: University of California Press, 1978.

Corwin, Edward S. *Constitution of Powers in a Secular State*. Charlottesville, Va.: Michie Co., 1951.

Curry, James E. *Public Regulation of the Religious Use of Land*. Charlottesville, Va.: Michie Co., 1964.

Davis, Kenneth C. *Administrative Law*. St. Paul: West Publishing Co., 1973.

Dworkin, Ronald. *Taking Rights Seriously*. Cambridge: Harvard University Press, 1977.

Eckenrode, N.J. *The Separation of Church and State in Virginia*. Richmond: Virginia State Library, 1910.

Erickson, Donald A., ed. *Public Controls for Nonpublic Schools*. Chicago: University of Chicago Press, 1969.

Field, David D. *American Progress in Jurisprudence*. New York: Martin B. Brown, 1893.

Foote, W. H. *Sketches of Virginia, Historical and Biographical*. Philadelphia: n.p., 1850.

Ford, D. R. *Writings of Thomas Jefferson.* New York: G. P. Putnam's Sons, 1892.

Forer, L. G. *The Death of the Law.* New York: David McKay, 1975.

Freemont-Smith, Marion R. *Philanthropy and the Business Corporation,* New York: Russell Sage Foundation, 1972.

Glazer, Nathan. *American Judaism.* Chicago: University of Chicago Press, 1957.

Greeley, Andrew and Peter Rossi, *Education of Catholic Americans.* Chicago: Aldine Press, 1966.

Hanna, Mary T. *Catholic and American Politics.* Cambridge: Harvard University Press, 1979.

Hart, H. M., and A. Sacks. *The Legal Process: Basic Problems in the Making and Application of Law.* Cambridge: Harvard University Press, 1958.

Higham, John. *Strangers in the Land: Patterns of American Nativism 1860-1925.* New York: Atheneum Press, 1965.

Horwitz, Robert H., ed. *The Moral Foundations of the American Republic.* Charlottesville: University Press of Virginia, 1977.

Howe, Mark D. *The Garden and the Wilderness.* Chicago: University of Chicago Press, 1965.

Humphrey, Edward F. *Nationalism and Religion in America, 1774-1789.* Boston: Chipman Law Publishing Co., 1924.

Hunter, T. Willard. *The Tax Climate for Philanthropy.* Washington, D.C.: American College Public Relations Association, 1968.

Jefferson, Thomas. *The Writings of Thomas Jefferson.* Edited by Andrew A. Lipscomb. Washington, D.C.: Thomas Jefferson Memorial Association of the United States, 1903.

Jordan, Wilbur K. *The Development of Religious Toleration in England.* London: Allen and Unwin, 1940.

Kauper, Paul G. *Religion and the Constitution.* Baton Rouge, La.: State University Press, 1964.

Kelley, Dean M. *Why Churches Should Not Pay Taxes.* New York: Harper & Row, 1977.

Kinzer, Donald L. *An Episode in Anti-Catholicism: The American Protective Association.* Seattle: University of Washington Press, 1964.

Kraushaar, Otto F. *American Nonpublic Schools.* Baltimore: The Johns Hopkins University Press, 1972.

_____. *Private Schools: From the Puritans to the Present.* Bloomington: The Phi Delta Kappa Educational Foundation, 1976.

Kurland, Philip B., ed. *Church and State: The Supreme Court and the First Amendment.* Chicago: The University of Chicago Press, 1975.

_____. *Politics, The Constitution and the Warren Court*. Chicago: University of Chicago Press, 1970.

_____. *Religion and the Law*. Chicago: Aldine Publishing Co., 1962.

Lakoff, Sanford A. *Equality in Political Philosophy*. Boston: Beacon Press, 1964.

LaNoue, George R., ed. *Educational Vouchers: Concepts and Controversies*. New York: Teachers College Press of Columbia University, 1972.

Larson, Martin A. *Church Wealth and Business Income*. New York: Philosophical Library, 1965.

_____. *When Parochial Schools Close*. Washington, D.C.: Robert B. Luce, 1972.

Larson, Martin A. and Stanley C. Lowell. *The Churches: Their Riches, Revenues and Immunities*. Washington, D.C.: Robert B. Luce, 1969.

_____. *Praise the Lord for Tax Exemption*. Washington, D.C.: Robert B. Luce, 1969.

_____. *The Religious Empire*. Washington, D.C.: Robert B. Luce, 1976.

Lee, Robert and Martin E. Marty, eds. *Religion and Social Conflict*. New York: Oxford University Press, 1964.

Love, Thomas T. *John Courtney Murray: Contemporary Church-State Theory*. Garden City, N.J.: Doubleday & Co., 1965.

McLoughlin, William G. *Isaac Backus on Church, State and Calvinism*. Cambridge: Harvard University Press, 1968.

McLoughlin, William G. and Robert N. Bellah. *Religion in America*. Boston: Beacon Press, 1968.

Malone, Dumas. *Jefferson and the Rights of Man*. Boston: Little, Brown, and Co., 1951.

_____. *Jefferson The President, First Term: 1801-1805*. Boston: Little, Brown, and Co., 1970.

Mayer, Frederick E. *Jehovah's Witnesses*. St. Louis: Concordia Publishing House, 1952.

Mead, Sidney E. *The Nation with the Soul of a Church*. New York: Harper & Row, 1975.

Meyers, Marvin. *Mind of the Founder: Sources of the Political Thought of James Madison*. New York: Bobbs-Merrill, 1973.

Miller, Howard S. *The Legal Foundations of American Philanthropy 1776-1844*. Madison: The State Historical Society of Wisconsin, 1961.

Mitchell, Basil. *Law, Morality and Religion in a Secular Society*. New York: Oxford University Press, 1965.

Morgan, James N.; Martin H. Daird; Wilbur J. Cohen; and Harvey E. Brazer. *Income and Welfare in the United States.* New York: McGraw-Hill, 1962.

Morgan, Richard E. *The Politics of Religious Conflict.* New York: Pegasus Books, 1968.

_____. *The Supreme Court and Religion.* New York: The Free Press, 1972.

Murray, John C., ed. *Religious Liberty: An End and a Beginning.* New York: The MacMillan Co., 1966.

_____. *We Hold These Truths.* New York: Sneed and Ward, 1960.

O'Dea, Thomas. *The Mormons.* Chicago: University of Chicago Press, 1957.

Padover, Saul K. *The Complete Jefferson.* New York: Duell, Sloan and Pearce, 1943.

Parsons, Wilfred. *The First Freedom: Considerations on Church and State in the United States.* New York: F.X. McMullen Co., 1948.

Pattillo, Manning M. Jr. and Donald M. MacKenzie. *Church-Sponsored Higher Education in the United States.* Washington, D.C.: American Council in Education, 1966.

Pechman, Joseph A. and Benjamin A. Okner. *Who Bears the Tax Burden?* Washington, D.C.: The Brookings Institution, 1974.

Peters, Ronald M., Jr. *The Massachusetts Constitution of 1780.* Amherst: University of Massachusetts Press, 1978.

Pfeffer, Leo. *Church, State and Freedom.* 2d ed. Boston: Beacon Press, 1967.

Raab, Earl, ed. *Religious Conflict in America.* Garden City, N.J.: Anchor, Doubleday and Co., 1964.

Robertson, D. B. *Should Churches Be Taxed?* Philadelphia: Westminister Press, 1968.

Ryan, John and Francis Boland. *Catholic Principles of Politics.* New York: The MacMillan Co., 1948.

Sanders, Thomas G. *Protestant Concepts of Church and State.* New York: Holt, Rinehart and Winston, 1964.

Smith, Donald E., ed. *Religion, Politics and Social Change in The Third World.* New York: The Free Press, 1971.

_____. *Religion and Political Development.* Boston: Little, Brown and Co., 1970.

Smith, Elwyn A. *Religious Liberty in the United States: The Development of Church-State Thought Since the Revolutionary Era.* Philadelphia: Fortress Press, 1972.

Sorauf, Frank J. *The Wall of Separation.* Princeton: Princeton University Press, 1976.

Stokes, Anson P. *Church and State in United States*. Vols. 1 and 2, New York: Harper & Row, 1950.

Story, Joseph. *Commentaries on the Constitution*. Vol. 3. Boston: Hilliard, Gray and Co., 1833.

Sullivan, Daniel J. *Public Aid to Nonpublic Schools*. Lexington, Mass.: D.C. Heath, 1974.

Swomley, John M., Jr. *Religion, The State and The Schools*. New York: Pegasus, 1968.

Tanner, Andrew D. *The Question of Tax Exemption for Churches*. New York: National Conference of Christians and Jews, n.d.

Tax Institute of America. *Tax Incentives*. Lexington, Mass.: Heath Lexington Books, 1971.

Tawney, R.H. *Religion and the Rise of Capitalism*. New York: New American Library, 1947.

————. *Equality*. 4th ed. London: George Allen & Unwin, 1952.

Tewksbury, Donald G. *The Founding of American Colleges and Universities Before the Civil War*. New York: Arno Press, 1969.

Twain, Mark. *The Adventures of Huckleberry Finn*. New York: Washington Square Press, 1960.

Verduin, Leonard. *The Anatomy of a Hybrid*. Grand Rapids, Mich.: Erdmans Publishing Co., 1976.

Wechsler, Herbert. *Principles, Politics and Fundamental Law*. Cambridge: Harvard University Press, 1961.

Wolf, Donald J. *Toward Consensus: Catholic-Protestant Interpretations of Church and State*. Garden City, N.J.: Doubleday and Co., 1968.

Zollman, Carl. *American Civil Church Law*. Studies in History, Economics and Public Law. Vol. 77. 1917. Reprint. New York: AMS Press, 1969.

CHAPTERS IN BOOKS

Aaron, Henry. "Federal Encouragement of Private Giving." In *Tax Impacts on Philanthropy*, pp. 210-13. Princeton, N.J.: Tax Institute of America, 1972.

Arons, Stephen. "The Peaceful Uses of Education Vouchers." In *Educational Vouchers: Concepts and Controversies*, edited by George R. LaNoue. New York: Teachers College Press of Columbia University, 1972, pp. 70-97.

Bittker, Boris I. "The Propriety and Vitality of a Federal Income Tax Deduction for Private Philanthropy." In *Tax Impacts on Philanthropy*. Princeton, N.J., Tax Institute of America, 1972, pp. 145-70.

Bridge, Gary. "Citizen Choice in Public Services: Voucher Systems." In

Alternatives for Delivering Public Services. Edited by E. S. Savas. Boulder, Colo.: Westview Press, 1977, pp. 51-109.

Fey, Harold E. "An Argument for Separation." In *The Wall Between Church and State.* Edited by Dalin Oaks. Chicago: University of Chicago Press, 1963, pp. 26-40.

Ginsberg, Eli. "The Economics of the Voucher System." In *Educational Vouchers: Concepts and Controversies.* Edited by George R. LaNoue. New York: Teachers College Press, 1972, pp. 98-108.

Greenawalt, Kent. "All or Nothing at All: The Defeat of Selective Conscientious Objection." In *Church and State: The Supreme Court and the First Amendment.* Edited by Philip B. Kurland, Chicago: The University of Chicago Press, 1975, pp. 168-231.

Howe, Mark D. "The Constitutional Question." *Religion and the Free Society.* New York: Fund for the Republic 49, 1958.

Katz, Wilbur. "The Case for Religious Liberty." In *Religion in America.* Edited by John Cogley. New York: Meridian Books, 1958, pp. 95-115.

Leone, Robert A. and John R. Meyer. "Tax Exemption and Local Property Tax." In *Local Public Finance and the Fiscal Squeeze: A Case Study.* Edited by John R. Meyer and John M. Quigley, Cambridge, Mass.: Ballinger, 1977, pp. 41-67.

Nelson, Susan. "Financial Trends and Issues." In *Public Policy and Private Higher Education.* Edited by David W. Breneman and Chester E. Finn, Jr. Washington, D.C.: The Brookings Institution, 1972, pp. 63-142.

Pfeffer, Leo. "The Case for Separation." In *Religion in America.* Edited by John Cogley. New York: Meridian Books, 1958, pp. 52-94.

Sunley, Emil M. Jr. "Federal and State Tax Policies." In *Public Policy and Private Higher Education.* Edited by David W. Breneman and Chester E. Finn, Jr. Washington, D.C.: The Brookings Institution, 1978, pp. 281-320.

LEGAL AND SOCIAL SCIENCE JOURNAL ARTICLES

Askin, Steve. "Higgins on Church as 'Boss'." *National Catholic Reporter* 16, 17 (22 February 1980), 1.

Bartholomew, Raymond. "Religion and the Public Schools." 20 *Vanderbilt Law Review* 1078 (1967).

Bittker, Boris I. "Churches, Taxes and The Constitution." 78 *Yale Law Journal* 1285 (1969).

Blum, Virgil C. "Is the Supreme Court Anti-Catholic?" 79 *Homiletic and Pastoral Review* 7 (1974).

Bordon, Morton. "Federalists, Antifederalists, and Religious Freedom." 21 *Journal of Church and State* 469 (1979).

Brandt, Irving. "Madison on Separation of Church and State." 8 *William and Mary Quarterly* 3 (January, 1951).

Brown, Ernest J. "Quis Custodiet Ipsos Custodes? The School Prayer Cases." 1963 *Supreme Court Review.*

"Church Property Disputes." 75 *Harvard Law Review* 1142 (1962).

Clark, J. Morris. "Guidelines of The Free Exercise Clause." 85 *Harvard Law Review* 327 (1969).

Clear, John M. "Political Speech of Charitable Organizations Under the Internal Revenue Code." 41 *The University of Chicago Law Review* 352 (1973-1974).

Coleman, James S. "Social Clearage and Religious Conflict." 12 *The Journal of Social Issues* 44 (1956).

"Constitutionality of State Property Tax Exemptions for Religious Property." 66 *Northwestern University Law Review* 118 (March-April 1971).

Corwin, Edward S. "The Higher Law Background of American Constitutional Law." 42 *Harvard Law Review* 149 (1928).

———. "The Supreme Court as National School Board." 14 *Law and Contemporary Problems* 3 (1949).

Cox, Kenneth. "The FCC, The Constitution, and Religious Broadcast Programming." 34 *George Washington Law Review* 197 (1965).

Davidson, Joel E. "Comment: Religion in Politics and the Income Tax Exemption." 42 *Fordham Law Review* 397 (1973).

Feldstein, Martin. "The Income Tax Charitable Constitutions: Part I—Agreement and Distributional Effects." 28 *National Tax Journal* 81 (March 1975).

Figinski, M. A. "Military Chaplains: A Constitutionally Permissible Accommodation Between Church and State." 24 *Maryland Law Review* 377 (1964).

Fleet, Elizabeth. "Monopolies, Perpetuities, Corporations. Ecclesiastical Endowments." In "Madison's Detached Memoranda." *William and Mary Quarterly* 534 (1946).

Freund, Paul A. "Public Aid to Parochial Schools." 82 *Harvard Law Review* 1680 (1969).

Giannella, Donald. "Lemon and Tilton: The Bittersweet of Church-State Entanglement." 1971 *Supreme Court Review* 147.

———. "Religious Liberty, Nonestablishment and Doctrinal Development, Part I: The Religious Liberty Guarantee." 80 *Harvard Law Review* 1381 (1967).

_____. "Religious Liberty, Nonestablishment and Doctrinal Development: Part II—The Nonestablishment Principle." 81 *Harvard Law Review* 513 (1968).

Gilbert, D. A. "Property Tax Base Sharing: An Answer to Central City Fiscal Problems?" 59 *Social Science Quarterly* 681 (March 1979).

Golden, Cornelius J. "Educational Vouchers: The Fruit of the Lemon Tree." 24 *Stanford Law Review* 687 (1972).

Golding, Joanne. "State Aid to Nonpublic Schools: A Legal-Historical Overview." 19 *Journal of Church and State* 231 (Spring 1977).

Hager, Donald J. "Religious Conflict in the United States." 12 *The Journal of Social Issues* 7 (1956).

Herrmann, Klauss J. "Some Considerations on the Constitutionality of the United States Military Chaplaincy." 14 *American University Law Review* 24 (1964).

Higgins, George H. "Unions and Catholic Institutions." *America* 142, 3 (26 January 1980).

Jencks, Christopher. "Is the Public School Obsolete?" 2 *Public Interest* 18 (1966).

Jones, J. P. " 'Religion' in the Religion Clauses." 19 *Journal of Public Law* 283 (1970).

Karst, Kenneth. "Equality as a Central Principle in the First Amendment." 43 *University of Chicago Law Review* 20 (1976).

Katz, Wilbur. "Radiations from Church Tax Exemptions." 1970 *Supreme Court Review* 93.

Kauper, Paul G. "Church and State: Cooperative Separatism." 60 *Michigan Law Review* 1 (November 1961).

_____. "The Churches and the Public Order." *Chicago Theological Seminary Register* (December 1965).

_____. "Prayer, Public Schools and the Supreme Court." 61 *Michigan Law Review* 1031 (1963).

_____. "Public Aid for Parochial Schools and Church Colleges: The Lemon, Dicenso and Tilton Cases." 13 *Arizona Law Review* 567 (1971).

_____. "The Walz Decision: More on the Religion Clauses of the First Amendment." 69 *Michigan Law Review* 179 (1970).

Kelley, Dean M. "Operational Consequences of Church-State Choices." 57 *Social Progress* 15 (January-February 1967).

Knoles, George H. "The Religious Ideas of Thomas Jefferson." 30 *The Mississippi Valley Historical Review* 187 (1943-1944).

Kurland, Philip B. "The Regents' Prayer Case: Full of Sound and Fury, Signifying . . ." 1962 *Supreme Court Review* 1.

––––––. "The Supreme Court, Compulsory Education and the First Amendment Religion Clauses." 75 *West Virginia Law Review* 241 (1973).

LaFontaine, Charles V. "God and Nation in Selected U.S. Presidential Inaugural Addresses, 1789-1945: Part One." 18 *Journal of Church and State* 39 (1976).

Lippy, Charles H. "The 1780 Massachusetts Constitution: Religious Establishment or Civil Religion." 20 *Journal of Church and State* 533 (1978).

Loeringer, Lee. "Religious Liberty and Broadcasting." 33 *George Washington Law Review* 631 (1965).

Lumdquist, John. "The Constitutionality of Church Property Exemptions Upheld by the 'Benevolent Neutrality' of the Supreme Court." 20 *DePaul Law Review* 252 (1971).

Miller, Arthur S. and Ronald F. Howell. "The Myth of Neutrality in Constitutional Adjudication." 27 *University of Chicago Law Review* 683 (1960).

Moore, John H. "The Supreme Court and the Relationship Between the 'Establishment' and 'Free Exercise' Clauses." 42 *Texas Law Review* 142 (1963).

Morgan, Richard E. "The Establishment Clause and Sectarian Schools." 1973 *Supreme Court Review* 57.

Murray, John C. "The Problem of Religious Freedom." 25 *Theological Studies* 503 (December 1964).

––––––. "Law or Prepossession?" 14 *Law and Contemporary Problems* 23 (Winter 1949).

Oppenheim, Felix E. "The Concept of Equality." 5 *International Encyclopedia of the Social Sciences* 103 (1968).

Palmer, Kenneth T. and Roy W. Shin. "Compensatory Payment Plans in the States." 48 *State Government* 216 (Autumn 1975).

Pfeffer, Leo. "The Becker Amendment." 6 *Journal of Church and State* 344 (1964).

––––––. "Freedom and Separation: America's Contribution to Civilization." 2 *Journal of Church and State* 100 (1960).

––––––. "Religion Blind Government." 15 *Stanford Law Review* 389 (1963).

Quigley, John M. and Roger W. Schmenner. "Property Tax Exemption and Public Policy." 23 *Public Policy* 259 (Summer 1975).

Rhys, Isaac. "Religion and Authority: Problems of the Anglican Establishment in Virginia in the Era of the Great Awakening and the Parson's Case." 30 *William and Mary Quarterly* 3 (January 1973).

Rimlinger, Joseph G., Jr. "Comment: Demilitarizing the Chaplaincy: A Constitutional Imperative." 19 *South Dakota Law Review* 351 (1974).

Rosenfeld, Marguerite S. "Comment: Religious Rights of Public School Teachers." 23 *UCLA Law Review* 763 (1976).

Schwartz, Alan. "No Imposition of Religion: The Establishment Clause Value." 77 *Yale Law Journal* 692 (1968).

_____. "The Nonestablishment Principle: A Reply to Professor Giannella." 81 *Harvard Law Review* 1465 (1968).

Schwartz, Robert A. "Personal Philanthropic Contributions." *Journal of Political Economy* 1264 (November-December 1970).

Siegel, Martin. "Revamping the Military Chaplaincy." 79 *The Christian Century* 959 (6 August 1962).

Sorauf, F.J. "Zorach V. Clausen: The Impact of a Supreme Court Decision." 53 *American Political Science Review* 777 (1959).

Stagg, Frank. "Rendering to Caesar What Belongs to Caesar: Christian Engagement With the World." 18 *Journal of Church and State* 95 (Winter 1976).

Stahmer, Harold. "Defining Religion: Federal Aid and Academic Freedom." 1 *Religion and Public Order* 116 (1963).

Taft, Roger A. "Tax Benefits for the Clergy: The Unconstitutionality of Section 107." 62 *Georgetown Law Journal* 1261 (1974).

Taussig, Michael K. "Economic Aspects of the Personal Income Tax Treatment of Charitable Constitutions." 20 *National Tax Journal* 1 (March 1967).

"Title I Benefits to Public Schools Outweigh Those to Private Schools, NIE Study Shows." 59 *Phi Delta Kappa* 727 (June 1978).

VanAltstyne, Arvo. "Tax Exemption of Church Property." 20 *Ohio State Law Journal* 461 (1959).

Warren, Alvin C. Jr.; Thomas G. Krattenmaker; and Lester B. Snyder. "Property Tax Exemptions for Charitable Educational, Religious and Governmental Institutions in Connecticut." 4 *Connecticut Law Review* 181 (Fall 1971).

Weber, Paul J. and Olson, Janet R. "Religious Property Tax Exemptions in Kentucky." 66 *Kentucky Law Journal* 651 (1978).

Wechsler, Herbert. "Toward Neutral Principles of Constitutional Law." 73 *Harvard Law Review* 1 (1959).

Whelan, Charles M. "'Churches' in the Internal Revenue Code: The Definitional Problems." 45 *Fordham Law Review* 885 (March 1977).

Wolf, Donald. "The Unitary Theory of Church-State Relations." *Journal of Church and State* 4 (May 1962).

DOCUMENTS, DISSERTATIONS, AND REPORTS

Advising Commission on Intergovernmental Relations. *The Property Tax in a Changing Environment.* M-83. Washington, D.C.: Government Printing Office, 1974.

American Association of Fund-Raising Counsel, *Giving U.S.A.: A Compilation of Facts and Trends on American Philanthropy for the year 1977.* New York: American Association of Fund Raising Counsel, 1978.

Boileau, Raymond G. "Moving Into the 70's: The Status of American Nonpublic Education." A report to the President's Commission on School Finance, November 1971.

Commission on Private Philanthropy and Public Needs. *Giving in America: Toward a Stronger Voluntary Sector.* n.p.: Commission on Private Philanthropy and Public Needs, 1975.

————. *Research Papers.* Vol. 3: *Special Behavioral Studies, Foundations, and Corporations.* n.p.: Department of the Treasury, 1977.

————. *Research Papers.* Vol. 4: *Taxes.* n.p.: Department of the Treasury, 1977.

————. *Research Papers.* Vol. 5: *Regulation.* n.p.: Department of the Treasury, 1977.

Common Cause. *Gimme Shelters: A Common Cause Study of the Review of Tax Expenditures by the Congressional Tax Committees.* Washington, D.C.: Common Cause, 1978.

Council for Financial Aid for Education. *Voluntary Support of Education 1975-76.* New York: Council for Financial Aid to Education, n.d.

Erickson, Donald; George Madaus; and Joseph P. Ryan. "Summary of Local Cooperative Programs Between the Public and Nonpublic Schools." In *Report of the Archdiocesan Advisory Committee on the Financial Crisis of Catholic Schools in Philadelphia and Surrounding Counties,* John T. Gurash, Chairman. Philadelphia: Archdiocesan Advisory Committee on the Financial Crisis of Catholic Schools in Philadelphia and Surrounding Counties, 1972.

Eulau, Heinz; Harold Quinley; and David D. Henry. *State Officials and Higher Education.* A general report prepared for the Carnegie Commission on Higher Education. New York: McGraw-Hill, 1970.

Falcon, James. "An Inventory of Federal Programs in Aid to Elementary and Secondary Education." A Report to the President's Commission on School Finance, January 1972.

Fleischman Report. By Manly Fleischman, Chairman, New York State Commission on the Quality, Cost and Financing of Elementary Education. Vol. 1. New York: Viking Press, 1973.

Freeman, Roger A. Tax Loopholes: *The Legend and the Reality.* AEI— Hoover Policy Study 5. Washington, D.C.: American Enterprise Institute for Public Policy Research, 1973.

Golladay, Mary A. *The Condition of Education. 1977 Edition.* A Statistical Report on the Condition of Education in the United States. Vol. 3. Washington, D.C.: Government Printing Office, 1977.

Kramer, William A. *Public Aid to Church-Related Nonpublic Schools.* St. Louis: Board of Parish Education, The Lutheran Church—Missouri School, April 1970.

Levi, Julian H. and Sheldon E. Steinbach. *Patterns of Giving to Higher Education III.* n.p.: American Council in Education, n.d.

McFarland, William H.; A. E. Dick Howard; and Jay L. Chronister. *State Financial Measures Involving the Private Sector of Higher Education.* n.p.: National Council of Independent Colleges and Universities, 1974.

Mintz, Steven. "Education Vouchers: Proposals and Prospects." A staff report to the President's Commission on School Finance, 1972.

National Center for Education Statistics. *Nonpublic School Statistics, 1976-77—Advance Report.* Washington, D.C.: U.S. Department of Health, Education, and Welfare, 1977.

National Science Foundation. Division of Science Resources Studies, Universities and Nonprofit Institutions Study Group. *Federal Support to Universities, Colleges, and Selected Nonprofit Institutions, Fiscal Year 1975,* by J. G. Huckenpahler. Surveys of Science Resources Series NSF 77-311. Washington, D.C.: Government Printing Office, 1977.

National Tax Association—Tax Institute of America. Report of the Property Taxation Committee. "The Erosion of the Ad Valorem Real Estate Tax Base." 40 *Tax Policy* 1 (1973).

President's Commission on School Finance. Economic Problems of Nonpublic Schools. A report prepared for the Commission by the University of Notre Dame Office of Educational Research. Washington, D.C.: President's Commission on School Finance, 1972.

President's Commission on School Finance. *Public Aid to Nonpublic Education.* A staff report prepared for the Commission by Janet S. Foerster. Washington, D.C.: The President's Commission on School Finance, 1971.

President's Panel on Nonpublic Education. *Nonpublic Education and the Public Good.* Washington, D.C.: Government Printing Office, 1972.

Quigley, John M. and Debra Stinson. *Levels of Property Tax Exemption.* Exchange Bibliography No. 840. Monticello, Ill.: Council of Planning Libraries, July 1975.

Report of the Archdiocesan Advisory Committee on the Financial Crisis of Catholic Schools in Philadelphia and Surrounding Counties, John T. Gurash, Chairman. Philadelphia: Archdiocesan Advisory Committee on the Financial Crisis of Catholic Schools in Philadelphia and Surrounding Counties, 1972.

Stauffer, Alan C. *Property Assessment and Exemptions: They Need Reform.* Research Brief No. 3. Denver: Education Commission of the States, 1973.

U. S. Congress. House Committee on Ways and Means. *Hearings on H.R. 9332.* 95th Cong., 2d sess., 1978.

U.S. Department of Commerce, Bureau of the Census. *1972 Census of Governments,* Vol. 2. *Taxable Property Values and Assessment—Sales Price Ratios,* pt. 2. Assessment-Sales Price Ratios and Tax Rates.

U.S. Department of Health, Education, and Welfare. Education Division. *The Condition of Education:* 1976 Edition, by Mary A. Golladay. National Center for Education Statistics. NCES 76-400. Washington, D.C.: Government Printing Office, 1976.

————. Education Division. *Digest of Education Statistics 1976 Edition,* by W. Vance Grant and C. George Lind. National Center for Education Statistics. NCES 77-401. Washington, D.C.: Government Printing Office, 1977.

————. Education Division. *Projections of Education Statistics to 1984-85,* by Kenneth A. Simon and Martin M. Frankel. National Center for Education Statistics. NCES 76-210. Washington, D.C.: Government Printing Office, 1976.

Vitullo-Martin, Thomas. Testimony on Tuition Tax Credit Bill, S-2142 before the Subcommittee on Taxation and Debt Management of the Senate Finance Committee, 18 January 1978.

Weber, Paul J. "Religion and Equality: Understanding the First Amendment." Ph.D. dissertation, University of Chicago, 1977.

NEWSPAPERS AND POPULAR JOURNALS

Cohn, Marcus. "Religion and the FCC." *Reporter,* 14 January 1965, pp. 32-34.

Cusick, Dennis. "Misplaced Faith?" *Louisville Times,* 15 June 1979.

Friedman, Milton. "The Voucher Idea." *New York Times Magazine,* 23 September 1973.

Gollin, James. "There's an Unholy Press in the Churchly Economy." *Fortune*, May 1976, p. 223.

Himmelfarb, Milton, "How High a Wall?" *Commentary*, July 1966, p. 23.

Koten, John. "Faith Under Test: Some Church Bonds Plunge Into Default; Investor Losses Mount." *The Wall Street Journal*, 27 February 1978.

Lekachman, Robert M. "Education Report: Vouchers and Public Education." *New Leader*, July 1971, p. 9.

Hunt, Gaillard. "Aspects of Monopoly One Hundred Years Ago." *Harpers*, March 1914, p. 489.

Moynihan, Daniel P. "Government and the Ruin of Private Education." *Harpers*, April 1978, p. 28.

Muskie, Edmund A. "Muskie Says Benefits of Many Tax Breaks Go Mostly to the Wealthy." *Muskie News*, press release, 13 February 1978.

Weber, Paul J. "Bishops in Politics: The Big Plunge." *America* 134 (1976): 220.

INDEX

About the Authors

PAUL J. WEBER is Associate Professor of Political Science and Chairman of the Social Science Division, at the University of Louisville, Louisville, Kentucky. He has contributed to such publications as *The Kentucky Law Journal*, *Creighton Law Review*, *The Jurist* and *Assessors Journal*.

DENNIS A. GILBERT is Associate Professor of Political Science at the University of Louisville, Louisville, Kentucky. His articles have appeared in such journals as *Social Science Quarterly*, *Public Administration Review*, and *Assessors Journal*.